Karolina Karr

Democracy and Lobbying in the European Union

Campus Verlag
Frankfurt/New York

Distribution throughout the world except Germany, Austria and Switzerland by

The University of Chicago Press
1427 East 60th Street
Chicago, IL 60637

Bibliographic Information published by the Deutsche Nationalbibliothek.
Die Deutsche Nationalbibliothek lists this publication in the Deutsche Nationalbibliografie;
detailed bibliographic data are available in the Internet at http://dnb.d-nb.de.
ISBN 978-3-593-38412-2

Zugl.: Erfurt, Univ., Diss., 2006

Printed on acid free paper.
Printed in the United States of America

For further information:
www.campus.de
www.press.uchicago.edu

Contents

Acknowledgements

The successful completion of this dissertation in 2006 is owed in no small part to the support and advice of the following people:

I wish to thank my advisor Prof. Dr. Dietmar Herz at the Universität Erfurt. The core ideas and the final structuring of this work profited greatly from a perfect mixture of academic freedom and support which I experienced over the past three years. The discussions triggered in his doctoral seminars helped spark new ideas as much as keep up the academic motivation – not always an easy matter over such a long period of time.

On the practical side, it was Prof. Herz' team at the Department for Comparative Political Studies (Lehrstuhl für Vergleichende Regierungslehre) – in particular Stefanie Steuber and Kathrin Eisenhauer – who ensured a smooth administrative process without which the academic process would have come to no satisfactory end. Thank you

Prof. Dr. Maria-Theresa Wobbe, Universität Erfurt, acted as a supportive second advisor. Her academic work on gender questions in the EU context brought up interesting new perspectives on the more generalist approach of this work.

The topics of democracy and lobbying were guaranteed to provoke heated debate in my general surroundings. Many of the more valuable discussions I owe to colleagues at McKinsey & Co. as well as to my brother Daniel and various friends – in particular Christoph Heumann, the first to read Part I and offer criticism. Special thanks goes to Tim Lawrenz who was always ready to remind me that there is a life apart from (and after) the dissertation.

Last but not least, this work would have never been completed without the unfailing belief my parents showed in my ability to master the task at hand, including that of disciplining myself. Representative for my whole family I dedicate this work to my grandfather Orren Leslie Karr (*1909–†2005).

Introduction

All representative systems have had to confront the opportunities offered as well as the threats posed by the formation and activities of interest groups.[1] Up until the mid twentieth century the anticipated threats dominated the assessment of interest groups and their activities, giving rise to such descriptive phrases as »the anonymous empire« (Finer 1960) or »the rule of associations« (Eschenburg 1955). James Madison's definition and judgment of interest groups is simply one of the better known ones:

> By a faction I understand a number of citizens, whether amounting to a majority or a minority of the whole, who are united and actuated by some common impulse of passion, or of interest, adverse to the rights of other citizens, or to the permanent and aggregate interests of the community. There are two methods of curing the mischiefs of faction: the one, by removing its causes; the other, by controlling its effects. (2003, orig. 1787-88: 51)

Several developments have since come to bear on societal and political perception and have decreased the fear of faction. First, the view of interest groups and their role within a representative system has become more differentiated, driven mainly by pluralist theory and new political concepts such as participatory and associative democracy. Second, heightened awareness and technological developments have increased public transparency on interest groups and have in some cases lead to a better regulation of their influence on political decision-making. Yet, the underlying question remains the same: How are interest groups to be integrated into repre-

---

1 While this works concentrates on those activities aimed primarily at political institutions and decision-making officials and termed lobbying, interest groups usually have a broader range of activities including the organization and information of their members and – if they are not constituted for the sole purpose of representing their members' interests – may also follow a primary purpose, e.g., community work done by charitable organizations.

sentative democratic systems without destroying the legitimatory grounds of democratic decision-making?

This question can be posed both in the context of political theory and in the practical, empirical setting of an existing representative system. Accordingly, this work intends to explore the possible role of interest groups and the impact of their involvement on a democratic representative system both in theory and in the context of the experience of democracy and lobbying in today's European Union.

Not even the greatest critics of European democracy and its interest group system negate the important role of interest groups within representative democracies. The role of groups has supposedly always been to provide representatives with information on diverging interests within the population, which in turn enables officials to balance all interests to the advantage of the whole. In today's system of, on the one hand, heightened complexity of policy issues calling for technical expertise and, on the other hand, of growing distance between the representatives and the European people the supporting role of interest groups is magnified. At the same time, the complexity and centralization – also characterized by a pronounced intransparency of the decision-making process – give rise to questions as to the complementarity or opposition of lobbying and democracy in the European Union:

Is lobbying complementary to the other forms of institutionally formalised representation, such as the European Parliament, the Social and Economic Committee, the Committee of the Regions? Does it support them by the production of expertise? Or does it destabilise them, short-circuit them through the play of competing intervention mechanisms? Does the predominance of technical expertise not conflict with the very nature of universal suffrage? (Gobin et al. 1998)

In other words, is there a real threat that the democracy of citizens could be replaced by a »democracy of organizations« (Andersen et al. 1996a: 230) or has EU democracy indeed already been transformed into a »lobbycracy«, *Lobbykratie* (Bode 2003: 208), by the dominating influences of special interests?

Since the early 1990s both Anglo-Saxon and German academic research and writing have shown an increasing interest in topics concerning lobbying in the European Union. Much effort has been made to compile information on and analyses of the workings of the relevant EU institutions from the point of view of the various types of lobby groups working in Brussels (Mazey et al. 1993c, Buholzer 1998, Teuber 2001). A vast library of how-to guides (e.g., Cassidy 2000, Vandenberghe 1995) and, mainly, industry case studies has accumulated. Many of these works are marked by an interdisciplinary approach combining political science with communication science (Fischer 1997, Geißler 2002) and sociology (Lahusen et al. 2001).

At the same time there exists a long tradition of critical works dealing with the almost proverbial lack of democratic legitimacy of the European Union, its processes and institutions (Abromeit 1998b, Decker 2002, Greven 2000a, Schmuck 1993, Veit 1989, Zürn 1996, Zweifel 2002). The question of interest lobbying is but one of many aspects constituting this so-called democratic deficit.

The increasingly widespread criticism of the EU is not a result of political manipulation which can be corrected by neutral information but stems mainly from the discrepancy between the prevailing normative model of political organization (i.e. the democratic state) and perceived deficits of the EU with reference to this model. [...] the public political debate is in desperate need for models of the European polity which give a realistic analytical image of the EU and at the same time serve as normative guideposts for feasible reforms balancing democracy and governance. (Jachtenfuchs 1997: 11)

In the years since Jachtenfuchs' appeal many such models have been suggested though most authors continue to focus on state-centric approaches. Some models – such as that of the multi-level governance system relying to a large part on policy networks – go beyond official institutions in their consideration of political players shaping EU democracy and offer a wider range of solutions. The present work aims at adding to current models by choosing an interest group focused and lobbying-centric approach. In this it joins the comparatively short list of works combining the question of European democratic legitimacy with the question of the role of public and private interest groups. A collection of essays resulting from a 1997 conference and compiled by the Groupe d'étude de Lobbyisme Européen at the University of Brussels was one of the first substantial attempts at »the connection between democracy and lobbying, ethics [and] the evolving political system of the EU« (Claeys et al. 1998a: cover text).

Considering the various demands to address the questions of lobbying legitimacy as well as the broader aspect of EU democracy, the challenge at hand, thus, is the design of a balanced integration of interest lobbying into the processes and structures of representative democratic governance. This integration would, on the one hand, have to ensure that the variety of interests present in society can organize and represent themselves vis-à-vis the decision-making institutions and officials in a meaningful way and contribute to the problem-solving of a growing number of complex issues. On the other hand, the principles of democracy would have to be safeguarded from the dominance of special interests, which would otherwise mock the freedoms granted them by democracy and which could lead to policy decisions that neither balance all interests nor consider the common interest in any other form. Whether such a balanced integration is possible, both in theory and in the reality of the European Union, is the main question this work sets out to explore.

Structurally, the approach to this question is divided into two parts, the first creating a theoretical base and various frameworks which are subsequently employed in the second part and its examination of EU reality. An overview of the two parts and their main chapters as well as a first understanding of the argument unfolded throughout is offered in the following. It should be mentioned that Parts I and II are both headed by a short introduction recalling the main points made here and going into further detail where necessary to facilitate an easy overview of the two-part structure and the parts' parallels and interconnections.

Part I develops the theoretical concept of a sustainable integration of lobbying in a representative democracy. For this purpose it first deals separately with the key concepts of democracy and of interest groups and interest representation. Chapter 1 creates a normative model of democracy based on the principles of political equality and self-determination and delineated by four cornerstones that act as normative democratic standards. While the four cornerstones enable a normative assessment of democratic governance in general and of its integration of lobbying in particular, the normative model is supplemented with a second, descriptive model of democracy based on a comparative empirical approach. This second model offers a view of the compromises struck between democratic norms and practical politics in a functioning system of governance. Its choice of consociational democracy is informed by the need in Part II for a descriptive model that best grasps the particulars of the EU system. For the same reason, Chapter 1 concludes with an examination of the challenges facing democracy beyond the nation-state.

Chapter 2 unfolds the terminology and systematics needed to deal with interest groups and interest representation. This includes a classification of groups, a framework separating lobbying addressees from interest lobbies and other intermediaries involved in the process of interest intermediation, and a broad examination of lobbying methods and resources. Furthermore, the key concept of the common good is analyzed, which appears to be omnipresent in the context of interest lobbying and democracy. Similarly, the debate on the best system of interest representation or intermediation, on the vices and virtues of pluralism and corporatism, is recaptured and synthesized for its later application to the EU context.

Chapter 3 combines the frameworks developed in the two previous chapters in order to examine the range of positive and negative impact interest group lobbying can have on a system of representative democracy. This includes a consideration of the mutually reinforcing influences of interest representation and consociationalism; both share a preference for proportional, consensual decision-making and a tendency towards informal and intransparent processes. Based on the anticipated effects of lobbying on the democratic processes Part I is rounded off with an examination of the possibilities for curbing negative lobbying impact and develops a list of institutional and regulatory recommendations, which can inform the later development of measures aimed at reconciling democracy and lobbying in the European Union.

Part II applies the models and systematics developed in Part I to the reality of EU democracy and lobbying. The normative democratic standards outlined in Chapter 1 structure the examination of the so-called democratic deficit of the European Union in Chapter 4 as well as the suggestions offered for its alleviation. The consociational character of EU democracy is outlined, making use of the earlier descriptive model, and its understanding is further deepened by an analysis of the particulars of European multi-level governance and the policy networks driving its processes. Finally, Chapter 4 takes into consideration possible challenges to democracy posed by the latest developments, i.e., the 2004 enlargement and the pending ratification of the EU Constitution.

Chapter 5 undertakes an in-depth examination of the EU lobbying landscape. The development and current situation of representative offices in Brussels is analyzed and searched for indications of the distribution of power and influence between the different types of lobby groups. These different types of groups, as well as their methods and resources, also play a role in understanding the interaction between institutional addressees and lobby groups. The access to EU lobbying addressees is strongly determined by the different access goods the groups have at their disposal. The chapter concludes with an overview of the heterogeneous systems of lobbying regulations in place in the European Commission and the European Parliament and offers an assessment of their impact on the European system and style of lobbying.

In an attempt to answer the main question driving the investigation throughout both parts, Chapter 6 combines the insights gained on the system of European governance and lobbying in Part II with the theoretical concept suggested in Chapter 3. An examination of the impact of lobbying on European democracy and an outlook on probable developments expected for the near future of EU lobbying lead up to the formulation of opportunities for and limits to a democratically integrated system of EU lobbying, which wraps up this work's argument.

Table 1: Structure of argumentation

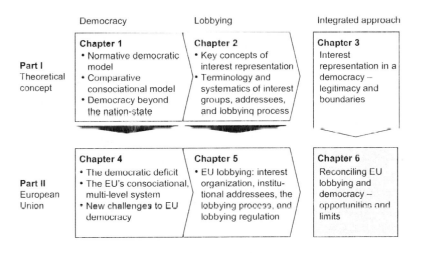

	Democracy	Lobbying	Integrated approach
Part I Theoretical concept	**Chapter 1** • Normative democratic model • Comparative consociational model • Democracy beyond the nation-state	**Chapter 2** • Key concepts of interest representation • Terminology and systematics of interest groups, addressees, and lobbying process	**Chapter 3** Interest representation in a democracy – legitimacy and boundaries
Part II European Union	**Chapter 4** • The democratic deficit • The EU's consociational, multi-level system • New challenges to EU democracy	**Chapter 5** • EU lobbying: interest organization, institutional addressees, the lobbying process, and lobbying regulation	**Chapter 6** Reconciling EU lobbying and democracy – opportunities and limits

Source: Own framework

A final point to be considered here before moving on to the theoretical concept in Part I is the question as to the broader context of academic theory and analysis into which this work might be placed. Various authors attempt to structure literature on the European Union by considering the different underlying theoretical approaches (among others Jachtenfuchs et al. 2003, Wallace 2000a). Jachtenfuchs et al., for example, differentiate between three classical approaches: integration theories covering intergovernmental institution-building (i.e., neofunctionalism and intergovernmentalism), policy analysis focusing on individual areas of the EU, and constitutional debate combining normative and analytical questions and often seen as relating to the field of political consulting. Such structuring exercises often reach the conclusion that no single approach yields a well-rounded picture of the object under scrutiny and that examinations of the EU should best consider the various points of views offered by different schools of theory. Along similar lines, the choice of analytical approach – of macro, meso, and micro categories (Wallace 2000a: 70f) – also demands an awareness of the limits to each approach, e.g., a meso-level examination of policy processes not necessarily being able to transfer its conclusions to other policy areas.

An approach as broad as that envisaged by this work – integrating a number of areas in political science from democracy theory and theories of interest representation to the large field of European integration research – is not easily placed within a single theoretical or analytical context. Lead by the idea that a combination of different points of view and their variety of insights into the EU is most likely to produce a new and better understanding of democracy and lobbying in the European Union, the chosen approach does not explicitly follow a particular school of thought. Notwithstanding, this work exhibits tendencies towards macro-level analysis and what Jachtenfuchs et al. term the constitutional debate dealing both normatively and analytically with the process of constitutionalization in the EU and addressing concepts such as legitimacy and democracy found less frequently in other theoretical approaches (Jachtenfuchs et al. 2003: 13f). These tendencies will no doubt become obvious throughout the following chapters.

I. Theoretical concept

Combining insights gathered through an investigation of democracy theories as well as theories of interest group representation and intermediation, Part I develops a concept of legitimate interest lobbying for a modern democracy. This concept, which pays special attention to the challenges of a consociational democracy, functions as foundation and point of reference for the examination of democracy and lobbying in the European Union in Part II.

Chapter 1 introduces two contrasting but, in a way, also complementary models of democracy, derived from different schools of thought. The normative model argues in favor of two underlying principles of democracy in a representative system, namely political equality and freedom of self-determination. From these it derives four so-called democratic cornerstones – equality of vote, equality of voice, authorization, and accountability – responsible for the realization of the two principles. By contrast, the comparative empirical model does not aspire to declare normative standards. With the strong elements of consociationalism in the European Union in mind, it uses the experiences from actual democratic systems to create an abstract but nevertheless descriptive model of consociational democracy. The advantage of combining the two models in a single work lies in the different roles they play in examining the EU. While the normative model allows for a top-down assessment of democratic standards, the comparative empirical model enables a detailed and bottom-up examination of the strengths and weaknesses of practical democracy with a consociational nature. Thus, the understanding of EU democracy in Part II becomes more complete than it could have been from the single viewpoint of either an idealized, unrealistic condemnation of the EU reality and its democratic shortcomings or a relativist, apologetic acceptance of the current EU democracy as a given. Chapter 1 closes with a discussion of the possibilities and limits of transferring models developed from mainly nation-state experiences of democracies to a supranational system such as the European Union.

Chapter 2 examines several concepts that are key to an understanding of the debate on interest representation and lobbying in a democracy, these concepts being the common good as well as pluralism and corporatism, the two most common systems of interest intermediation. This is followed by an exploration of the terminology and systematics of interest groups and lobbying. Based on this, Chapter 2 suggests a system of interest group classification useful in the context of this work's objective, develops a framework for the examination of lobbying addressees, and structures the multitude of methods and resources employed in the lobbying process.

Synthesizing the preceding examinations of both democracy and interest theories, Chapter 3 considers the possible impact of lobbying on representative democracy. In addition, it analyzes the particular combination of lobbying and consociationalism and the mutual reinforcement of their positive and negative characteristics. Finally, Part I wraps up with institutional, regulatory and other recommendations for the reduction of negative lobbying impact, a prerequisite for a concept of lobbying as a legitimate part of and not a threat to democracy.

1. Democracy

Though global belief in and commitment to democracy as the preferred or even only legitimate form of governance is a recent development after centuries of oligarchic, monarchic, and tyrannical rules, political actions today widely obtain legitimacy when taken within a framework of democratic rules (Fukuyama 1989, 1992, Held 1993, Schmidt 2000a). Yet, when it comes to a detailed definition of what makes up democratic governance, political theory and practice and empirical analytic approaches to it have generated diverse and sometimes contradictory models. Most authors agree only that there is no agreed definition of democracy; »the diversity of elements involved in the idea of a self-governing community is sufficient to ensure that ideas of democracy are many and various« (Hindess 1991: 191).

Over time so many issues and open questions have been attached to the concept of democracy that it has become hard to identify possible core elements or cornerstones of such a concept. These issues include among others the reconciliation of individual freedom and self-determination with the need for community imposed rules and order, the question of the boundaries of a democracy, i.e., of its *demos*, the balance between participation and representation, and questions centering around the legitimacy and shortcomings of majority rule.[2] At the same time, there exists the need for many authors to attempt a definition in the form of normative principles which may guide an institutional and organizational outlook on modern democracies:

[…] democracy will be defined as a form of government characterized by political equality […] democracy in this sense will be justified by the principle of personal autonomy […] An attempt will be made to deduce organizational consequences from this principle. (Midgaard 1998: 193)

---

2 For an in-depth discussion of these and further issues surrounding the concept of democracy and a comparison of different schools of theory see Abromeit (2002).

Others again chose to employ empirical comparative models as starting points of analysis in lieu of a normative model. Instead of selecting a set of democratic principles from the different schools of theory, the empirical comparative approach examines existing systems and designs comparative models through the systematization of observed characteristics.

Both the normative and the empirical approach have their advantages and disadvantages in the definition and analysis of democratic governance. A normative model defining cornerstones or core elements does not limit the outlook in the relativistic manner of which empirical models are often accused (Schneider 2000: 261). However, the shortcomings of an empirical model can also constitute its strengths since the experiences of existing systems in different developmental stages hold valuable information for the analysis of a related system.

Chapters 1.1 and 1.2 use both a normative and a comparative empirical approach to define, on the one hand, cornerstones of democratic governance which can later inform a discussion of the alleged democratic deficits of the European Union and, on the other hand, to outline a comparative empirical model with which to develop a substantial outlook on the EU system and its possible mid-term perspectives. The normative approach is minimalist in the sense that it tries to draw only basic and more or less agreed principles from the different schools of democratic theory. The empirical model systematizes the debate on consociational democracy as the form lending itself most clearly to a comparison with the existing system of the European Union.

Chapter 1.3 presents an excursus on the question of democracy beyond the boundaries of a nation-state. The goal here is to examine and justify the use of principles and models in the analysis of a supranational system such as the EU. Is it possible to simply transfer principles, models, and experiences? What deviations are to be expected and what characteristics remain valid?

1.1 Cornerstones of democratic governance – a normative model

Political theory since Aristotle has spanned a multiplicity of ideas concerning the ideal system of social organization and has been based on a range of concepts of human nature. While it cannot be my goal here to produce an even synoptic review, it should be possible to draw from some of these writings a set of principles or cornerstones able to define a democratic system by which modern governance might be analyzed.

Democracy theory generally chooses as its starting point the individual and the basic rights assigned each individual. From these are derived the two basic principles underlying most all concepts of democracy since Aristotle: Freedom of self-determination and political equality.[3] The first principle is both the foundation and the limitation of popular sovereignty, the second leads to the concept of universal suffrage and majority rule; though what defines a majority and which role minority rights play remains open to debate.[4]

While the principles of freedom of self-determination and political equality have remained constants in the historical evolution of democracy theories, developments such as the enlargement of territories or growing social, technological, and other complexities have caused shifts in other basic assumptions on democratic governance. One major shift is that from the understanding of democracy as a mainly direct, participatory governance system to the recognition of the need for a system of territorial (and functional) representation.[5] Such a shift from participation to representation brings with it the question of how to ensure the preservation of political equality. A representative system has to ensure a satisfactory implementation of the principles of self-determination and political equality. The two key factors leading to a reconciliation of the two basic principles with the idea of representation are those of authorization and accountability of the representatives. This entails free, fair, and frequent elections, process

---

3 These principles of democracy can be found in Aristotle's *Politics*, Book VI Chapter 2 (1994). For general agreement on the two basic principles of freedom and equality see, among others, Held (1993), Dahl (1998), Hindess (1991), Midgaard (1998), Abromeit (2002), Schmidt (2000a), Offe (1972, 1996), Fishkin (1997).

4 For a comprehensive argument why majority rule – understood as simple majority – is not required for democratic process see Dahl (1989).

5 Some authors go as far as to dismiss participatory possibilities altogether. For instance, Held who lists three basic variants of democracy (direct/participatory democracy, liberal/representative democracy, and one-party democracy) dismisses the possibility of direct/participatory democracy as a variant unable to succeed in circumstances of »social, economic and political differentiation« (1993: 223). He praises liberal representative democracy for having solved the dilemma between sovereign power and its limits vis-à-vis its members by introducing citizen equality and representation.

transparency and formality allowing citizens access to all information in order to make informed decisions.

However, even in modern mass democracies citizen participation is seldom confined to regular elections. The degree to which participation is to be extended beyond the election cycle is strongly debated. Liberal democracy theory generally agrees that representative governance – and with it the rule of reason – is desirable both for purely practical reasons as well as for reasons of moderation and avoidance of tyranny of the majority. While to such authors as Locke and J. S. Mill participation remained a core element of democratic governance (Locke 1966, orig. 1689, Mill 1971, orig. 1861), the authors of the *Federalist Papers* indeed preferred a system of representation limiting participation. Its advantages were seen in the possibilities of deliberation (of the representatives) and the avoidance of tyranny of the majority; however, the anti-federalists criticized such a system for its lack of equality and participation (Fishkin 1997). The so-called empirical or realist school of modern democracy theory limits citizen participation even more explicitly to participation in elections:[6]

Democracy does not mean and cannot mean that the people actually rule in any obvious sense of the terms »people« and »rule«. Democracy means only that the people have the opportunity of accepting or refusing the men who are to rule them. [...] The voters outside of parliament must respect the division of labor between themselves and the politicians they elect [..] they must understand that, once they have elected an individual, political action is his business and not theirs. (Schumpeter 2000, orig. 1942: 284f, 295)

Any system that does not limit opportunities of citizen participation to elections, where political equality might be secured through the principle of »one man, one vote«, has to take into account possible inequalities in political participation beyond elections. Participation between elections includes activities as an individual, a member of an interest group, a member of a political party, etc. Political inequalities can arise through unequal access to (political) resources. As Dahl and others point out, this is the paradox presented by liberal democracies that flourish best when paired up with modern market economy. Whilst political governance is based on

---

6 For a discussion see Hindess (1991: 179) and Abromeit (2002: 90ff). Apart from classical liberal theory and empirical realist theory of democracy, Abromeit examines a third school, that of deliberative democracy theory. Since its main focus lies well beyond the simple question of representation and on the communication and self-organization of (civil) society, the interested reader is referred to Abromeit (2002: 100ff).

equality, modern market economy leads to economic and, therefore, often to political inequality, i.e., unequal access to political resources (Dahl 1998, Schneider 2000). Thus, there is not only a balance to be struck between participation and representation, between self-determination and representation but also between political equality and participation.

Representation is not the only major topic debated as to its role in a concept of democracy. Another balance that authors try to establish is between the principle of self-determination and the concept of social justice and welfare. One key term here is that of the common good. As such, the common good is examined in the context of interest groups in Chapter 2.1. Presently, the discussion is briefly broadened from the idea of social welfare and the common good to the idea of general political output – an expression coined by Scharpf in his »model of a political system that takes in political *inputs* (notably articulated interests) from its societal environment and turns them into political *outputs* (notably binding decisions)« (1970: 21, own translation).

Scharpf's model separates concepts of democracy into two parts, input legitimacy and output-legitimacy. The input-oriented theories look at the design of the political system and processes which receive and process political input; the system is then judged by the fairness and openness of this process. Output theories, in contrast, judge the system by its outputs, the effectiveness and efficiency with which demands for social and economic performance are fulfilled (1970: 24f, 1999). While the idea of separating concepts into these two parts might have been new at the time, the notion of democratic governance having to supply the democratic framework for political decision-making and to achieve acceptable results was not. The classic definition of a democracy provided by Lincoln in his Gettysburg address of a »government of the people, by the people, for the people« (1995, orig. 1863) has been used by many as a base for their definition of democracy. Scharpf himself quotes this definition (1999: 16).

The three parts of Lincoln's definition, 1) government of the people, 2) for the people, and 3) by the people, can be subsumed under the individual concepts of *identity* (the existence of a somewhat united people), *political input* and *political output*. Those who use this definition might test a democracy to see whether there is a people, whether the decision-makers have been authorized by and are accountable to the people, and whether decisions reflect the people's wishes and needs, possibly described as the common good.

Table 2: Conceptual dissection of Lincoln's definition of democracy

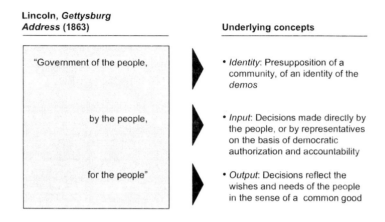

Lincoln, *Gettysburg Address* (1863)	Underlying concepts
"Government of the people,	• *Identity*: Presupposition of a community, of an identity of the *demos*
by the people,	• *Input*: Decisions made directly by the people, or by representatives on the basis of democratic authorization and accountability
for the people"	• *Output*: Decisions reflect the wishes and needs of the people in the sense of a common good

Source: Lincoln (1995, orig. 1863), in parts suggested by Scharpf (1970)

Two of many authors whose concepts fit quite well into this systematization are Lord and Schneider. Lord demands »certain tests that *any* democratic system will have to satisfy, even if it is entirely reasonable for answers to be conditioned by values and constraints defined in a historical context« (1998: 15). He suggests the terms authorization, representation, accountability, and identity to circumscribe his tests. While authorization through elections and accountability through transparency and election cycles are empirically confirmable, representation in the form of decisions for the common good and identity of the people are less easily decided, and judgement has to be based on qualitative observations. Similar conclusions can be reached for Schneider's criteria of equality of vote, authorization, accountability, and common good orientation; there seems to exist no way of definitive measurement, especially for the last. Rather, as Schneider himself remarks, the criteria rely on qualitative evaluations of governance situations (2000: 258ff).

The concept of identity is new to the discussion; it is more closely examined in Chapter 1.3 with its excursus on democracy beyond the nation-state and, thus, beyond the customary boundaries of national or state identity. At this point suffice it to say that an identity of the people in the strict sense of a unified community does not function as a cornerstone of the concept of democratic governance used in this work. In short, the argument explored in Chapter 1.3 sees the identity of a *demos* not as a static given in a democratic system but instead as a dimension that develops and changes in quality over time. To make a fully developed *demos* a prerequisite would negate the possibility of democracy in more heterogeneous societies.

As to the output criteria suggested above – e.g., Lord's representation or Schneider's common good orientation – it has already been remarked that it is highly improbable that the results of political process can be measured as to their common good realization (see also discussion of the concept in Chapter 2.1). Even if it were possible to measure and judge political output, is output-legitimacy sufficient for the definition of democratic governance? Would a system that is by no means a democracy when it comes to political input, i.e., not a government »by the people«, be called a democracy due to its realization of certain goals »for the people«? And thirdly: Is it necessary to require an output dimension for a definition of democracy? A clear design of the political system, of institutions and processes, on the input side should ensure the democratic character of the system's output. In this light, democratic output-legitimacy or »government for the people« appears neither a possible, nor a necessary or, even less, a sufficient criteria for the definition of democratic governance.

Having dismissed both »government of the people« and »government for the people« as parts of a definition of democracy, the cornerstones of democratic governance suggested in this work concentrate on the so-called political input, the »government by the people«. The approach is both high level and minimalist. It considers the demands which the basic principles of freedom of self-determination and of political equality have vis-à-vis a representative system and leaves aside several issues, e.g., majority rule, which instead is picked up by the empirical comparative model in Chapter 1.2. The following cornerstones serve as a normative standard in the analysis of the political system of the European Union in particular with regard to its alleged democratic deficit and its interface with interest group lobbying:

–   Equality of vote
–   Equality of voice: Equal influence on representatives and decision-making during terms, equal participation opportunities, proportional representation of interests in important non-elected bodies

- Authorization: Election of key representative bodies, election of further bodies by those directly authorized
- Accountability: Control of representatives through process transparency and formality, regular election cycles.[7]

Table 3: Cornerstones of democratic governance in a representative system

Political equality	Freedom of self-determination

1. Equality of vote	3. Authorization
2. Equality of voice	• Election of representatives
• Equal influence and participation opportunities	• Election of further bodies by those directly authorized
• Proportional representation in important non-elected political bodies, e.g., commissions and committees	4. Accountability
	• Process transparency and formality
	• Regular election cycles

Source: Own framework

1.2 Comparative model of consociational democracy

Comparative political theory has identified several pairs of political systems that lend themselves to empirical and analytical examination, such as presidential versus parliamentary democracy (Steffani 1979). Depending on the pair selected the emphasis of examination may lie on different systemic features – institutions, processes, etc. One such pair is competitive versus consociational democracy (Lehmbruch 1969, Lijphart 1993) or majority-

---

7 With a few differences it is possible to map Dahl's defining criteria of a democratic system to the four cornerstones suggested here. He lists equality of voting, inclusion of all adults, opportunity for effective participation, possibility to gain enlightened understanding, and exercising final control over the agenda (1998).

rule versus consensus democracy as Lijphardt calls this pair in some of his works (Lijphart 1999, Lijphart et al. 1991). As the terms indicate, this pair lends itself in particular to the analysis of decision-making processes and of the accommodation of societal segments or interest groups. The following introduces the model of consociational democracy to the reader and clarifies the reasons for using it as a comparative empirical backdrop to the system of the European Union.

The revival of the term consociational democracy and the development of its present-day meaning has at least two independent sources in the late 1960s: Gerhard Lehmbruch and Arend Lijphart both presented their ideas on stable non-majoritarian systems at the 1967 Brussels Congress of the International Political Science Association (Lijphart 1968, Lehmbruch 1974).[8] What Lehmbruch first called *Proporzdemokratie* – proportional democracy – in his analysis of the Swiss and the Austrian political systems, he later renamed *Konkordanzdemokratie* (lat. *concordantia* – agreement, concord) or consociational democracy (1969, 1975). Another term which is used synonymously in Lehmbruch's works is *Verhandlungsdemokratie*, negotiatory or bargaining democracy (1996). Similarly, Lijphart's works use a variety of terms to describe the same concept, e.g., consensus democracy, consociational democracy. The latter term is most common to literature of political science and sociology in English while *Konkordanzdemokratie* and *Verhandlungsdemokratie* are the most common in German literature – and consociational democracy is therefore used here.[9]

As pointed out above consociational democracy is joined in a comparative pair with majority-rule democracy. The latter was long believed to be the only legitimate form of democratic rule, embodied in the Anglo-American systems of Great Britain and the United States.[10] Lijphart's empirical studies show a growing degree of majoritarianism with the pres-

---

8 See several sources on the two authors' independence and simultaneity (McRae 1974, Czada et al. 1993, Czada 2000).

9 Though the terms are conveniently called synonymous here, McRae has pointed out that the choice in terms points to the authors' emphasis of different aspects of the political system such as social structure, processes of (elite) decision-making, and historical circumstances of political culture (McRae 1974: 5f).

10 Pluralist theory of the late 1960s (e.g., Almond et al. 1966) argued that only majoritarian democracies whose competitive procedures mirrored modern market economy processes could achieve sustainable stability. This required a more or less homogenous and secularized political culture and stands in stark contrast to models of consociational democracy.

ence of Anglo-American political culture and traditions (e.g., Lijphart 1984: 221); he interchangeably uses the terms majoritarian and Westminster model without agreeing with the argument for exclusive legitimacy (Lijphart 1999). The most commonly cited examples of consociational democracies have been four smaller countries on the European continent: Switzerland, Austria, Belgium, and the Netherlands.

While more majoritarian models appear to develop in countries with a relatively homogeneous society in terms of ethnic, cultural, religious or economic background, consociational democracies occur in settings where society is segmented along ethnic, religious, or other lines and interchange between different segments, e.g., behavior such as *Wechselwahlverhalten* (cross-voting), is rare. Consociational democracy – as Bogaards points out – »originated as a deviant case from pluralist theory which held that political stability was impossible in societies characterized by mutually reinforcing cleavages, i.e., segments, instead of cross-cutting cleavages« (1998: 489) or overlapping memberships which are at the center of pluralist democracy. Some authors have therefore also spoken of consociationalism as segmented pluralism (Lorwin 1974).

Lijphart lists the characteristics of consociational democracy and the factors favorable to its establishment which were the findings of several empirical studies of democracies around the world (1993, 1999, Lijphart et al. 1991). The principle characteristics describe a quasi-federal and – where possible – decentralized system of political decision-making that accommodates autonomous segments with proportional power allocation including veto rights:
–   Shared decision-making in matters of common concern,
–   Autonomous decision-making on all other issues,
–   Proportionality of political representation, civil service appointments, and allocation of public funds, and
–   A minority veto for the protection of minority interests.
Lehmbruch (1992) lists many of the same or similar characteristics, which classify a consociational democracy. In addition he also mentions
–   All-party coalitions in government[11] and
–   Proportional access to public mass media.
In Lijphart's classification democracies move on a continuum between the ideal models of consociational versus majoritarian democracy or, as he

---

11 Basically, this constitutes an institutionalized form of Lijphart's shared decision-making.

suggests in *Patterns of Democracy* (1999), democracies can be located in a matrix of »federal-unitary« and »executives-parties« dimensions.[12] This helps to explain why Sweden has been termed a bargaining and consensus democracy (Stenelo et al. 1996, Sannerstedt 1996). Although Sweden is clearly a unitary state without autonomous societal segments, it has also developed a tradition of parliamentary bargaining and the corresponding committees.[13] Despite the mixture of majoritarian and consociational elements in political practice, shared decision-making, proportional power allocation, and minority rights should characterize a system to be termed clearly consociational. In this sense Lehmbruch agrees that,

generally, one only characterizes such systems as consociational democracies in which important decision-making processes on the level of central government are ruled by the principle of amicable agreement (amicabilis compositio), formally or informally through agreements outside parliament. (1992: 208, own translation)

The above characterizes and classifies an existing consociational democracy. In addition, there are factors favoring its establishment and preservation. Lijphart and other authors after him identified such factors, several or all of which seem to have favored the development and maintenance of consociational democracy over majoritarian democracy in many countries (e.g., Switzerland and Belgium) and enabled the establishment of democratic rule in societies heretofore regarded as rather adverse to it (e.g., Colombia, Malaysia). These factors include absence of a majority segment, absence of large socioeconomic inequalities, segments of similar size, small population, foreign threats,[14] (national) loyalties spanning all segments, and consensus traditions – the last point meaning in particular the willingness

---

12 Tsebelis has suggested another classification through the calculation of what he calls veto players. Again, political systems move on a continuum of few versus many veto-players affecting political decision-making (1995).

13 In the case of Sweden, Tsebelis, too, sees a unitary political system that for the sake of increased policy stability chooses to include addititional veto-players such as the unions (308).

14 However, Lehmbruch points out that the survival of a consociationl democracy is more probable if foreign policy loads remain small and do not weigh too heavily on internal conflicts, e.g., if the state can remain neutral on the international scene. For him this is a possible explanation as to why consociational democracy is more sustainable and mostly found in small countries (Lehmbruch 1969, 1975). Daalder, on the other hand, debates this statement as to whether small country means small load in international politics and instead suggests that many small European consociational democracies survived because consociationalism taught them how to handle foreign imposed loads (1971: 369f).

of the segments' elites to cooperate. Lijphart even called this elite cooperation »the essential characteristic of consociational democracy« (1968: 21).

The key role of elite cooperation has been emphasized by most authors and might be explained by the following: While the above list of favorable factors in general speaks of socio-political determinism,[15] the factor of elite cooperation assigns an active role to the elites – a role they assume when there are no or only lower benefits to be achieved from majoritarian strategies (Lehmbruch 1992: 210). So while Lijphart claims that in several examples – Austria, the Netherlands, and Luxembourg – the model worked so well that the need for consociationalism declined and the system moved to a more majoritarian model,[16] Lehmbruch has remarked »that continued existence of fundamental cleavages is not an absolute condition for the persistence of [consociational democracy]« (1974: 94) when elites choose to uphold political segmentation and cartelized decision-making.

Benefits, however, reach beyond society's elites. One main advantage is consociational democracy's ability to integrate a large variety of societal groups into a political system and process that, partly as a result of this integration, reaches a high level of acceptance and government stability (Luthardt 1997). Scharpf goes even further to say that the logic of consociational democracy – when fully realized – not only integrates all groups into one »collective self« but also distributes political responsibility so that any negotiation leads to the best possible results and its participants are not split into »winners and losers« but instead all groups »win« (Scharpf 1993).[17] In summary, the benefits can be subsumed under system stability, problem solving, and policy formation powers.

Interestingly, a list of consociational democracy's disadvantages would include the same points. The main point of criticism is a claimed low effectiveness and efficiency of the decision-making process and a weak ability to quickly adjust to new problems (Luthardt 1997, Abromeit 1993). Instead, there is a strong bias towards the status quo (some call it policy

---

15 For a detailed critic of the so-called favorable factors in writings of political and social science dealing with consociational democracy and their deterministic and voluntaristic implications see Boogards (1998).

16 Compare also Lorwin who sees the success of consociationalism as partly responsible for its decline in the Netherlands (1974: 57).

17 He underlines his idea of the collective self by pointing to the logic of pluralist theory and its »overlapping membership« and »potential groups« (Bentley 1908, Truman 1951) – a point many would dispute who see the main difference between consociationalism and pluralism in the former's lack of overlapping memberships.

stability). Policy stability, in turn, is said to destabilize government (Tsebelis 1995). This paradox of system advantages also being system disadvantages could explain why some see consociational democracy as feasible mainly for newly formed systems that profit from its potential for conflict resolution and stability and – as a *Schönwettersystem* (good-weather system) – for old, saturated systems that can allow themselves the luxury of slow decision-making (Abromeit 1993: 177).

Lijphart has continuously compared the effectiveness of consociational and majoritarian democracies concerning macroeconomic factors such as unemployment and rate of inflation. Contrary to the critics, he has come to the conclusion that

the evidence with regard to economic growth and economic freedom is mixed, but with regard to all the other indicators of economic performance [unemployment, strike activity, budget deficits], the consensus democracies have a slightly better record and a significantly better record as far as inflation is concerned. (1999: 270)

More recently, these findings have been contested. Anderson shows that the positive development of inflation and unemployment in consociational democracies can be exclusively attributed to two factors: the presence of an independent central bank and a high level of corporatism.[18] However, he strongly questions the integration of these two factors into a measure of consociationalism (2001: 443ff). The question of corporatism versus pluralism as the system of interest intermediation in consociational democracy is discussed in Chapter 1.2.1.

Another point of criticism launched at consociational democracy is that of the domination of political processes by elites. This is said to lead to the frustration of the ordinary citizen, who lacks the »functional channels for the articulation of dissent«, and it is also responsible for a lower learning capacity of the system which receives less feedback (Steiner 1974: 104). According to Abromeit this aspect of elite cartels can be ameliorated by the implementation of »mass-participatory valves« such as referenda or the Swiss *Verfassungsinitiative* (constitutional initiative) and the principle of subsidiarity (1993: 183). Yet, with or without the possibilities of mass participation, consociational democracies tend towards low election turn-

---

18 To Lijphart both of these are defining characteristics of consociational democracies as opposed to a dependent central bank and pluralism in majoritarian democracies (1999: 3f).

outs,[19] a good indicator for what Lorwin calls »a peculiar blend of democracy and elite decision making [...] of *leadership and passivity*« (1974: 51).

Frustration is also experienced by the elites who have to translate a co-operative result into a zero-sum game for their political group and often find legitimation only in the show of power, e.g., strikes (Scharpf 1993). At the heart of these frustrations lies the intransparency of many negotiatory systems – often needed to reach results but harmful to democratic legitimation. Intransparency and informality are main characteristics of the many committees, which have acquired key roles in consociational democracies as negotiatory bodies[20] and often include not only political representatives but also technical experts and representatives of special interest groups.

Table 4: Advantages and disadvantages of consociational democracy

⊕	⊖
• Political stability in segmented, heterogeneous societies	• Policy immobilism, conservative/status-quo bias
• Conflict resolution/problem solving capacities	• System instability due to limited crisis reaction capacities
• Accommodation of segment autonomy	• Elite domination and citizen passivity/frustration
• Strong protection of minority rights	• Intransparency and informality of decision-making process
• Proportionality of interest representation in institutions, processes, and decisions	• Intransparent and often informal integration of special interests
• Policy stability	

Source: Compiled from Abromeit 1993, Anderson 2001, Daalder 1971, Lijphart 1993, 1999, Lijphart et. al. 1991, Lorwin 1974, Luthhard 1997, Scharpf 1993, Steiner 1974, Waschkuhn 1998

---

19 On this topic see, e.g., Abromeit (1993: 185) and Waschkuhn (1998: 446).
20 »The typical consociational devices in these democracies are the advisory councils and committees, which, in spite of their very limited formal powers, often have decisive influence« (Lijphart 1974: 77).

The above lists of praises and criticisms of consociational democracy identify obvious areas of strengths and weaknesses. These can be further systematized by a comparison of the empirical model with the four cornerstones (equality of vote and of voice, authorization, and accountability) defined in the normative discussion in Chapter 1.1. What is revealed by a mapping of the model for consociational democracy onto the democratic cornerstones? How does the trade-off between, on the one hand, the proportional representation of heterogeneous interests and, on the other, the informality and lack of transparency of the decision-making process affect political equality, in vote and voice, and the freedom of self-determination ensured by the authorization and accountability of representative bodies?

The basic principle of political equality was said to be ensured both by the equality of vote and the equality of voice. Preference for unanimity in decision-making and autonomy in areas that do not touch common interest score positively with these cornerstones: Minority votes are not lost in majority decisions but are proportionally heard, the consideration of all interests is institutionalized, and minority interests are accommodated in areas of autonomous rule and subsidiarity. Yet, political equality is frustrated by the domination of elites in the political process as well as by the inclusion of non-elected decision-makers. If this inclusion is unbalanced in the sense that certain special interests are disproportionately represented, the equality of voice can be negatively affected.[21]

The basic principle of freedom of self-determination is provided for in the two cornerstones of authorization and accountability. In general these cornerstones are satisfied in a system of consociational democracy – as in any other democratic system – by the election of representatives and their accountability to the voter in regular election cycles. However, intransparency, informality, and negotiations in non-elected bodies, such as committees including special interest representatives, score badly in the area of accountability: Decisions cannot be traced to the decision-makers which means these cannot be controlled by the public; in some cases the proportionality system does not even allow for corrections in regular election

---

21 On the risks for political equality Schneider is very explicit: »The inherent selectivity of bargaining and negotiatory arrangements and the disregard of the rule of political equality is very problematic. Only such actors are included that command relevant resources« (2000: 260, own translation).

cycles as in the case of the Swiss *Zauberformel*.[22] Authorization is similarly affected by the inclusion of non-elected persons in crucial stages of decision-making.

While political equality is particularly emphasized by the proportional representation in a consociational system, freedom of self-determination is negatively affected by the informality and intransparency of the decision-making process as is political equality where an elite negotiatory system dominates. Some deficits are obviously inherent in the consociational process of decision-making; they are further aggravated by the inclusion of non-elected players, e.g., representatives of interest groups, into the system. This receives special attention in Chapter 3 where the possibilities and limitations of interest intermediation in a democratic system with consociational traits are examined.

1.2.1 Corporatism and consociational democracy

Interest intermediation is common to all models of modern democracy. Consociational democracy, however, is often said to possess a special form of interest intermediation: corporatism. While it is taken up in depth in Chapter 2.2, a short look at corporatism as the system of interest intermediation in consociational democracy is helpful at this point.[23]

Corporatism is most commonly explained in comparison with or in opposition to pluralism as a form of interest intermediation in a political system. There are those that claim it as a mere »variant of democratic pluralism« (Dahl 1993: 706), »a variety of pluralism – to be distinguished from a more disaggregated competitive variety of pluralism at one extreme, and a state-controlled variety at the other« (Almond 1983: 251). Authors in-

---

22 The *Zauberformel* has frozen the proportional distribution of seats in every *Bundesrat* to a static 2-2-2-1 (FDP-CVP-SP-SVP) independent from the outcome of elections (Abromeit 1993: 184).

23 The question might arise as to the difference between the terms interest intermediation and the more commonly used interest representation, which here is used mainly in Part II in the context of the EU. Though the two terms are often used synonymously, interest intermediation insists on a more active role of interest groups in organizing interest organization and articulation and is used by advocates of corporatism to differentiate it from pluralist interest representation (Streeck 1994: 12). In the case of this work, however, an evaluative differentiation is not intended and interest intermediation is simply used in any context dealing with corporatism.

volved in the renaissance of corporatist theory and study claim the two to be – in their pure forms – rival labels, while in political practice interest associations may well operate in both fashions depending on the negotiatory partner (Schmitter 1993: 196). For the sake of this work it is important to keep in mind these relativistic tendencies observed in political practice while recognizing clear-cut differences emphasized between the two in their theoretical conceptions.[24]

Though it has been often debated since its first publication in 1974, Schmitter's juxtaposition of pluralism and corporatism is a helpful starting point for a definition of terms. The following table groups the characteristics proposed by Schmitter into a numerical, a structural, and a state-related dimension:

Table 5: Schmitter's juxtaposed concepts of interest representation through corporatism and pluralism

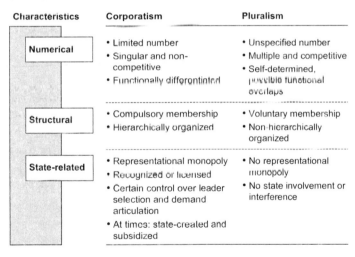

Characteristics	Corporatism	Pluralism
Numerical	• Limited number • Singular and non-competitive • Functionally differentiated	• Unspecified number • Multiple and competitive • Self-determined, possible functional overlaps
Structural	• Compulsory membership • Hierarchically organized	• Voluntary membership • Non-hierarchically organized
State-related	• Representational monopoly • Recognized or licensed • Certain control over leader selection and demand articulation • At times: state-created and subsidized	• No representational monopoly • No state involvement or interference

Source: Adapted from Schmitter 1979

To sum up and elaborate on the above table, corporatism is characterized by an institutionalization of interest intermediation, an official incorpora-

---

24 In practice, systems of interest intermediation and the operations of individual groups within might best be categorized along a continuum with the ideal forms of pluralism and corporatism representing its opposite ends. Some authors would, however, object to this since they see the two systems as discontinuous rather than porous (e.g., Marques-Pereira 1998).

tion into state-moderated or state-initiated processes. The official character partly necessitates other corporatist characteristics which help simplify such processes, i.e., the »limited number of singular, compulsory, noncompetitive, hierarchically ordered and functionally differentiated categories« (Schmitter 1979: 13) of interest groups. Particular to such corporatist arrangements is a trilateral character best known through processes of wage bargaining in which the state typically assumes the role of a moderator between the conflicting parties of labor and capital. In an ideal corporatist system this trilateralism goes well beyond simple wage bargaining and is seen as a system of class relations able to negotiate »structural changes in the economy« (Lehmbruch 1979a: 61) with the historical – though failed – precedent of the German *Konzertierte Aktion* in the 1960s.

Clearly, corporatism and consociational democracy share defining characteristics such as elite cooperation, societal segmentation restricting overlapping membership, and a preference for bargaining versus competitive, majoritarian processes of decision-making. Lehmbruch speaks of a »structural isomorphy« (1979a: 59) and points out mutually reinforcing experiences and learnings in consociational and corporatist processes. While he states that extreme examples of corporatism can be found in consociational democracies, Lehmbruch does not go as far as Lijphart to say that corporatism is a defining feature of consociational democracy:

> Our main hypothesis is that corporatism is the interest group system that goes together with the consensual [consociational] type of democracy and that its opposite, the »pluralist« interest group system, goes together with majoritarian democracy. (Lijphart et al. 1991: 235)

Lijphart and Crepaz's study goes on to show that in accounting for the existence of corporatism 22 percent of the variance is explained by the prevailing type of democracy – consociational democracy favoring corporatism.[25]

---

25 Altogether the study finds two main explanations for the existence of corporatism. The regression procedure yields a 53 percent explanation of the variance through the dominant tendency in government – social democratic dominance favoring corporatism – and a 22 percent explanation through the type of democracy – consociational favoring corporatism. All other variables analyzed add only insignificant explanation (Lijphart et al. 1991: 244). A later answer to criticism launched against their incorporation of corporatism into the concept of consociational democracy reinforces and elaborates on the arguments (Crepaz et al. 1995: 285f).

Lane and Ersson, after their examination of several quantitative studies including Lijphart and Crepaz's, come to the conclusion that corporatism »is neither a sufficient nor a necessary condition for Konkordanzdemokratie« (1997: 14).[26] Instead they see the two as simply sharing a characteristic notion of power distribution. When it comes to sources of support and policy outputs, consociational democracy and corporatism differ considerably. While the first is supported by centrist governments and favors higher market allocation and slightly lower redistributive public spending, the latter is supported by left governments and favors allocative state programs and redistributive public spending (Lane et al. 1997: 16, 18). Anderson follows a similar line of argument when he says:

Regardless of whether elite-level behavior is sufficient justification for integrating corporatism into consensus democracy, it is clear that institutionally, the two are not similar. The political institutions of consensus democracy involve the systematic disaggregation of political interests; indeed, the more consensual the system by Lijphart's measure, the more fragmented. Corporatism meanwhile, entails extreme aggregation of societal interests. (2001: 444f)

Czada, too, supports Lane and Ersson's view that consociational democracy and corporatism are alternatives rather than complementaries. He describes consociationalism, corporatism, and joint decision-making (*Politikverflechtung*) as three dimensions or expressions of *Verhandlungsdemokratie*, i.e., bargaining democracy (Czada 2000, 2002, 2003).[27] In parts, Czada's differentiation between consociational democracy and bargaining democracy lies in a slightly different use of terms; he takes consociational democracy and splits it into executive concordance/consociationalism and legislative or federal joint decision-making. Yet, he makes an important point when emphasizing that corporatism and a weak government cancel each other out since corporatism relies on a strong state counterpart to ensure its associational cohesion and monopoly (2000: 14). To Czada it is in particular joint decision-making which results in governmental weak-

26 On this point see also Reutter who states that one should not conclude as Lijphart has done that corporatism is only found in consociational democracies and pluralism only in majoritarian ones (2001: 21).

27 Yet another systematization of these terms can be found in Abromeit or Lehner who both arrange them along a continuum or axis where »the continuation and completion of federal and corporatist principles is concordance [consociationalism]« (Abromeit 1993: 177, own translation) or where corporatism lies between the extremes of pluralism and concordance (Lehner 1986: 153f).

ness. However, both joint decision-making and executive concordance, a government relying on the mechanisms of consociationalism, do not seem to provide the governmental strength and unity prescribed for a functioning of corporatism.

In summary, it has become clear that an examination of a consociational democracy is well advised not to make biased assumptions as to its system of interest intermediation. Theory of interest intermediation is again taken up in Chapter 4.2, which deals further with the relationship of pluralism and corporatism important for a classification of the EU system of interest intermediation.

1.3 Democracy beyond the nation-state

In Part II of this work the democratic cornerstones and the consociational model introduced in Chapters 1.1 and 1.2, based mainly on the experiences of modern nation-state democracies, are applied to the reality of the EU system. This makes it necessary to contemplate the possibilities and limitations that may crop up when applying concepts, which normally presuppose a nation-state, to a supranational, non-state system.

To begin with, it should be pointed out that the idea and experience of transposing the concept of democracy from a smaller onto a larger scale political system is by no means a historical first. Dahl indeed calls the present European and global transformation the third transformation (1989: 317ff). He counts first a transformation from nondemocracy to the city-state democracies of Greece, Rome, and medieval and Renaissance Italy, then a second transformation from city-scale to nation-state democracies. A transformation that increased both the size and the heterogeneity of the people had been ruled out before by such writers as Rousseau and Montesquieu to whom small scale and homogeneity represented the base for a sustainable polity (Schmidt 2000a: 438). However, while stating the disadvantages of the second transformation, Dahl insists that they are clearly outweighed by the advantages and opportunities of democracy on a larger scale:

Even while the second transformation drastically reduced the opportunities for direct political participation in the decisions of the national government, and virtually eliminated prospects that all citizens might be committed to a harmonious vision of the common good, it prodigiously increased the number of people who lived within a common legal and constitutional system and enjoyed a comprehensive body of equal rights. (1989: 318)

The opportunities of yet a third transformation, this time from a nation-state to a transnational scale, are less convincing in their probable realization since transnational political structures and what Dahl calls consciousness are seen as weak and a transformation onto a scale and quality beyond the nation-state might be neither sustainable nor democratic. This raises the question as to what role concepts of state, nation, and identity – similar to Dahl's term consciousness – play in creating and nurturing a democratic polity.

Historically, democracy is seen as embedded in the state as guarantor of the individual's rights. The Westphalian state system limits power and makes it accountable to the people thus enabling the trust and solidarity necessary as a social base for democracy.[28] Legitimacy and sovereignty are bound to a definite territory. Matláry differentiates between state-based and nation-based legitimacy claiming that state-based definitions have been favored but that this is gradually changing:

Nationhood appears to have become more important than statehood as the basis of legitimate government, although regions basing their claim to sovereignty on ethnicity have so far only been semi-recognized by their own and other states. Yet the European Union represents an area for making such claims. (1995: 108)

However, many authors make no clear differentiation between the concepts of state and nation. Others chose to speak of the nation-state as the *locus* of stable democracy. To them this includes a dimension seen as prerequisite to democracy which they in turn call identity (Fukuyama 1992, Lord 1998), consciousness (Dahl 1989), *demos* (Offe 2000, McGrew 1997), or common destiny (*Schicksalsgemeinschaft*) (Kaiser 1996).[29] It is the nation-state that is seen as providing the political system with cultural affirmation. To this effect Offe quotes Habermas: »It is only the sense of belonging to a »nation« that establishes an interrelation of solidarity between persons

---

28 For discussion of the role of the state or the nation-state and the Westphalian system for democracy see for example Kaiser (1996), Matláry (1995), McGrew (1997), Offe (2000).

29 Hindess calls it a presupposition. To him the idea of a self-governing community »presupposes identification in terms of a clear political demarcation and of population« (1991: 176).

who up to that point had been total strangers to one another« (1996: 135, translation Offe 2000).

If there is truly no democracy without a *demos* – a political identity of the people considered possible only in a national state context – where does such a *demos* originate and why is its development not possible outside a nation-state context? A strong argument can be made that the *demos* is not a given, is not the same as an *ethnos* and should not be treated as a static or maybe not even as a prerequisite but, rather, as a dimension of democracy that develops and changes over time. While it may need boundaries within which to constitute itself, it is not necessary for these to be national borders. As long as the space within which the *demos* defines itself is more or less identical to the constitutional, legal space in which government power can be made accountable to the people,[30] it is not the aspects of a nation but rather the aspects of a state which form the basis for the development of a *demos*.[31]

With the *demos* as an important component of a sustainable democratic system and the *demos* needing a defined space in which it can constitute itself and hold its representatives accountable, what are the chances of democracy in a multi-state system like the European Union or even in the current nation-states faced with globalization? Albert (1998) recognizes both a »glocalization« and a »de-territorialization« trend in what is generally described as globalization. These trends question current models of democracy requiring a territorial reference point, preferably that of a nation-state. Glocalization means a relocation of political processes to both a global and a local level whilst de-territorialization addresses the fact that territory as reference point of political and other decisions is being replaced, e.g., by functional context.

As was pointed out by Dahl's remark at the beginning of this chapter the current political structures and processes make a transformation of

---

30 Held refers to this as the direct and symmetrical correspondence between government and the governed, the accountability of all power systems (1995, 1996).

31 This view is shared – among others – by Abromeit (1998a: 33), Fukuyama (1992: 222), and Zürn (2000: 98f). The latter puts it thus: »A *demos* is not a prepolitical quantity, the result of cultural or ethnic homogeneity. On the contrary, cultural pluralism is, logically speaking, a precondition for a democratic process. […] A *demos* is thus necessary only in the sense that, in addition to the plethora of differences, a basic public-interest orientation must exist. A fully cultivated public-interest orientation, nevertheless, need not obtain [sic] from the outset. As the development of democratic nation-states has shown, community and democracy are mutually reinforcing.«

democracy onto a global level seem less possible, but with decision-making structures outpacing the usual boundaries of sovereign nation-states it appears at the same time all the more necessary.

Although the nation-state generates the relations of trust and solidarity upon which democracy and the welfare state depend, it is structurally a suboptimal formation. [...] It is politically suboptimal because it tends to priorize narrowly defined national interests over transnational interests, even to the point of accepting the collective harm of war. (Offe 2000: 69)

Different authors have argued, either out of real or theoretical necessity, for democratic models and practical solutions that work around and beyond the current embedding of democracy in the nation-state. Many such appeals for a »globalization of democracy« (McGrew 1997: 15) go beyond the scope of this work. However, suggested improvements or solutions to democratic deficits caused by a broadening of political decision-making beyond a system of nation-states can inform a model examining the European Union in particular. The following takes a look at suggested solutions counteracting the problems faced by democracy in a non-nation-state system with what may be called at the most a *demos in development*.

At first glance there are three main areas in which solutions to the lack of democracy in a political system beyond that of the nation-state are suggested. The first area of suggestions targets the supranational level and a strengthening of democracy through democratic channels which are also key to democracy on a national level; for this purpose a constitution, institutions, and parties are to be fully translated to the supranational level. The second area seems to suggest quite the opposite: democracy beyond the nation-state, where the distance between the people and their representatives has become larger, is to be revived by more channels of direct involvement for the people. The third area of possible solutions takes into account the heterogeneity of a supranational system and suggests the accommodation of pluralism through consensus decision-making, subsidiarity, and the involvement of supranational civil society in the form of NGOs (non-governmental organizations).

»The act of establishing a constitution implies not only that a legal, ordered, and limited authority of the state exists but also that a political community of the »people« exists« (Offe 2000: 64). This implies that a constitution could strengthen a supranational system by granting it a degree of unity and a status usually reserved for nation-states. It could play a part in initiating the formation of a *demos*. In the context of the EU a con-

stitution would establish a contract between the citizens instead of a contract between governments as in the current treaties (Matláry 1995: 117). In
the eyes of Offe a constitution furthermore guarantees the control of the
citizens over their representatives and the political institutions (2000: 72).
Yet, concerning the control of institutions Grande insists that in a complex
supranational system there exists, more than ever, the need for an institutional checks and balances that relieves the individual citizen of this task
(2000b: 133). At the same time it is suggested that the link between political institutions and the people can be strengthened by the existence of such
intermediaries as political parties – not national parties elected into a supranational representative body but genuine supranational political parties
that unite the people behind shared political interests that are no longer
dominated by national interests (Abromeit 1998a: 34, Zürn 2000: 107).

While some authors believe that a constitutionalization and institutionalization of the supranational system is key to closing the democracy gap,
others believe that what is needed is a step in the direction of a more direct
democracy: »The answer to the riddle of European democracy is not the
basically statist one of constitutionalisation-cum-parliamentarisation, but
the more flexible one of supplementing the European decision-making
process with various direct-democratic instruments« (Abromeit 1998a: vii).
Instruments suggested include regional vetos, sectoral vetos (in the form of
optional referenda), public petitions, and mandatory referenda in certain
areas (Abromeit 1998a: 134f).[32] These instruments are seen as having the
dual purpose both of allowing those groups most affected by supranational
decisions to be heard and have a real say in such decisions and of strengthening citizen ties beyond national boundaries by highlighting common
concerns. Another suggestion aiming at a more direct link between the
demos and the supranational system – though more in the classical sense of
parliamentarization – is that of shortening the chain of legitimation from
the citizen to the bodies on supranational levels by installing direct elections of all bodies instead of indirect delegation through national bodies
(Zürn 2000: 104).

As outlined above there is a third area of suggestions on democratizing
a supranational system which tries to account for the strong heterogeneity
within such a system. Most of its buzz words such as consensual decision-
making (Abromeit 1998b, Grande 2000b) or subsidiarity of decision-mak-

---

32 On the point of referenda see also Zürn (2000: 104ff) and Grande (2000b: 133).

ing (Abromeit 1998a, Dahl 1989) need little explaining. These suggestions
aim at locating the decisions as close as possible to those affected by them
– naturally this is not possible for all levels and areas of legislation – or in
cases where several groups are affected to encourage compromise and
problem-solving. Some authors even see non-elected bodies such as international NGOs as playing an active role in the strengthening of both functional and supranational consensual decision-making, though such options
give rise to a debate on legitimacy that is picked up in Chapter 2.

**Table 6: Challenges for and paths towards democracy and a *demos*
beyond the nation-state**

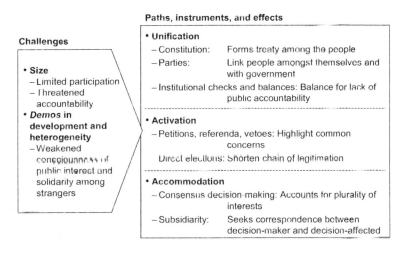

Challenges	Paths, instruments, and effects
	• **Unification**
	– Constitution: Forms treaty among the people
• **Size**	– Parties: Link people amongst themselves and with government
– Limited participation	– Institutional checks and balances: Balance for lack of public accountability
– Threatened accountability	
• ***Demos* in development and heterogeneity**	• **Activation**
– Weakened consciousness of public interest and solidarity among strangers	– Petitions, referenda, vetoes: Highlight common concerns
	Direct elections: Shorten chain of legitimation
	• **Accommodation**
	– Consensus decision-making: Accounts for plurality of interests
	– Subsidiarity: Seeks correspondence between decision-maker and decision-affected

Source: Abromeit 1998a, b, Dahl 1989, Grande 2000, Habermas 1996, Held 1995,1996, Mallàry 1995, Offe 2000, Zürn 2000

Clearly, the three areas introduced above can overlap – both unification
and activation include measures that help build a politically active people, a
demos; activation and accomodation suggest regional and functional subsidiarity, since this means both a more direct involvement of the citizen
and accommodates the heterogeneity of a supranational system. Depending on the supranational system examined, an individual mixture of different instruments might be required. This is analyzed in Part II when the so
called democratic deficit of the European Union is discussed. What this
chapter, however, makes clear is that the translation of democracy onto a
level beyond the nation-state carries very specific challenges and may well
require the development of new models of democracy and of instruments,

institutional and procedural, with which to develop and stabilize such systems in practice.

Chapter 1 introduced both a normative and a comparative empirical model of democracy. The first is built on the two underlying principles of political equality and freedom of self-determination in a representative system and consists of four so-called cornerstones of democracy ensuring the realization of the two principles. These cornerstones have been named equality of vote, equality of voice, authorization, and accountability. The second model fills the space between these cornerstones with the concept of consociational democracy. This choice is prompted by the strengths of a consociational system in view of a strongly segmented, heterogeneous society such as that of the European Union. In the third part of Chapter 1 the peculiarities of the EU were further considered in an exploration of the questions concerning a translation of democracy from a nation-state bound idea to the concept of a supranational polity.

2. Interest groups

This chapter examines the basic concepts necessary to understand interest groups and their role in a modern political system. First, an outline of the debate on interest groups in political theory and practice is given, i.e., its development from an etaistic, state-dominated, to a pluralist understanding of interest intermediation, and the key questions concerning the control and balancing of special interests are summarized. The concept of the common good and its link to important questions of interest representation are discussed as well as are the two main systems of interest intermediation, corporatism and pluralism. This is followed by a development of the basic terminology and systematics of groups to be used throughout this work. This naturally includes a basic framework of addressees, methods and resources.

»En peu de mots, le *lobbying* jouit d'une légitimité, d'autant que son exercice repose sur la *liberté* reconnue en démocratie de faire valoir ses opinions et ses intérêts« (Hudon 1998: 196). »[The] legitimacy of interest representation in our political culture stands out of question [...]« (Teuber 2001: 17, own translation). These observations are typical of many recent descriptive works on lobbying – here taken from an essay on Canadian lobbying and from the introduction to a work on interest associations and lobbying in the European Union. Lobbying has established itself as part of the modern political system. This is reflected in the use of the term »fifth power« as a synonym for lobbying (Hildebrandt 15.02.2006, Leif et al. 2003, 2006, Vowe 2003, Zick 08.10.2003). Vowe does point out that the term »fifth power« is not yet widely established as compared to the term »the fourth power« as a synonym for the press and media. However, its use has become frequent as has that of other terms that signal a certain institutionalization of lobbying and related activities in state processes. The former German Secretary of the Interior Schily coined the term »consultative« (commissions, committees, consultants) which some authors declare to be the fifth power (Bolz 27.01.2004) and which represents one of the playing fields of interest intermediation.

It is true that since the advent of modern pluralism and its systematic integration of interest groups into political theory, the idea of a purely etatistic articulation and representation of interests has been superseded by the acceptance and – for the most part – appreciation of non-state interest organization.[33] Yet, the new belief in interest intermediation and groups was accompanied by two phenomena: Firstly, the idea of a constitutional or otherwise institutionalized control of interest group activities was replaced – if at all – by purely normative appeals to the groups' subscription to the common good. Secondly, the equality of the individual's interest articulation and representation, formerly seen as resting in universal suffrage, was now assumed to be a given in interest group pluralism.

Earlier pluralists did not restrict themselves to normative appeals. One of the best known arguments for control over the power of factions, i.e, interest groups, was Madison's Federalist No. 10. »The inference to which we are brought, is, that the *causes* of faction cannot be removed; and that relief is only to be sought in the means« of controlling its *effects*« (Hamilton et al. 2003, orig. 1787–88: 54). The means of control were twofold: A system of representation was to be installed aiming at removing the decision-makers from exposure to immediate interests, enabling the chosen representatives to act independently; and a geographical dispersion of interests to be achieved through the size of the suggested republic.

Many after Madison have insisted on the importance of independent state powers, though they have been disillusioned when it comes to the possibilities of interest dispersion in a large system. Instead of weakening the influence of interest groups, mass democracies and the ensuing political apathy create power vacuums open to and easily filled by interest groups (Weber 1970: 131f). Thus, while these authors do not deny the importance of interest groups for a democratic system, they have emphasized strong state institutions removed from the influence of interest groups (Eschenburg 1955, Weber 1957, 1970, Fücks 2003).[34] Others have

---

33 As one pluralist argued against the wholesale disapproval of interest groups: »To assert that the organization and activity of powerful interest groups constitutes a threat to representative government without measuring their relation to and effects upon the widespread potential groups [i.e., unorganized interests] is to generalize from insufficient data and upon an incomplete conception of the political process« (Truman 1985: 34).

34 Eschenburg, e.g., demands a monocratic state administration which does not allow for the employment of interest group functionaries (1955).

since joined with variations on this topic, e.g., von Arnim has suggested what he calls »due-process-pluralism« in which regulation of political process ensures the independence of democratic institutions (Arnim 1977). To this he adds mass participatory components which are to serve to reinstate the sovereign (Arnim 1993, 2000).

Modern pluralism replaced arguments for a certain independence of institutions with a strongly group-centered concept of democracy.[35] The control of interests in the name of the common good was delegated to all institutions and groups involved and their expected adherence to societal norms. Hence, legitimate groups are those that acknowledge »fundamental regulative ideas of fairness and justness« (Fraenkel 1972: 181, own translation). Due to the lack of (effective) control mechanisms in his theory, Fraenkel has been accused of a *laissez-faire* pluralism. While his critics are not wrong about this gap in his theory, Schütt-Wetschky has since pointed out that Fraenkel's focus lay not on the effects of interest group activities but on a legitimate foundation of these activities (1997: 35). Fraenkel was well aware that a purely normative control would not always lead to socially just results, though he remained vague on the process of modification of such results (1973).[36]

Other pluralists' belief in the self-controlling capacities of the pluralist system went further in that they saw no need even for such modifications or corrections as Fraenkel mentioned. Truman identified two elements both of which were said to have a balancing effect on the articulation and representation of interests. »These are, first, the notion of multiple or overlapping membership and, second, the function of unorganized interests, or potential interest groups« (1951: 25). According to Truman the multiple memberships of one group's members – e.g., an individual can be a taxpayer, a parent, a union member, etc. – leads to an internal process in which each group has to reconcile its goals to a certain extent with those of other groups. Potential interest groups further reinforce political stability. They remain potential as long as the interests concerned are not violated.

---

35 Typical for this group-centered approach is Bentley's definition: »Government is the process of the adjustment of a set of interest groups in a particular distinguishable group or system« (1908: 260).

36 In a frequently cited passage Fraenkel states: »In no open society is there a guarantee that the social and economic parallelogram of power will automatically yield a result that is tolerable both to public opinion and from the point of view of social justice. It is often in need of modifications and corrections reflecting considerations which we usually term »the common good«« (1973: 339, own translation).

In the case of violation, however, they will organize to oppose and balance out such an infringement. Widely held interests of such potential groups thus function mainly as »rules of the game« (Truman 1985: 30), similar to Fraenkel's regulative ideas of fairness and justness.

The idea of overlapping membership and potential groups has been frequently adopted. Scharpf, for instance, uses the concept of overlapping membership to argue in favor of negotiatory systems of democracy; overlapping membership is said to ensure a certain degree of output satisfaction and legitimacy (Scharpf 1992). Potential interest groups have often been picked up under different names: anomic groups (Almond et al. 2004), slack resources (Dahl 1961), quasi-groups (Dahrendorf 1957), or latent groups (Olson 1965). Not all adoptions have, however, come to Truman's optimistic conclusions on the self-correcting powers of overlapping membership and potential groups in a pluralist system. Olson's application of the ideas of the new political economy and its concept of human nature to group theory leads him to believe that large groups will remain latent and ineffective if not mobilized by selective incentives:

> Indeed, unless the number of individuals in a group is quite small, or unless there is coercion or some other special device to make individuals act in their common interest, rational, self-interested individuals will not act to achieve their common or group interests. (Olson 1965: 2)

Dahl shares neither Truman's optimism nor Olson's pessimism. While arguing for the benefits of a pluralist democracy he also points out the unequal distribution of influence among individuals and among associations (1989: 195ff).[37] Others challenge the idea of overlapping membership: where it existed, it has lead to opportunism and misled adaptation (Beyme 1969: 206); where it was lacking, this has not lead to the political instability Truman predicted (Lijphart 1974).

Today, the integration of interest groups into the political system, in theory and practice, has become the norm. While the fear of factions such as expressed by Madison, Eschenburg, or Olson[38] has diminished, the need

---

37 Similarly von Arnim in his »Kritik der Gleichgewichtslehre« (criticism of the equilibrium theory) (1977).

38 In his *The Rise and Decline of Nations* (1982) Olson follows through with the implications of *The Logic of Collective Action* (1965) and concludes that interest groups will lead to the decline of stable systems which allow for the accumulation of networks of distributional coalitions (interest groups) in the first place. As the name implies, the coalitions aim at

for boundaries of interest group influence that go beyond normative appeals or a *laissez-faire* of the »invisible hand« of self-corrective pluralism is also broadly acknowledged. »[…] not only do politics without ties to societal interests not function, they need them for legitimating reasons. Not the *If* of interest intermediation is thus the problem but the *How*« (Abromeit 1993: 8, own translation and emphasis). For Abromeit the legitimatory potential of interest group involvement is based on the justness and balance of interest consideration. This consideration depends both on the political system (majoritarian/consociational, central/federal, elite/mass participation, etc.) and on the interest group system (number of groups, type of groups, group resources, link to political system, etc.) in place. These are examined in Chapters 1.2, 2.2, and 3. Legitimacy of interest group involvement is also often linked to the concept of the common good which is therefore briefly examined in the following.

2.1 The common good

The legitimacy of interest intermediation in a democracy is often linked to its consideration of the so-called common good. Many authors have thus made the common good, the *volonté générale*, the public interest (as opposed terminologically to the special interest, the *volonté particulière*, the private interest) a focal point of their evaluation of interest group involvement in interest representation and public policy.

Interest representation in a democracy cannot be evaluated by reference to principles of pluralist politics of representative theory alone. The policies that arise as a consequence of group interventions in politics must be justified according to explicit criteria of public welfare and common good. (Anderson 1979: 297)

Accordingly, the common good has also become the basis on which such authors construct suggestions for checking and possibly regulating the influence of individual groups and special interests.

The common good is a reference point well beyond the narrower discussion of interest groups and interest intermediation; as a key concept it is present in or deliberately absent from all theories of political systems. One

---

distributing economic gains to their benefit. This leads to a macroeconomically suboptimal distribution unless the coalition is in some way encompassing.

of many examples is found in the following quote taken from Madison's Federalist No. 45: »[…] the public good, the real welfare of the great body of the people is the supreme object to be pursued; and [.] no form of Government whatever, has any other value, than as it may be fitted for the attainment of this object« (2003, orig. 1787-88: 280). But how exactly is the common good defined and what consequences do the various definitions carry for the political system in general and the representation and intermediation of interests in particular?

It seems that while the term is widely used and has a buzz-word effect, there exists no one agreed definition:

There is obviously no authority today that would be able to perform a binding definition of the common good. The state that was ascribed this function in earlier societal models has decidedly lost its definitorial monopoly. At the same time, every effort for a concrete determination of the common good appears contestable: there is no consensus on what the bonum commune consists of exactly. (Mayntz 1992: 18, own translation)

Instead there is an array of questions the answers to which inform a definition of the common good. The first such question deals with the genesis of the common good: When does the common good come into existence? Does it precede societal organization or does it only define itself within societal processes? The second question – depending on the answer to the first – asks either how the common good manifests itself or how it is established. This question then triggers a subset of follow-up questions concerning the possibility of influencing the definition of the common good, the mechanisms for ensuring a common good orientation in public policy, etc. The following gives an overview of the different sets of answers to these questions and the definition(s) of the common good resulting from them.

Concerning its origin the common good might exist either *a priori* or *a posteriori* (Fraenkel 1972: 160f), it is either a natural given or the result of a process. If the common good is a given, then the question of how it manifests itself is also a question as to who recognizes and interprets the manifestation. If it is a result of a process, can this process be designed, is it a repeat process, and does it produce a definite, empirically verifiable common good?

To Rousseau in his work *Du Contrat Social* (1977, orig. 1762) the origin of the *volonté générale* was clear; it precedes societal organization in the sense that it exists as the true interest of all people and simply has to be understood correctly and then implemented. The problem thus lies not in the definition of the common good but in the right understanding thereof, i.e., its interpretation. The *volonté générale* is not to be confused with the *volonté de tous* which is simply the sum of all special interests (II, 3).[39] In order to differentiate between the two *volontés*, Rousseau suggests that the people be educated so as to make well informed decisions in the interest of the common good (II, 7). In addition, the state should be limited in size making it easier for all to recognize the *volonté générale* and not be led astray by special interests embodied by individual groups so common to a larger society and state (III, 4; II, 3).[40] The consequence of these suggestions seems to be that the common good as understood by Rousseau could not be realized in a modern mass-democracy. Even if the problem of size could be eliminated, an education favoring a realization of the *volonté générale* »leads, in the extreme case, to a form of educational dictatorship« (Herz 1999: 177, own translation).

Similarly, etatist writers imply a preexisting common good embodied by the state alone which therefore is to be shielded from the influence of special interests (e.g., Schmitt 1972). To strengthen the state authority acting in »public responsibility« (Weber 1970:141) a neutral power is required, e.g., a civil administration backed by a patron — the British crown, the U.S. president, a redefined, strong German Bundespräsident — that can act independently from special interests. None of the etatist writers questions the realization of the common good since they do not question the authority of state decisions. However, critics have questioned the neutrality of the state and its implied understanding of the common good:

Where does the state gain its concrete understanding of the contents of the common good? [...] It may be suspected that in reality it is no more than a »fauned common interest oriented etatism« (H. Grebing) which simply wishes to enforce conservative special interests with the help of the state. (Rudzio 1977: 61, own translation)

Criticism of the consequences of an etatist understanding of the realization of the common good deems the insulation of state authority from special interests and groups unrealistic, reminds us of the positive effects group involvement in state processes can have and, last but not least, points out

---

39 Parentheses indicate corresponding book and chapter.
40 The argument for an education of the citizen (IV, 5) and the restriction of the size of the community (VIII, 16) in the interest of the common good could already be found a decade and a half earlier in Montesqieu's *De l'Esprit des Lois* (1994, orig. 1748).

that, instead of constructing around groups in order to preserve a common good orientation, groups could and should be safely included in the design (Cohen et al. 1992: 408ff).

A constitutional and institutional design targeting the balancing, or rather the control of groups and interests, is proposed in *The Federalist Papers* – though not in the sense of an associative democracy intended by Cohen et al. (1992). In Federalist No. 10 Madison argues in obvious opposition to Rousseau's understanding of the nature of the *volonté générale* and his suggestions for citizen education for the common good and small size of community.[41] It is not the common good that is seen as lying in human nature but the tendency towards faction, »thus sown in the nature of man. [...] the human passions, have in turn divided mankind into parties, inflamed them with mutual animosity, and rendered them much more disposed to vex and oppress each other, than to cooperate for their common good« (2003, orig. 1787-88: 52). The common good is not considered an *a priori* given as it is in Rousseau or by the etatist authors. It may merely come into existence through a control of factions and special interests by an institutional design and a geographical size that allows for a very large number of groups which control each other and prevents the bundling of power.

Joseph A. Schumpeter is another author who argues against the possibility of a preexisting common good as »the motive power of the political process« (2000, orig. 1942: 263):

There is, first, no such thing as a uniquely determined common good that all people could agree on or be made to agree on by the force of rational argument. This is due [...] to the much more fundamental fact that to different individuals and groups the common good is bound to mean different things [...] because ultimate values – our conceptions of what life and society should be – are beyond the range of mere logic. (251)

Again groups are said to play a decisive role in fashioning the will of the people, the *volonté générale*. Schumpeter calls it a »manufactured will« (263)

---

41 Madison's disagreement with the kind of education suggested by Rousseau is expressed in the following: »The second expedient [giving to the citizen the same opinions, the same passions, and the same interests] is [.] impracticable [...]. As long as the reason of man continues fallible, and he is at liberty to exercise it, different opinions will be formed. [...] The diversity of faculties of men from which the rights of property originate, is not less an insuperable obstacle to a uniformity of interests« (2003, orig. 1787-88: 52).

placing far less trust in the possibilities of controlling the influence of groups. It is a distrust in human nature and groups or factions which echoes that of earlier writers such as Hobbes. It was the authors of pluralist theory who first attempted a positive inclusion of groups in the process of defining the common good.

In a pluralist understanding of the concept the common good is the result of the democratic process; according to Fraenkel it is recognizable only »a posteriori« (1972: 160f). As Dahl puts it, it is what democracy's members choose if they have access to all parts of what defines a democratic system and process — thus the common good is both substance and process (1989: 306ff). It is in this process that groups and interests are to enter into competition and balance each other. Some assign so much importance to the design of the process – von Arnim speaks of due-process-pluralism (1977: 183ff) – that they criticize Fraenkel for promoting a simple *laissez-faire* pluralism.

Others, however, insist that »politics is more than process« (Cohen et al. 1992: 415f) and criticize pluralism and its concept of a common good that is the result of a procedure of fair bargaining. The *a posteriori* declaration of the common good to be whatever is the result of a conflict or bargaining of interests — interests deemed to have great differences in power base in the first place – to them seems euphemistic (Offe 1972). Theories of participatory or associational democracy demand a more substantive conception of the common good; yet, a precise definition of the common good is again avoided and substituted with a list of democratic norms such as political equality, distributional fairness, etc. (Cohen et al. 1992).

In view of this unsatisfied demand for a substantive definition John Rawls possibly comes closest to defining the common good »as certain general conditions that are in an appropriate sense equally to everyone's advantage« (1971: 217). He sees the appeal to the common good as a political convention in democracy and his suggested difference principle as a reasonable extension thereof; thus the furthering of the least advantaged individual's long-term perspectives is a furthering of the common good (280f, 65ff). Even this leaves us with a fairly abstract sense of what the common good might consist of. The starting point of this exploration, i.e., the statement by Mayntz that there exists no binding, concrete definition of the common good still appears to hold true. The question is whether such a clear definition is necessary?

»[The common good] is of no use as an analytical model for empirical research« (Beyme 1969: 18, own translation); does it exist on a normative level alone? For Fraenkel the common good has purely normative qualities as a desirable target, a regulative idea, based on common values but also taking into account current social and economic necessities (1964, 1973: 339). Yet, this seems to defer the problem of definition simply to the next level: What (or who) defines the common values and how (or why) are utilitarian considerations of the social and the economic to be integrated? Is the common good a wholly arbitrary concept?

The concept proposed for further reference in this work is that of an *a posteriori* common good. In accordance with the four democratic corner-stones this concept does not expect to predefine and measure democratic output and common good orientation. Instead it proposes a democratic definition of the political input side, i.e., of processes and institutions that admit and consider all interests and aim »at maintaining conditions and achieving objectives that are similarly to everyone's advantage« (Rawls 1971: 205). As Dahl puts it: »Our common good [...] rarely consists of specific objects, activities, and relations; ordinarily it consists of the prac-tices, arrangements, institutions, and processes that [...] promote the well-being of ourselves and others« (1989: 307).[42]

2.2 Systems of interest intermediation

With the achievement of common good oriented, democratic decision-making so closely linked to the design of political process and institutions, it is relevant to take a close look at the possible systems of interest inter-mediation. The respective system in place determines the type and number of interest groups, the form and intensity with which they interact with government officials, and the overall role they may play in political deci-sion-making.

---

42 This would include such dimensions as discussed above in Chapters 1.1and 1.2, e.g., the choice of decision rule. Schütt-Wetschky (1997: 15f) argues that the majority rule is the rule of the common good. Referring back to the discussion of majoritarian versus consociational democracy, it might be said that the decision-making rule appropriate to the achievement of the common good – as well as most other details of the democratic process and institutions – quite certainly depends on such factors as, e.g., the homogeneity or heterogeneity of the society concerned.

Most accounts of systems of interest intermediation are bipolar: ideal pluralism versus ideal liberal corporatism (e.g., Lijphart 1999: 171). Some authors may add a third pole such as a controlled interest group system (Almond et al. 2004: 69) or a participatory interest group system (Reutter 2001: 9, 15). The third pole often indicates historical experiences or newer developments in political science: the controlled interest group system was dominant in the Soviet Union and has continued to exist in some countries after the end of the Soviet Union; the participatory interest group system is central to the normative theories of associative or discursive democracy (e.g., Dryzek 1990, Hirst 1994). For the sake of clarity and focus the following examination concentrates on pluralism and corporatism.

This picks up the examination in Chapter 1.2.1 of the supposed link between consociational democracy and corporatism. It served to show that pure corporatism is by no means the system of interest intermediation to be expected in the European Union in the long run. With the formation of interest intermediation in Brussels still under way, it is instructive to compare the ideal systems of pluralism and corporatism and understand their implications for the process of political decision-making.

Without wanting to repeat the depiction in Chapter 1.2.1, the characteristics of the two systems can be grouped into numerical, structural, and state-related characteristics (see Table 5). The corporatist system, on the one hand, is defined by a limited number of non-competitive, hierarchically organized interest groups operating as monopolists within institutionalized state-group relations. The pluralist system, on the other hand, has an unlimited number of competing, voluntary, non-hierarchical interest groups interacting with the state without a formal framework. The obvious polarity is the outcome of a construction of ideal systems. While the benefits of a pluralist system of interest groups are widely accepted, its alleged drawbacks are also multiple and have lead to the formulation of the corporatist system. It specifically addresses many of the drawbacks of the pluralist system and is seen by some as a possible solution to problems of modern states such as inflation, negative growth, and unemployment (Almond 1983: 259). However, corporatism in turn is seen as possessing drawbacks of its own.

An outline of the advantages and disadvantages of both systems must begin by acknowledging the benefits of a liberal system of interest representation and intermediation in general. Advocates of pluralism have emphasized that interest groups provide for a stronger inclusion of the public into political processes, serve to educate on political matters, counteract the dominance of single interests, provide specialized information to government institutions, etc. (Dahl 1993). These benefits are by and large claimed to be shared by both systems of interest intermediation. However, critics of the pluralist system have indicated several drawbacks, some of which could counteract positive effects. The pluralist system of interest intermediation with its multiplicity and competitiveness is seen as a winner-take-all system often entailing the mutual blocking of interests (Czada 1994, Lijphart 1999). Its informal and volatile nature can make it a system of simple interest articulation focused mainly on political input instead of effective output (Jochem et al. 2003, Reutter 2001). Also, it is accused of repeatedly favoring the same groups and ignoring interests which are less easily organized (Teuber 2001).

Corporatism in its ideal form is said to avoid the drawbacks of the pluralist system through the encompassing nature of its organizations and the supposed ideology of social partnership between all parties involved (Lijphart 1999: 172). While special interest lobbying is termed the main occupation of pluralist interest groups, concertation targeting the common good as a main goal is seen as that of corporatist, trilateral systems (Jochem et al. 2003, Streeck 1994, Traxler 1990). Trilateral concertation is also said to balance interests and give them equal influence. At the same time, corporatism supposedly supplies major relief to the state by bundeling and checking interests, supporting the implementation of government programs, and altogether positively affecting governability (Czada 1992, 1994, Schmitter 1993, Streeck 1994). All these benefits are the result of monopolistic representation of interests through a limited number of non-competitive, overarching, hierarchical organizations, sometimes even with compulsory membership. Of course, these characteristics have also triggered criticism of corporatist systems.

The first point of criticism is the hierarchical structure combined with the monopoly of representation vis-à-vis the state. Participation of the individual is low – the corporative organizations and not the citizen becomes the state's subject (Schmitter 1993) – and the hierarchical organization favors traits of an »elite-cartel« (Abromeit 1993, Lehmbruch 1979b). Reduced levels of participation are, however, not the only source of frustration: the trilateral relations – best known through the triangle of employers, labor unions, and the state – signal an inclusion of all major interests while in fact leaving out less easily organized interests and potential groups such as the unemployed or the consumers. In many cases even these trilateral arrangements fail either due to the lack of a third organized party or because of inherent power asymmetries between the three, especially between capital and labor (Abromeit 1993, Traxler 1990).[43] Moreover, where a functioning institutionalized relationship is in place, i.e., between the interest organization and state bureaucracy, there is the danger of special interests gaining control over the supposedly neutral decision-makers thus undermining democracy and the pursuit of the common good (Czada 1992).

Table 7: Benefits and drawbacks of corporatism and pluralism as systems of interest intermediation

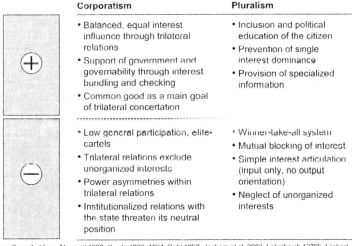

	Corporatism	Pluralism
⊕	• Balanced, equal interest influence through trilateral relations • Support of government and governability through interest bundling and checking • Common good as a main goal of trilateral concertation	• Inclusion and political education of the citizen • Prevention of single interest dominance • Provision of specialized information
⊖	• Low general participation, elite-cartels • Trilateral relations exclude unorganized interests • Power asymmetries within trilateral relations • Institutionalized relations with the state threaten its neutral position	• Winner-take-all system • Mutual blocking of interest • Simple interest articulation (input only, no output orientation) • Neglect of unorganized interests

Source: Compiled from Abromeit 1993, Czada 1992, 1994, Dahl 1993, Jochem et al. 2003, Lehmbruch 1979b, Lijphart 1999, Reutter 2001, Schmitter 1993, Streeck 1994, Teuber 2001, Traxler 1990

It has already been pointed out in Chapter 1.2.1 that the comparisons of pluralism and corporatism as systems of interest intermediation are for the most part based on the ideal forms which exist only in normative theory. Empirical studies of political practice have revealed many possible combinations of the two systems and their individual features. Yet, this work does not agree with those authors who detect merely normative differences

---

43 Abromeit even claims that the frustration of underdeveloped participation, of lacking or mis-representation destabilizes corporate systems in the long run and condemns them to an existence as a mere transitory system of interest intermediation (1993).

between the two schools (compare Buholzer 1998: 89). The drawbacks and benefits of the ideal forms discussed above can also be found in the practice of combined systems. One such combined system in place is the system of interest intermediation prevalent in the European Union.

Some authors state that the amalgamation of pluralist and corporatist elements in the European Union is the consequence of the endurance of pluralism as a meta-system of which corporatism was a historically dominant subform (Aleman 2000, Leif et al. 2003). At the same time, it has been remarked that the degree of corporatism in the EU has been decreasing in favor of pluralism (Lahusen et al. 2001: 22f) or – more to the point – in favor of lobbying as »the original naked manifestation of pluralism« (Aleman 2000: no page numbers, own translation). The analysis of the EU system in Part II tests these statements and examines the consequences of the EU-specific system for both interest intermediation and democracy.

2.3 Interest group terminology and systematics

The following clarification of terminology is necessary to ensure a common understanding of such widely used terms as lobbying or interest group. The clear definition of terms forms the base for the development of a general systematics of interest groups including a classification of groups, of their addresses, and the examination of the more widely spread methods and resources of lobbying. This chapter serves as an introduction on an abstract level and later informs a customized systematics introduced for and used in the investigation of EU lobbying in particular.

2.3.1 Interest groups and lobbies, intermediation and lobbying

The term interest group as it is being used in this work spans a wide variety of more or less organized interests. For the normative and abstract discussion preceding the examination of the EU system its use is preferred to terms related to lobbying so conspicuously used in this work's title. The preference stems from the neutral, non-judgmental connotation of the term interest group and the bias possibly attributed to such terms as lobby or lobbying group.

Outside the Anglo-American political realm and culture from which the term lobbying originates – the activity of special interest pursued in parliamentary or hotel lobbies[44] – the term and often the thus identified groups and activities conjure up negative images of illegitimate or even illegal influencing of government officials by narrow, special interests (e.g., Anderson 1979: 277f). Similarly, the terms pressure group or grassroots organization carry judgmental connotations. However, the use of the term lobbying in the context of the European Union has become customary in the process of which it has lost much of its negative undertone (Schütt-Wetschky 1997: 103, note 24). For this reason, the terms lobbying and lobby groups are used mainly in the examination of the EU.

Any negative connotation aside, there is a general understanding of what defines a lobby and its lobbying activities. A group that focuses its efforts on influencing government officials and institutions in their interests without aiming at taking over direct government responsibilities through participation in elections is considered a lobby (Finer 1960, Rudzio 1977, Schütt-Wetschky 1997). This implies that an interest group whose activities typically focus on internally organizing its members, e.g., a sports club, can turn into a lobby group when trying to influence government policy design favoring the group's interests.

The above points to a second reason for using the term interest group in a first general approach to the integration of interest in a representative democracy. The term interest group accommodates a broad variety of groups differing in their underlying interests, their form of organization, their choice of activities and methods. While this is not the place to expound a history of the group as a basic concept in sociology and, later, political science,[45] it is of interest to note some of the terms and definitions covered by interest group and how they may differ from lobby. Grassroots organizations, social and sports clubs were mentioned above, other terms like Olson's distributional coalitions and encompassing organizations is examined in Chapter 2.3.2 and its typology of groups. Terms like associa-

---

44 Buholzer, among others, points out the two most commonly cited sources of the term: one is an anecdote in which U.S. President Grant was approached by interest group representatives while residing at a hotel after a fire at the White House; the second refers to the lobby of the U.S. congress in which interest group representatives waited for the opportunity to approach members of congress (Buholzer 1998: 6).
45 For an introduction see Beyme (1969: 26f).

tion, faction, and pressure group all of which are subsumable under the term interest group are briefly surveyed below.

Association is one term often found in literature dealing with the phenomenon of groups and their relationship to the state. Though not as widely used in English language works, its German equivalent *Verband* is more common than any other term including interest group itself. The use of association or *Verband* is prompted by the system of interest intermediation in place. The broader term interest group often signals a pluralist understanding. *Verband* conjures an image of more strictly organized groups and a structured group system as a whole that are associated with corporatist systems of interest intermediation. While the emphasis of the group's organization is seen as a merit of *Verband* compared to interest group (Schütt-Wetschky 1997: 10), it is generally more strict than the term lobby when it comes to the type of interest or group included. Thus state agencies, regional or national representative offices as they can be found pursuing lobbying activities in Brussels would in most cases not be covered by the term association or *Verband* (Vieler 1986: 11).

Just as association may hint at the underlying assumption of a corporatist system of interest intermediation, the terms faction and pressure group can imply either a liberal or a republican concept of state and its alleged or at least desired independence from special interest (Cohen et al. 1992). Such a term as grassroots organization can signal an author's commitment to a pluralist society and state organization. Even this small selection shows the difficulty of finding terms relating to the subject of interest groups and their relationship to the state that do not in one way or the other connote a preference for a certain political or interest group system.

This work employs the passably neutral term of interest group when speaking in general terms of interest organization and articulation by bodies other than those of representative government. This encompasses all functions of the group, i.e., those internal to the organization and its members as well as those in which interests are carried outward and represented to the public and to the government. A lobby, on the other hand, shall be defined as such a group that sets up lobby offices or sends representatives to lobby government institutions and officials or that otherwise employs lobbying capacities, e.g., professional lobbyists or consultants. This has the twofold advantage of more clearly focusing on a certain aspect, the lobbying aspect, of interest group activities as well as conforming to the choice of terms generally encountered in literature on the European Union.

A group is defined by the combination of structure and function, of organizational form and activities pursued. For this reason, depending on the activities under attention, this work speaks either of interest intermediation or of lobbying. Interest intermediation signals a two-way process in which the interest group functions as intermediary between its members and the state and vice versa. While lobbying is by no means a one-way street in which communication flows solely in the direction of the state, it does emphasize the interface between the lobby group and the state or other representative institutions and slightly disregards the interface between the group and its individual members.[46]

While the term lobbying group in the above definition may seem to suggest a certain homogeneity of defining characteristics, it actually covers an astounding variety of groups and organized interests. These can include individual companies, industry sector associations, employer umbrella organizations, labor unions and their respective umbrella organizations, as well as non-profit organizations ranging from human rights, to welfare interests, environmental issues, consumer interests, or cultural interests. Furthermore, lobbies are not by definition non-governmental. They can also comprise governmental agencies and bodies, mainly regional or local, but also national as in the case of the EU, and various other associations under public law. In short, as a general term lobby includes all groups or bodies that organize themselves with the goal of representing their interests vis-à-vis decision-making governmental institutions.

2.3.2 Classification of interest groups

The wide variety of possible lobbies suggests a need for classification. This allows for an easier handling of the large number of heterogeneous groups when it comes to, e.g., examining lobbying processes or specifying lobbying regulation. Interest group and lobbying literature, with and without a focus on the EU, suggests a large variety of group classifications or typologies. Criteria of classification depend on the questions pursued or the argument made or sometimes on no apparent reason at all. Criteria used

---

46 Interest intermediation involves such questions as to where original interests arise, how they are aggregated, and which role group functionaries carry out regarding group members, the state, and themselves (compare, e.g., Abromeit 1993, Steinberg 1985, Herder-Dorneich 1979).

include the degree of organization and institutionalization (Almond et al. 2004) or the preferred channels of intermediation (Leif et al. 2003), but the most commonly used criterion of group classification is, not surprisingly, the type of interest represented (Finer 1960, Rudzio 1977, Vieler 1986, Van Schendelen 2003a). Taking group classification to the next level of complexity some authors suggest matrixes of two or more criteria allowing for a greater differentiation (e.g., Buholzer 1998). The following takes a look at the most frequently applied classification criteria before introducing the typology chosen for this work and the reasoning behind it.

Classifying by degree of organization or by channels of influence is of interest when asking about the ability of certain interests to be heard and reminds us of the arguments made by Mancur Olson and others that not all interest will organize in the same manner or to the same degree and that there exists a bias towards smaller groups as well as towards groups that wield special individual incentives inducing member-cooperation. The phenomenon is attributed to individual rational behavior; thus, even the philanthropist will focus his efforts where they are perceived and not where they disappear in incrementality (Olson 1965: 64).[47] The degree of organization and, thus allegedly, of power wielded is certainly of interest to a work dealing with the relationship between democracy and lobbying. However, with regard to the examination of lobby groups in the European Union organization and representation in Brussels is considered for the most part a prerequisite and is of secondary interest for a classification of existing groups. Those groups and interests not represented on a European level at all are reflected on outside the framework of classification. Similarly, factors such as group power and influence are acknowledged in a different context, e.g., the question of lobbying resources.

The most common criterion of interest group classification is that of the represented interest itself. Though even here there exist telling differences. Finer (1960) lists seven main interests: businesses, workers, cooperatives, free professions, civil groups, churches, cultural interests, and special issues. Similarly, Vieler (1986) and Rudzio (1977) list the following five: groups of the economic and labor system, of the social sphere, of leisure, of culture, religion, politics, and science, and associations/institutions un-

---

47 Obviously, Truman's theory of latent groups and their controlling function in society, which Olson's theory refuted, is also based on a classification by degree of organization. However, to him the degree was by no means a measure of a group's power (Truman 1951).

der public law.[48] These lists are unbiased and groups are easily assigned to the generic captions. However, many authors avoid such lists that, though unbiased, run the risk of being neither mutually exclusive nor collectively exhaustive. Also, such lists as the above seldom bring substantively new information to the author's argument.

Instead of using generic lists of interests many works opt for a simple interest dichotomy which often more strongly underlines the author's argument. This dichotomy might be summarized under the terms public and private interests and its first-glance simplicity hides other problems which are discussed later on. Here are examples of such dichotomous terms and interests suggested: common – special (Bode 2003), promotional – economic (Beyme 1969), encompassing – distributional (Olson 1982).[49]

Bode differentiates between non-governmental organizations (NGOs) or advocacy groups representing common or public interests and economic and industry lobbies representing special interests (2003: 158f); yet, he fails to mention how a group is identified as an advocacy group in the first place.[50] Beyme includes a variety of interests in his category of promotional groups that primarily pursue non economic goals (1969: 31ff). However, he points out that many may also have economic interests (e.g., religious groups), involve personal interests (e,g., the American ALRA, the Abortion Law Reform Association), or may in general be hiding economic interests behind a promotional group name (Civic Liberty League, lobbying the interests of breweries during Prohibition). Along similar lines, Olson identifies encompassing groups, their membership covering substantial parts of society, that while remaining special-interest groups have »some incentive to make the society in which they operate more prosperous« (1982: 53) and thus differ from distributional groups of small, vested interests that merely distort the distribution of income and slow down the growth rate for innovation and productivity (1982: 44ff).

---

48 Both are referring back to the classification introduced by Ellwein (1974).
49 As will become clear in the following, these examples go beyond the simple differentiation between public and private interests as van Schendelen suggested. To him all non-governmental interests are private interests, e.g., companies, trade associations, NGOs, and all governmental interests are public interests, e.g., local, regional, national governments and agencies (2003a: 301).
50 Bode does point out the problem of using NGO as a synonym for non-profit advocacy group due to the fact that it can include all non-governmental groups, i.e., also such interests as companies or labor unions (2003: 159).

This short overview has already identified several problems which a classification of interest groups into public and private interests faces. Where exactly is the line along which public and private interests can be separated? How can one differentiate between primary and secondary economic interests? Does a long membership role guarantee public interest orientation? Where does one place labor unions that primarily pursue economic interests of their members but that may also encompass large parts of the population? Where does one place consumer groups concerned with both economic and non-economic interests, with both prices and non-material issues like health risks? And could it not be argued that the lobbying of automotive companies for lower environmental standards profits the money-purses of many consumers and thus such lobbying is in the public interest?

This can be taken back one step to the discussion of the common good in Chapter 2.1. It was noted that the common good is best defined as the *a posteriori* result of a democratically designed decision-making process. Is it thus possible to differentiate between public and private interest groups by looking at the way they are constituted and how they reach their decisions? Many authors have argued in favor of the democratic organization of interest groups and some have gone as far as to say that only such democratically organized groups can hold a legitimate role in democracy.[51] In a corporatist system, where due to the monopolistic character of the interest group system membership is encompassing and compulsory, the reasoning behind this is more obvious (see Anderson 1979: 291). However, in a pluralist or a mixed system of interest intermediation a need for internal democratic structures and decision-making cannot be argued. An interest group is by definition a sub-group of society voluntarily organized behind a special interest, and while the manner in which they interact with society as a whole is or should be democratically regulated, they rest internally free to choose an organizational form and processes of decision-making best suited to the achievement of their interests. Thus one can find hierarchical, non-democratic organizations both in industry interest groups and in in-

---

51 For a discussion on internal democracy in interest groups see among others Anderson (1979), Vieler (1986), Hirst (1992). Internal democracy is often suggested as a means of avoiding disjunction between group leaders and simple members, oligarchic tendencies seen as »sources [...] of negative-sum relations between the powers of association and egalitarian-democratic order« (Cohen et al. 1992: 443).

ternational advocacy groups such as Greenpeace.[52] Since it seems neither possible nor desirable to differentiate along the lines of organizational form, are there other possible indicators of public interest orientation?

Clearly, there are a range of similarities between all interest groups or lobbies; these cannot serve as differentiating criteria between public and private interests:

- Legitimate role in a democracy: Under democratic rule all interests have the right to assemble and present themselves and their demands to the public and the government.[53]
- Representation of members' special interests: In as far as they are not elected to represent the public, all interest groups can be called special interest groups; they represent the interests of their members which in some cases may coincide with public interests.
- Lobbying tools and methods: Whether they are industry or non-profit lobbies, lobby groups generally employ similar methods to voice and assert their interests.

Apart from these common characteristics shared by all interest and lobby groups there are several dimensions which allow for or even strongly suggest a differentiation between public and private interests even if the differentiation is a preliminary one and might have to be opened to review in individual cases:[54]

- Lobbying resources: While there is a large overlap in lobbying methods employed by all types of groups, there is strong evidence that the resources deployed and used for bargaining within these methods are far from equally distributed. When it comes to personnel, financial, and organizational resources, economic interest groups clearly outweigh non-profit organizations.[55]

---

52 One exception to this are government bodies – acting as lobbying bodies, e.g., regional representation on the EU level in Brussels – in the sense that they are for the most part directly or indirectly constituted through a democratic process and are subject to democratic control

53 For one of many discussions of legitimacy of interest groups see Beisheim (1997).

54 E.g., see the somewhat ambiguous examples, e.g., the Civic Liberty League, quoted earlier from Beyme (1969).

55 This point is examined in Chapter 2.3.4 on lobbying methods and resources. One source that has examined and confirmed the unequal distribution of lobbying resources and power between different types of lobby groups is Eising & Kohler-Koch (1994: 191ff).

- Material versus ideal interests: Though there are those groups that may exist in a grey zone between material and ideal interests, most groups' goals can be identified in their mission and vision statements or the statements of the organizations they represent. This allows for a separation of mainly material and mainly ideal interests; the latter in general being seen as public interest oriented.
- Status with governments and international organizations: Yet another strong point allowing for a differentiation between public and private interest orientation is the status differentiation already successfully practiced by many governments and international organizations. In such cases public interest status grants groups certain advantages such as special tax benefits or consultative association with decision-makers. This is examined in greater detail in the following.

Table 8: Similarities and differences between public and private interest groups

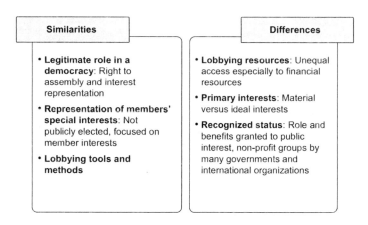

Similarities	Differences
• **Legitimate role in a democracy**: Right to assembly and interest representation • **Representation of members' special interests**: Not publicly elected, focused on member interests • **Lobbying tools and methods**	• **Lobbying resources**: Unequal access especially to financial resources • **Primary interests**: Material versus ideal interests • **Recognized status**: Role and benefits granted to public interest, non-profit groups by many governments and international organizations

Source: In parts compiled from Eising et al. 1994, Alhadeff et al. 2002, UN DPI 2004

The definition of public interest or common good orientation provided by German tax law is an example for the implementation of a special status granted public interest groups. According to German regulation a group's common interest orientation has to be based on the three principles of *selflessness* (no contributions to individuals, small restricted groups, or parties), *exclusiveness* (no other than the common interests defined in the mission are to be pursued), and *directness* (the organization does not delegate its tasks). German *Abgabenordnung* § 52 then lists in detail all such interests generally considered common interests. These include groups operating in the following areas: education, science, research, sports, arts, culture, environment, religion, welfare, etc. The main reason for organizations in Germany to aspire to such status are the tax and related benefits granted to recognized common interest organizations.

The EU itself has divided non-state actors into three groups: 1) private sector, 2) economic and social partners including trade unions, and 3) civil society organizations (Alhadeff et al. 2002). However, its definition of civil society or non-profit organizations is still vague compared to the definition in use at the United Nations. The definition in use at both UN ECOSOC and the UN DPI for NGOs speaks of non-profit, voluntary citizens' groups that are eligible for consultative or associational status only if they fulfill a list of criteria including »an established headquarters, a democratically adopted constitution, authority to speak for its members, a representative structure, appropriate mechanisms of accountability and democratic and transparent decision-making processes« (United Nations Department of Public Information 2004, United Nations Non-Governmental Liaison Service 2004). These organizations must derive the main part of their funding from national affiliates or individual members, and they cannot have been established by a government or intergovernmental agreements.

The German and the UN examples do not wish to suggest an exact replication in the European Union. They do, however, demonstrate that existing systems currently already practice a public/private differentiation. This point further underlines the other similarities and differences listed above and suggests a similar classification for this work and the analysis of the European Union in Part II. Singular cases that carry both characteristics of a public and a private interest group remain, of course, to be classified individually.

What can be gained by the suggested classification? So far the differentiation between public and private interests points to an asymmetry in the distribution of – mainly financial – resources and thus possibly of power and voice. If a system of interest intermediation is to reflect the democratic principles and cornerstones outlined in Chapter 1, it is of interest to recognize resource imbalances and the suggested classification can serve as a first source of evidence. If Olson's theory holds true, the classification will prove a certain underrepresentation of so-called encompassing, public interests which in turn could trigger suggestions for changes in process and regulation.

A second dimension suggested for this work's interest group classification is that of national or unilateral versus an international or multilateral interest representation. In the context of a supranational system such as the European Union it is important to understand which groups consolidate and leverage EU-wide interests and which remain focused on their (traditional) national or regional member and interest base. National or unilateral interest representation can imply a relative narrowness of the interest represented by, e.g., national advocacy groups, regional government bodies, individual companies, or national trade unions. International or multilateral interest representation, by contrast, can hint at a certain degree of interest consolidation throughout Europe in such groups as international advocacy groups, industry sector associations, or trade union umbrella organizations. Under different scenarios the narrowness or broadness of interest representation can signal different influence and power constellations. This is explored further in the later examination of EU lobby groups.

Table 9: Proposed classification of interest and lobbying groups

	Public interest	Private interest
National or unilateral focus	• National advocacy, non-profit groups • Local, regional, and national government bodies	• Individual companies • National associations
International or multilateral focus	• International advocacy, non-profit groups • International organizations of governments	• Supranational associations • Umbrella organizations

Source: Own framework

2.3.3 Addressees

Having defined and classified interest and lobby groups, it is necessary to take a look at the targets of their lobbying activities, at their addressees. The answer to the question of who is to be considered a lobbying target seems to be straightforward, namely all government officials and institutions that influence any part of the policy-making process, i.e.,

–   Executive branch: Members of government, in particular ministers and their administrative staff.
–   Legislative branch: Members of parliament and the main organizational units of parliament, such as party fractions, parliamentary committees and commissions.
–   Judicial branch: Judges involved in interpreting and, in some cases, reviewing policies.

However, a look at some authors' definitions of lobbying actors and their addressees shows that there is room for dispute in two areas. First, in several cases there seems to be an overlap between who is considered a lobbyist and who is considered an addressee. There is a fuzziness to the boundaries where special interest intermediation ends and government balancing for the common interest begins. Second, many lists of addressees acknowledge different levels of addressees without making explicit the differences between them, e.g., between the lobbying of a government minister and the lobbying of public opinion.

Abromeit makes no clear differentiation between lobbyists and addressees but instead speaks of the actors of interest intermediation (1993: 23). Listing citizens, political parties, associations, bureaucracy, and the judiciary she combines what this work, for the sake of systematization, tries to separate, namely lobbying actors and addressees. Yet, the fuzziness this produces may at times be an accurate picture of reality. Due to functional and personal overlaps it is often hard to differentiate between lobbyists and addressees. The example of the political party is an especially obvious one.

In his classification of interest groups Vieler lists political parties as a special form of interest group or association; special because they are generally characterized by their wish to gain direct political responsibility and by the integration of broader interests than normally typical of an interest organization (1986: 8ff). He argues in favor of such a classification – even though it finds few other supporters in interest group literature – by pointing out that there are enough examples of associations having put forward candidates in elections or of parties that have not participated in elections. Also, he names a number of parties representing very narrow interests and at the same time points out associations that cover very broad interests. These overlaps in Vieler's opinion do not allow for a clear separation of interest associations and political parties. One might add that apart from the organizational level, there is often no clear separation on the personal level where members of interest associations become party members or even members of parliament (compare Finer 1960: 152).[56]

Few authors, however, go as far as Vieler to classify parties as true interest groups. Abromeit sees the political party as an only unsatisfactory organizational form for the intermediation of interests since »parties are *not primarily* organizations for the intermediation of interests« (1993: 35, italics in the original); their »main goal [remains] the formation of government« (1993: 31, own translation). Yet, she remains unclear as to their role as interest groups or as addressees. Similarly, she sees bureaucracy and the judiciary partly as interest intermediators though for mainly status quo or resource-heavy interests.

Abromeit's categorizing of actors-addresses and their more or less effective roles in interest intermediation leads directly to the second point of debate mentioned above, the blending or confusion of different levels of interest intermediation and addressees. The majority of authors lists some or all of the following as addressees of lobbying: parliament, government, bureaucracy, judiciary, parliamentary fractions, and political parties; often added to this list are international organizations and public opinion (e.g., Beyme 1969, Rudzio 1977, Leif et al. 2003).

The ambiguous role of political parties is discussed above. The obvious role of the different branches as addressees of lobbying activities is evident; where possible, lobbyists try to influence such decision-makers that have direct access to decision-making during the different phases of the policy process. International organizations and public opinion seem oddly misplaced when considering direct influence on decision-makers. In most cases they play a more indirect role. In the lobbying process they are addressees only in the sense that they are addressed and mobilized by lobby-

---

56 In her examination of strategies for lobbying members of parliament Richter remarks that one such strategy is the use of a member of parliament itself as an internal lobbyist either in the plenary or in committees – here the distinction between lobbyist, addressee, and lobbying intermediary is clearly lost (Richter 1997: 21ff).

ists wishing to build up pressure on the actual decision-makers in government. They are intermediaries rather than real addressees. Table 10 offers a rather schematic systematization of the different players within the lobbying process from original, individual interests, to interest groups, to addressees, at times by way of secondary addressees or intermediary pressure builders such as the general public.

Table 10: Interests, intermediators, and addressees in the lobbying process

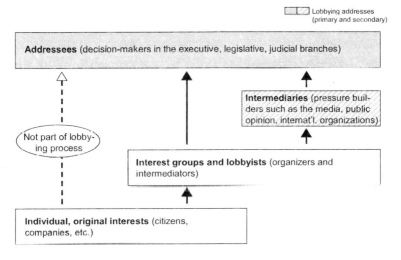

Source: Own framework

The definition of lobbying addressees chosen is in line with the definition of lobbying introduced earlier in Chapter 2.3.1. If lobbying seeks to influence government decisions, then its primary addressees are those institutions and officials in positions of direct decision-making responsibility. This definition is by no means new or innovative (compare, e.g., Milbrath 1963: 7). In his definition, in which he restricts lobbying to the influencing of government decisions, Milbrath also states that lobbying is an activity undertaken by an intermediating organization that brings together original, individual interests and expresses them in the direction of the decision-makers.

The differentiation of primary addressees and intermediaries, or secondary addressees, has several implications for the examination of the European lobbying system. It helps limit the number of addressees to be studied and ranks them in their level of effectiveness and importance. The detailed analysis follows in Chapter 5.2.[57]

2.3.4 Methods and resources

After defining the lobbying group as such, classifying its different manifestations, and systematizing its primary and secondary addressees, there remains an introduction to be given to the most common methods with which lobby groups strive to interact with their addressees and an overview of the resources they find helpful throughout the process. Though at first glance this may appear to be a mere technical debate, it will become clear that criticism of lobby groups and their influence on decision-makers is not seldom triggered by the coercive, illegitimate methods employed by some groups and by the differing amounts of lobbying resources available to the various interest groups.

Thinking along the lines of legitimate and illegitimate – or maybe even legal and illegal – lobbying, the methodological spectrum ranges from convincing with facts and values, to bargaining, to exerting pressure (Schütt-Wetschky 1997: 11f). Others, considering lobbying to be a special form of communication, differentiate between methods of direct and indirect communication, e.g., the direct approach of an addressee or an indirect approach through intermediary channels (Buholzer 1998: 59). Legitimate (or legal) methods then include direct communication through personal contacts at formal and informal meetings, participation in conferences, commissions, committees and the like. Also included are indirect communication and information through such channels as intermediary personal contacts, public opinion and mass media. At the negative end of the spectrum, which Schütt-Wetschky so mildly describes as exerting pressure, are located methods such as bribery, threatening, and coercion, which can be realized both through direct, personal channels or indirectly, e.g., through violent demonstrations.

---

57 In view of the lobbying methods discussed in Chapter 2.3.4 it can be noted that methods and activities also clearly differentiate between primary addressees and intermediaries. Buholzer points out that the lobbyist makes a basic choice in his method between direct or indirect communication. Indirect communication is an approaching of the addressee through secondary channels, through what is here called intermediaries, e.g., people close to the actual addressee, political parties or other public groups, public opinion, or scientific institutions such as think tanks (Buholzer 1998: 59).

Even if illegal methods could be dismissed, critics of lobbying would insist that there remains a large imbalance of resources used for lobbying between different groups. Much evidence has been collected and presented that supports the view that economic, private interests are strongly favored by a better supply of personnel, financial, and organizational resources (e.g., Eising et al. 1994: 191ff). The resources considered here have also been defined as bargaining resources (see in particular Buholzer 1998, Abromeit 1993, Rudzio 1977). They enter directly into the lobbying process, functioning as access goods, while resources such as personnel and organization have an indirect effect by influencing the quantity or quality of the bargaining resources. An overview is given in the following table.

Table 11: Financial and non-financial resources exchanged during lobbying process

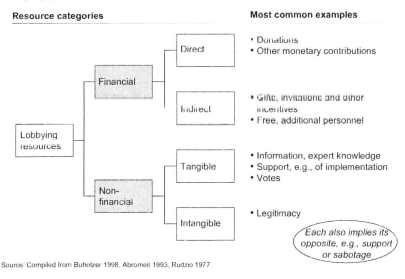

Source: Compiled from Buholzer 1998, Abromeit 1993, Rudzio 1977

Lobbying resources can be divided into those of financial and non-financial nature. Financial resources comprise, on the one hand, direct monetary contributions to the addressee institutions such as party and campaign donations and, on the other hand, indirect monetary levers such as gifts and invitations. An interesting form of an indirect financial resource is the provision of additional, free work force, e.g., an intern delegated to the addressee institution paid for by the lobbying group (Buholzer 1998: 233), or even regular staff delegated to government institutions for a certain period of time (Sassen 1999, Austermann 2003).

Non-financial resources that enhance a lobbying group's bargaining power can be both tangible and intangible. The most important instrument is the provision of information and expert knowledge. With limited resources within their own institution addressees can come to rely heavily on information provided by outside sources in order to make informed decisions. This use of outside information can extend to the point where large passages are adopted from lobby-financed studies or group position papers and included in official documents.[58] Tangible non-financial resources used in bargaining are, however, present during all phases of policy process. Support or, on its flipside, sabotage during implementation is a powerful resource as well. From a more general perspective, interest groups with large membership roles or with strong presence in mass media can also carry large numbers of votes to be mobilized for or against single issues or whole political agendas.

On the side of intangible lobbying resources legitimacy is the most visible resource. Where interest group influence can be interpreted as civil society engagement in democracy, policy decisions and the decision-makers receive additional credibility and legitimacy through the involvement of certain lobby groups. For a system such as the EU whose alleged democratic deficit remains a public issue this bargaining resource can carry heightened importance (Buholzer 1998: 238ff).

Chapter 2 summarized the debate and the key questions concerning interest groups and interest representation in a modern political system. It discussed the concept of the common good and the main systems of interest intermediation. Last but not least, it defined the terminology and developed the systematics of interest groups as they are used in the rest of this work. Together with Chapter 1 it laid the foundation on which Chapter 3 develops a theoretical model of balanced interest intermediation in a modern democracy.

---

58 One such example is an EU Commission draft on the regulation of patents for genetic sequences and cell functions that was issued in December 1995. Some of its passages were identical to passages found in a brochure distributed to members of the EU Parliament at the same time by the lobby of the biotechnology industry (Bode 2003: 134).

3. Legitimacy and boundaries of interest representation in a democracy

As was illustrated at the beginning of Chapter 2, lobbying has become more or less accepted as a pertinent part of modern political systems. The existence and meaningful participation of interest groups in decision-making processes is seen as a sign of a functioning democracy. Where the role of lobbying is discussed, the following quote applies: »Not the *If* of interest intermediation is thus the problem but the *How*« (Abromeit 1993: 8, own translation and emphasis). This chapter examines the role of lobbying with both its positive and negative impact on representative democracy and discusses lobbying regulation and »correction mechanisms« (Van Schendelen 2002) identified in current debate and their possible implications on system design. Then moving down from this level of abstraction, the insights are applied to the peculiarities of consociational democracy and interest representation within it. Overall, Chapter 3 provides the theoretical framework which informs and supports the analysis of democracy and interest representation in the European Union to follow in Part II.

The positive role played by interest groups can be traced throughout the entire process of decision-making from the formulation, to the discussion and acceptance, and the implementation of policies. During the individual phases the impact is seldom one-dimensional. Instead, it can be differentiated by taking into account three viewpoints: that of the individual citizen, that of government and the officials involved, as well as that of the corporate citizen, i.e., other interest groups. Underlying the whole are general effects on the quality of representation, democracy, and citizenship attributed to the existence and involvement of interest groups; these form the base for a sustainable policy process.

Seen from the logic of the policy process, interest groups can help set the political agenda and formulate policies by providing information both to citizens and to government officials, by facilitating deliberations and shaping opinions, and by acting as an interface between the citizens and representative government (Cohen et al. 1992). Similarly, they support the final acceptance of policies. During implementation they may act as agents carrying out decisions or as whistle-blowers monitoring correct implementation (Grant 1993). Where interest group support of the process works smoothly, there are gains both in efficiency and in effectiveness.

From the point of view of the citizen, interest groups also have a broader impact on strengthening sustainable representation and democratic participation. This can be mapped onto the two principles (political equality, freedom of self-determination) and the democratic cornerstones (equality of vote and of voice, authorization, accountability) introduced in Chapter 1.1. By providing information and thus also transparency groups support not only the policy process but also inform the authorization and accountability mechanisms essential to the principle of self-determination in a representative system (Schmidt et al. 1997, Cohen et al. 1992). However, interest groups can also help broaden the concept of self-determination as understood in the democratic cornerstones; they provide the means of political involvement in between and beyond elections. Involvement in between elections addresses a frequency of participation that is higher than that provided by the usual election cycle. Interest groups can enable a continuous feedback cycle between the citizens and representative government (Finer 1960: 125). Involvement beyond elections addresses participatory quality. »[Intermediary associations] provide a basis of representation that is more precise, more consistent with individual preferences [...] that appropriately supplements majoritarian and constituency interests« (Anderson 1979: 283). Group pluralism provides the possibility of refining the political agenda beyond the opportunities of, e.g., a party program aimed at uniting as many interests as possible (among others, Vieler 1986). In addition to this specification of political representation, some claim that groups positively effect the depth of involvement and representation also by reaching beyond territorial representation at a time when globalization is testing the limits of conventional representation (Voelzkow 2000). As regards the principle of political equality many authors speak of a furthering of political equality through the workings of interest groups. However, this opinion is limited to corporatist-like approaches to interest intermediation, in which groups receive encompassing, at least semi-public status, and seems based more on hypotheses than on observable facts (Cohen et al. 1992, Schmitter 1994).

The positive impact of interest groups from the point of view of government and its officials also goes well beyond the points mentioned above in the reflection on the policy process. As providers of information, experts, and public support, groups not only support decision-making in a technical fashion, but also strengthen the legitimacy of representative government by enhancing its output and its perception by the public (Van Schendelen 2002: 291ff). Another role attributed to interest groups is that they can function as »schools of democracy«, i.e., they can promote democratic values, civic integration, consciousness and deliberation and can underline the development of community feeling or identity. As van Schendelen points out, such values as tolerance and pluralism can be further emphasized by the competition between the groups themselves (2002: 299ff).

However, a democratic system can also easily be negatively impacted by the existence and involvement of interest groups and this is often due to the same characteristics that allow them to impact positively. The power wielded by some groups throughout the policy process might be abused in each of its stages in an effort to render the process unfair and overemphasize certain interests (Cohen et al. 1992, Vieler 1986). As van Schendelen argues, a balanced process in which all interests are heard and all groups admitted is only a group's second preference whilst an unlevel playing field to their advantage is the natural first preference (Van Schendelen 2002: 106). So, imbalance of interests can lead to an imbalance of process and ensuing ineffectiveness. What are the main sources of this often quoted unbalanced representation of interests? The most common explanation given is the inequality of resources available to different groups (see among others Cohen et al. 1992, Schmitter 1994, Van Schendelen 2002).[59] More imbalance can occur when groups are blocked out either by other interest groups or otherwise discriminated against by officials or the process design itself (Van Schendelen 2002, Cohen et al. 1992). The exclusion of interests can lie within the system, i.e., in a corporatist system, or in the logic of group formation itself and those interests that traditionally remain unorganized. Whatever the reason for interest imbalances, the effectiveness of the policy process will be negatively impacted when too many interests are left unconsidered.

---

59 This topic has been addressed before in Chapter 2.3.4.

Process inefficiency can be another negative effect. Applying his earlier *Logic of Collective Action* (1965) to the political and economic workings of nations Olson concludes that lobbying strongly increases the complexity of policies and government slowing down the policy process while at the same time diverting public resources to group interests (1982: 36ff). Depending on whether the system of interest intermediation shows characteristics of a pluralist or a corporatist system, efficiency and effectiveness are impacted differently. A pluralist multiplicity of groups can overload a system with the sheer number of groups and interests to be accommodated and explode the costs of bargaining and decision-making (Van Schendelen 2002, Vieler 1986). However, a corporatist limitation of groups included in the policy process, which may at first seem to lead to higher efficiency and effectiveness (Immergut 1992), can mean system sclerosis and a heightened misuse of what is then a semi-public status of those groups empowered, again leading to ineffectiveness and inefficiency.

From the citizen's point of view problems may arise from a disconnection between interest groups and their members (Hirst 1992). Where group leaders take control of the agenda and final decision-making while at the same time possibly reinventing group interests to match their personal interests, this can lead to such defects as identified by Dahl (1982): threats to political equality and civic consciousness, a loss of control over the public agenda and final decisions. Even if leaders represent group interests, power imbalances between groups can lead to overrepresentation of some and a »threat to public sovereignty« (Cohen et al. 1992: 423). Schmitter notes the same risks for self-determination both in a pluralist system with its further strengthening the interests of the strong as well as in a corporatist system with its privileged, bureaucratized rigidities (1994: 160f). Threats to self-determination and political equality are further heightened by lack of information and transparency as to the decision-making process and its results.

Negative impact of interest group lobbying as seen from the point of view of government and officials focuses on the alleged or real undermining of government competence and legitimacy in the eyes of the people. »If the people come to believe that [the system] is only a sort of republican court with lobbying groups and factions patronizing them, they may lose« some civic spirit and behavior and become more indifferent and passive« (Van Schendelen 2002: 301).

Table 12: Potential range of lobbying and interest group impact on democracy

$\oplus$	$\ominus$
• **Effectively and efficiently support policy process** – Agenda setting and policy formulation – Deliberation facilitation and opinion shaping – Implementation assistance and control • **Strengthen self-determination** – Provision of information and transparency – Quantitative enhancement of participation – Qualitative refinement of participation – Functional addition to territorial representation • **Further political equality*** • **Strengthen government legitimacy** – Output enhancement – "Schools of democracy"	• **Manipulate policy process effectiveness and cripple efficiency** – Resource and power inequality – Discrimination – Lack of interest organization – Lock-down of status quo – Heightened complexity – Explosion of bargaining costs • **Threaten self-determination and political equality** – Disjunction of citizens and leaders – Unbalanced representation of interests – Lack of information and transparency • **Threaten government legitimacy** – Appearance of faction domination

* This point may apply more to a corporatist system and be debatable for a pluralist system.

Source: Compiled from Anderson 1979, Cohen et al. 1992, Dahl 1982, Finer 1960, Grant 1993, Hirst 1992, Immergut 1992, Olson 1982, Schmidt et al. 1997, Schmitter 1994, Van Schendelen 2002, Vieler 1986, Voelzkow 2000

Institutional, regulatory and other recommendations focused on preventing or terminating potential negative effects of lobbying, i.e., the manipulation of political process as well as threats to citizen rights and government legitimacy, are extremely varied. There are the etatist and republican schools who speak of a complete insulation of government institutions from lobbying influences, e.g., by not allowing government officials any personal involvement in associations (Eschenburg 1955).[60] Others see the correction of possible negative impact already provided for in the system itself through group competition, the interests of government officials and in the control wielded by mass media and public opinion (Van Schendelen 2002: 305ff). In between these two more pronounced tendencies there can be found a medley of suggestions. The following gives a structured overview of the most common ones.

Recommendations aimed at reducing policy process manipulations seem to either tackle the process itself and the loopholes employed by lobbyists to their advantage or they address the inequalities among interest

---

60 Eschenburg refers mainly to government bureaucrats. Richter, however, shows that personal involvement of members of parliament can play an even bigger role in realizing group interests (1997: 17ff).

groups leading to an imbalance of influence on the policy process and its results. The latter efforts are focused mainly on strengthening underrepresented interests. Measures require anything from little to high government involvement: from resource balancing through taxes and compensation[61] to direct sponsoring and affirmative action to the establishment of a government agency committed to establishing and protecting the representation of underrepresented or unorganized interests (see, e.g., Cohen et al. 1992, Vieler 1986). While tax benefits for so-called common interest or non-profit groups is an established tool employed by governments today (see Chapter 2.3.2), affirmative action in pluralist systems aimed at integrating weaker interest groups is a measure still mainly employed at the discretion of individual government officials. Similarly, the activation of unorganized interests is essentially unexplored territory in political practice.

The measures suggested to close loopholes in the policy process can be divided into two main thrusts:

- Control and limit the activities of both interest groups and government officials;
- Curb potential negative lobbying impact through the institutionalization of interest group participation.

The keyword in controlling groups, government, and the overall process is, first and foremost, transparency. Authors that turn to the U.S. system as the system most well known for the influence of lobby groups on its workings regularly quote disclosure and its definition in the *Federal Regulation of Lobbying Act* (1946) as a minimal requirement for transparency of group facts and data (Saipa 1971: 196, Rudzio 1977: 43). However, others have remarked on the deficiencies of U.S. lobbying regulation; the data that lobby groups are required to disclose is both too much and too little to lead to real transparency on the influence and goals of the different

---

61 Cohen claims to be quoting pluralist suggestions when he speaks of resource balancing and affirmative action (1992). Vieler, too, speaks of tax rewards but wishes to target common interest representation in particular, the underlying premise being that common interests tend to be underrepresented (1986: 176ff). In contrast, Schmitter's suggestion »affirms that only self-interests can counter self-interests'« (1994: 169); he proposes a compulsory contribution to associations to be distributed through citizen vouchers. This, too, is an attempt to somewhat balance financial resource inequalities that can lead to influence imbalances.

groups.[62] In his examination of U.S. federal and individual state regulation of lobbying Lane concludes:

These laws lack precision, scope, and clear direction. They reach only individual lobbyists in an era of group politics. They reach only legislative lobbying in an era of expanding administrative power. They reach only personal confrontation in an era of indirect political persuasion. [...] These deficiencies are not irremediable, although there is no wide-spread clamor to correct them. Indeed, the germinal disclosure idea represents an approach to the central problem of government that should be worth every effort to conserve. (Lane 1964: 105f)

Even if real and complete transparency were possible – transparency of group data and facts as well as of the bargaining process and motivation – many authors are skeptical as to its contribution to a more balanced result of the policy process. Transparency of process and motivation can actually hinder an effective process that often relies on a willingness to compromise which is usually more easily gained behind closed doors (Schütt-Wetschky 1997: 58). Yet, the controlling function of transparency on actual financial or other tangible advantages gained by interest groups as a result of a policy process are rather convincing and not as easily dismissed (see Daumann 1999, Leif et al. 2003).

Regulation calling for transparency of lobbying group information may just as well target parliament and its members, government institutions and officials with an obligation to provide information on possible (financial) benefits gained through connections with lobby groups. At its simplest this can involve a disclosure of all additional earnings members of parliament and government have, e.g., through work as board members in associations, corporations, etc. (07.01.2005). While this may temper lobbying relations between lobbyists and more visible officials like members of parliament, this still ignores the power wielded by individual, often back-office bureaucrats whose relations with lobbyists can be just as close and much harder to disclose and regulate.

Another means of control is the introduction of sunset-legislation for policies that do not fulfill certain criteria of universality but instead favor certain groups (Daumann 1999).[63] Related to this are pluralist demands for

---

62 The »too much« means the pure quantity of financial and personnel reporting required that in turn obscures the »too little« of information provided on actual group influence and goals (Lane 1964).

63 To decide on the universality or the lack of the same in legislation Daumann suggests the installation of an independent institution (1999: 195f). Yet, in a sense this pushes the

judicial and administrative scrutiny of legislation with the goal of avoiding the discrimination of minority interests (Cohen et al. 1992: 413f). Imposing such requirements for transparency and legislation, however, raises questions of day-to-day feasibility and the consequences for process efficiency and effectiveness.

Eliminating policy process loopholes through transparency, control, and legislative review is one thrust suggested in literature. Another, which can also be seen as a special extension of the first, is the idea of institutionalization. This includes both an institutionalization of the participatory or bargaining process – which can mean anything from basic information and consulting committees to complex corporatist arrangements (Beyme 1969: 165ff, Vieler 1986: 180)[64] – and an official institutionalization of interest groups themselves granted semi- or quasi-public status and subject to regular review (Schmitter 1994, Cohen et al. 1992). Institutionalization is expected to lead to a »domestication« of lobby groups (Saipa 1971: 196). A quasi-public status entails the introduction of standardized, more in-depth disclosure on the part of the lobby groups and regular status reviews provide the means of enforcing this. Also, process effectiveness and efficiency gains are expected where participation is channeled and the main players develop more seasoned and professional interaction (Vieler 1986: 180ff). The flip-side, well known from the earlier discussion of corporatist arrangements, can be a lock-down of the status quo and a further weakening and exclusion of under- or unrepresented interests.

The bottom line goal in avoiding policy process manipulations is to ensure an open and fair policy process enabling interest groups' positive impact, balanced with regard to possible group inequalities, and organized as to ensure greatest possible effectiveness and efficiency while avoiding a lock-down of the status quo. The most promising approach seems to be that of careful process design; however, group inequalities may need special attention beyond the mere provision of an open and fair process. Altogether there will always remain a certain trade-off between balancing for fairness and process efficiency and effectiveness.

---

problem to the next level because an insulation of this institution from interests is both unrealistic and, to a certain extent, undemocratic.

64 Beyme sees the possibility of institutionalizing group participation at different levels of intensity and during several stages of the policy process: hearings involving government bureaucrats during the preparatory stages of policy development; hearings involving parliamentary committees during consultation; involvement in commissions; regular corporatist arrangements, e.g., standing committees (1969: 165ff).

Moving on beyond potential negative lobbying impact on the political decision-making process, there is an array of institutional and regulatory recommendations concerning possible threats to the more general principles of political equality and citizen self-determination as well as to legitimacy of representative government. In both the case of the citizen and of government the suggestions aim at keeping both in the driver's seat and in final control of decisions. Several of the suggestions made above to strengthen the democratic policy process – through balancing of power inequalities between different interests, through transparency and control – typically also serve to strengthen the democratic position of the individual citizen. In addition to these, many authors call for the introduction of some sort of (minimal) requirements for the internal organization of interest groups with the goal of reconnecting group leaders and individual members through stronger authorization and accountability (Rudzio 1977: 42f, Vieler 1986: 174ff). Different variations propose mandatory internal democracy for publicly licensed interest representation (Anderson 1979), benefits and special status for internally democratic organizations (Cohen et al. 1992), or an indirect constraint of peak organizations through a democratization of its subsidiaries (Hirst 1992).

While these suggestions may serve to reconnect leaders and group members and to empower the latter, the call for internal democratization ignores two facts of lobbying in today's democracies. The first is that many lobbies are not bottom-up citizen organizations but instead represent individual corporations; in these cases interest representation is based not on the principle of political equality but on an economic logic of power and the shareholder principle. The second is that in a pluralist system members of an organization already have the means of sanctioning unwanted leadership decisions and behavior by withdrawing their support in form of financial contributions, membership numbers, etc.[65] To demand internal democratic processes from member organizations would have a mainly negative effect on their effectiveness and efficiency further weakening them vis-à-vis the financially advantaged corporate lobbies.[66]

---

65 As mentioned before, Schmitter further develops this approach by suggesting a distribution of mandatory tax contributions to interest groups through a voucher system allowing the citizens to express their (proportional) interest preferences (1994).

66 Discussions of the pros and cons of internal democratization can be found in, among others, Finer (1960: 133ff), Beyme (1969: 187ff), or Rudzio (1977: 28ff).

Where the aim is to keep the government in the driver's seat by safe-guarding its legitimacy from such images as that of a mere puppet on the strings of so many lobbies or factions, several of the above mentioned recommendations reappear. Since the republican idea of the insulation of government institutions from lobby approaches (see Cohen et al. 1992) has in general been dismissed, the most commonly heard suggestion is that of transparency. This includes the provision of information on financial and other connections between government officials and lobby groups and could preemptively deal with allegations. Such measures could be flanked by a (financial) strengthening of legislators and bureaucrats who often depend on resources provided by lobby groups as was examined in Chapter 2.3.4 (Saipa 1971: 195, Leif et al. 2003: 28). Transparency could be extended to such debates held behind closed doors in parliamentary committees and party deliberations to further disclose possible interest affiliation (Finer 1960: 130ff). This might, however, prevent compromises that often rely on intransparency as to concessions and the like.

Table 13: Suggested balancing and correction of potential negative lobbying impact

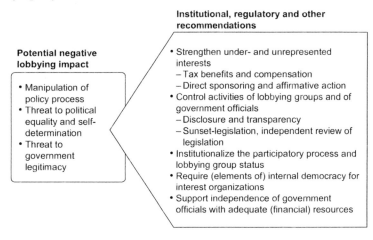

Institutional, regulatory and other recommendations

Potential negative lobbying impact

* Manipulation of policy process
* Threat to political equality and self-determination
* Threat to government legitimacy

* Strengthen under- and unrepresented interests
 – Tax benefits and compensation
 – Direct sponsoring and affirmative action
* Control activities of lobbying groups and of government officials
 – Disclosure and transparency
 – Sunset-legislation, independent review of legislation
* Institutionalize the participatory process and lobbying group status
* Require (elements of) internal democracy for interest organizations
* Support independence of government officials with adequate (financial) resources

Source: Compiled from Anderson 1979, Beyme 1969, Cohen et al. 1992, Daumann 1999, Eschenburg 1955, Finer 1960, Frankfurter Rundschau 07.01.2005, Hirst 1992, Lane 1964, Leif et al. 2003, Richter 1997, Rudzio 1977, Saipa 1971, Schmitter 1994, Schütt-Wetschky 1997, Vieler 1986

Van Schendelen has a rather different approach to the problem of balancing positive and negative lobbying impact. In his examination of lobby groups in the European Union he speaks less of regulation and more of

»system-bound correction mechanisms« (2002: 307), a self-regulation that can be reinforced »by the *activation, establishment* and *professionalisation* of many more interest groups in their capacity as EU lobby groups« (2002: 304). He sees three sets of players involved in this self-correction approach. First of all, there are the lobby groups themselves that keep the system open through constant competition, e.g., by reopening the arena for others in order to gain more support for their goals; and even where groups remain on the outside they add to the control of the process. Secondly, there are the EU officials and their wish to remain in the driver's seat. This leads to a power paradox to be examined in a later chapter: the larger the number of groups involved the stronger the position of the official on the EU side of the process; not only are there gains from the added resources and information but the large number of groups also places the official in a position of being able to make independent, balanced decisions while referring to the need to satisfy the diverse group demands. Thirdly, public opinion backed by mass media plays a key role in maintaining the self-correction described and the two principles on which they are based: open entry and fair competition.

Many of the recommendations summarized above point in the same direction as van Schendelen's »*activation, establishment* and *professionalisation*« (2002: 307). However, he sees all three sets of players equally involved in the process instead of laying it mainly in the hands of government as most of the other authors seem to do. In the end, it is most probably an interconnected process in which interest groups and citizens drive the activation and subsequently control the quality of the process while government is responsible for defining certain rules of the game that help establish and professionalize lobbying, i.e., input and consultation arrangements, codes of conduct, etc.

A balancing of interests and their impact on democracy certainly also depends on the characteristics of the individual political system in place. In view of the consociational character of the European Union system to be analysed in Part II a brief examination should concern itself with the special relationship between consociational democracy and lobbying. Do their effects on the basic democratic principles of political equality and self-determination reinforce each other or do they cancel each other out? Does the system allow for a self-correcting balancing of lobbying effects? Does a consociational democracy demand distinctive regulatory and other provisions for its lobby groups?

A mapping of consociational democracy's advantages and disadvantages onto the two democratic principles and the four cornerstones in Chapter 1.2 paints a heterogeneous picture. On the one hand, the consociational emphasis on unanimity as well as on subsidiary autonomy and on an overall proportionality supports political equality of both vote and voice. This holds true for all instances in which representation is either determined by vote or is otherwise formally controlled for proportionality. Similarly, consociational democracy allows for self-determination where it comes to institutionalized authorization and accountability. On the other hand, consociational weaknesses emerge where formality gives way to informality and intransparency, where non-elected persons and bodies are involved in the policy process and equal representation and citizen control of decisions can no longer be guaranteed.

The positive and negative impact of lobbying reinforces the tendencies of consociational democracy as summarized above. The pattern speaks of a strong correspondence between the decision-making processes of consociationalism and (pluralist) lobbying. Positive reinforcement is especially obvious when it comes to the actual method of decision-making; given the chance of undesirable outcome due to possible stronger influence of others most lobby groups prefer consensus, proportionality, and unanimity. »They prefer the large chance of winning a part of the game by consensus to the small chance of taking the full game by majority vote« (Van Schendelen 2002: 295). Groups that see no chance of winning anything at all will in particular push for unanimous decision-making. Thus, the lobby groups' desire to further their interests reinforces political equality of vote and voice as secured in the consensus principle of consociational democracy.

However, there exists the threat of a negative reinforcement of consociational democracy's tendency for unbalanced representation and its impact on political equality created by the inclusion into the process of non-elected decision-makers such as lobbyists, experts, etc. Where groups do not balance each other for influence as described or where certain interests remain unrepresented, a lack of institutionalization always bears the risk of unbalanced representation. Another possibility for negative reinforcement concerns the mechanisms of authorization and accountability underlying the freedom of self-determination in a representative system. The existence of non-elected persons and bodies throughout the policy process, something that is characteristic for a consociational system, is due to a large part also to the inclusion of lobby groups. They are not dependent on (re-)authorization by the public through elections and are thus beyond this form of control normally exercised in a democracy. This is underlined by the intransparency and informality of the lobbying process which profits from and reinforces the prevalence of informal and intransparent workings typical of consociational democracy. In contrast to this, what remains quite unaffected by the activities of lobby groups are the formalized aspects of self-determination, elections and their regular cycles.

Table 14: Lobbying may reinforce effects of consociational democracy on underlying democratic principles

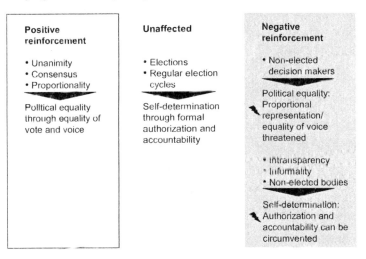

Positive reinforcement	Unaffected	Negative reinforcement
• Unanimity • Consensus • Proportionality	• Elections • Regular election cycles	• Non-elected decision makers
Political equality through equality of vote and voice	Self-determination through formal authorization and accountability	Political equality: Proportional representation/ equality of voice threatened
		• Intransparency • Informality • Non-elected bodies
		Self-determination: Authorization and accountability can be circumvented

Source: Own framework (see also Chapter 1.2)

The correspondence of positive and negative influences of consociationalism and lobbying on basic democratic principles suggests that mechanisms balancing for the effects of one will possibly also be applicable to a balancing effort for the other. This is a focus of the examination of the system in place in the European Union in Part II. For now the regulatory and other measures that seem most suitable to complete the self-correction conveyed in van Schendelen's examination are measures aimed at creating an open and fair process with balanced and transparent participation and representation of interests. Which of these are most suitable for European lobbying is a subject of Chapters 5 and 6.

Chapter 3 concludes Part I of this work. It synthesized the analyses of the two preceding chapters into a theoretical framework that integrates lobbying into modern democracy, in particular consociational democracy, while both profiting from its positive impact and controlling for its negative impact on the two basic principles and the four cornerstones of democracy introduced in Chapter 1.1. In Part II this framework functions as a theoretical backdrop for the in-depth examination of democracy and lobbying in the European Union today and in the future.

II. The European Union

Through an in-depth examination of the EU system of governance and a detailed analysis of the organization and processes of EU lobbying Part II develops an understanding of the interrelation between democracy and interest lobbying in the European Union. Based on this understanding it assesses the opportunities and limits to advancing the democratic sustainability of EU lobbying within the broader perspective of the continued democratization of European governance.

The examination of EU democracy in Chapter 4 makes extensive use of the frameworks offered by the normative and the comparative empirical models of democracy outlined in Chapter 1 and draws on that chapter's insights on democracy beyond the nation-state. The proclaimed European democratic deficit is put into perspective by the normative standards formulated as the two basic principles and the four cornerstones of representative democracy. The realities of the institutional backdrop and the policy process of the European Union further inform this perspective and are considered in the subsequent proposal for measures towards alleviating the EU's democratic deficit. This normative approach to the EU is complemented by an analysis of EU consociationalism and the multi-level system of governance characterized by a prevalence of horizontal and vertical policy networks. Chapter 4 concludes by acknowledging the latest challenges to EU democracy, i.e., the 2004 enlargement, which raised the number of member states to 25, and the proposed Constitution for the European Union stalled in its ratification process since May 2005.

Chapter 5 explores the complex system of EU lobbying covering the development and current composition of the lobbying landscape, the organization of different types of interest lobbies and their classification based on the two-by-two matrix developed earlier in Chapter 2. The main institutional addressees of EU lobbying are investigated as to their different points of access, their preferences in access goods and styles of approach as well as the types of lobby groups they most commonly interact with. The variety of access goods and methods of approach demanded by the European lobbying addressees strongly influences the lobbying process, its methods and the resources required to achieve its necessary breadth and depth, all of which are part of this chapter's examination. Finally, the regulatory environment of EU lobbying is reviewed and compared to the experience of different national lobbying regulations.

Combining the insights of the two previous chapters Chapter 6 analyzes the actual impact of lobbying on EU democracy and considers probable developments of the lobbying system expected for the near future. By exploring the opportunities and limits of a democratically integrated system of EU lobbying and placing them in the greater context of EU democracy and consociationalism Chapter 6 rounds off Part II and concludes what this work set out to accomplish.

4. Democracy in the European Union

»The EU is a polity. It does have a system of governance. But the polity does not yet conform to any existing model of liberal democratic, representative government« (Lodge 1996: 200). This quote expresses the two preoccupations dominating what will be called the *definition debate*. The first is the rather unsuccessful attempt to label the EU system with any of a large range of known definitions taken from nation-states, international organizations, etc. The second is the belief – revealed here by Lodge's use of the word yet – that this will some day be possible (and desirable) as the EU manages to install such a system.[67]

The most common as well as the most helpless of all labels is that of the political system *sui generis* – »of little use either for classification or for clarification« (Abromeit 1998a: 3f, see also Offe 2000). However, the broad *sui generis* statement is usually followed by a description or analysis of the current state of EU institutions and the policy processes. This often leads up to a more precise though not necessarily more accurate labeling of the system that sees the EU in a developmental stage between known models (e.g., Falkner 1994: 69ff). Beyond the *sui generis* definition Wallace (2000b: 9) identifies three camps that represent the range of labels used to define the EU system: the EU as 1) a transnational or international organization, 2) a state in the making[68], or 3) a governance rather than a government. Yet another, slightly different classification of the definition debate is offered by Goodman (1997: 172) who sees three dominating, ideal-type labels: Europe of nation states, federal Europe, Europe of the regions. All of these labels are based on the observation of EU system characteristics. Intergovernmental, transnational labels tend to emphasize unanimity rules,

---

67 There are more authors who turn to the generic term of polity avoiding the decision on a label, e.g., McGrew who calls the EU a »law-governed partially democratic international polity« (1997: 18).

68 Often further qualified as a federal state (see Schmidt 1997: 130f).

(inter-state) bargaining, and the representation of national interests. Supra-national, state-like labels quote majority rules, the binding authority of EU law, popular election of the European Parliament (EP), as well as the re-peat-game, problem-solving mode of decision-making as defining charac-teristics. Regional labels see a dominant role of the principle of subsidiarity in EU politics and of the representation of regional interests.

However, many authors agree that the European Union is unlikely to develop into any of the above clear-cut systems (Jachtenfuchs 1997, Benz 1998, Héritier 1999). Their view seems to be dominated by the governance rather than the government idea.

Almost fifty years after the creation of the first European institution it makes less and less sense to understand and judge the European Union by reference to one of these two ideal-typical models [federal state or international organization]. One possibility to deal with the present state of the EU without loosing its particular features out of site is to regard it as »dynamic multi-level system«. (Jachtenfuchs 1997: 2)

It is this definition that forms part of the comparative empirical analysis of the EU system in Chapter 4.2. The complexity expressed by the term of multi-level governance encompasses intra-level and inter-level interaction of supranational, national and regional as well as territorial and functional actors all of which, in addition to their official vertical and horizontal roles, tend to be part of multidimensional policy-networks.

Where the definition debate is an attempt to provide our understanding of the unique characteristics of the EU political system with a comprehen-sive supporting structure, the *efficiency dilemma* is a second topos shaping the discussion and understanding of democracy in EU. This alleged dilemma between efficiency and democracy describes the observed effect that strengthening EU democracy, e.g., by enhancing accountability or political equality (see Andersen et al. 1996b: 261), can add complexity to decision-making processes with a possible negative effect on process efficiency and effectiveness. The efficiency dilemma should in fact be called the effec-tiveness dilemma since it is mainly the ability to deliver results that is meant to be weighed against the fulfillment of democratic requirements. In con-trast, efficiency stresses the economical use of resources instead of the achieved results. However, a majority seems to refer to the efficiency ver-sus democracy dilemma (Héritier 2003, Benz 1998, Jachtenfuchs 1997) rather than to effectiveness (Andersen et al. 1996d). In a rare example

Neyer (2004) explicitly analyzes both the EU's decision-making efficiency, focusing on time lags, and its effectiveness, i.e., goal attainment.

In the discussion of democracy in the European Union it is often hard to tell apart normative and descriptive approaches both of which are frequently combined with practical consultative pointers as to how to heighten either the EU's efficiency or its democratic quality. Authors will further strengthen their arguments by referring to some concept of legitimacy. Depending on the direction in which the argument leans this will either be a legitimacy gained through the effectiveness and efficiency of the system (output legitimacy) or a legitimacy gained through the adherence to democratic norms (input legitimacy). In today's EU trade-offs are continuously being made between decision-making effectiveness, efficiency, and democratic norms. It is thus understandable that suggestions towards a solving of the dilemma or of at least balancing the trade-offs warn of the possibility »that too much democracy [...] will decrease the Union's institutional capacities« (Andersen et al. 1996b: 261), that »strengthening parliaments in the European multi-level system [...] threatens the efficiency of negotiations« (Benz 1998: 354).[69] Or more ominously put, »the problems of democracy, legitimacy and effectiveness in the EU can never be solved within the present set of constraints placed upon it by the member states« (Andersen et al. 1996d: 10)

An interesting take by public opinion on the relationship of the three concepts of democracy, efficiency, and legitimacy is expressed by the following: »Theorists of democracy will not like hearing this, but: not attending European elections means trusting Europe. Europe the way it works is not democratic. But it works« (Müller 11.06.2004, own translation). Referring back to the normative cornerstones developed in Chapter 1.1 and the refute of so-called output democracy it becomes clear that the efficiency or effectiveness argument is not one that can be normatively sustained by calling upon democratic legitimacy.[70] A lack of protest against results, i.e.,

---

69 Héritier (2003: 827) more specifically mentions a threat to the efficiency of bargaining should executive representation through the Council be systematically linked to parliamentary representation.

70 Arguments brought forward by Andersen et al. (1996d: 3f) point in the same direction: »In normative democratic theory effectiveness can, however, not replace representativity as an independent basis of legitimacy. On the contrary, democracy and effectiveness are often seen as contradictory terms. However, the tendency to emphasise effectiveness at the expense of parliamentary control is common in national political systems in Western Europe. This tendency has been paralleled by the diffusion of decision-making authority

government effectiveness, may be seen as an indirect granting of output legitimacy and may feed into the idea of so-called output democracy, but it can hardly be declared an expression of democratic support.[71]

A third topos that commonly appears in combination with the definition debate and the efficiency dilemma is the *identity question*. Chapter 1.3 examined the debate on democracy beyond the nation-state and the therein often stated question whether a shared identity, an established *demos*, is a prerequisite of democracy and if so whether such an identity is conceivable beyond the boundaries of a nation-state. The conclusion arrived at was that identity and *demos* are needed only in a very basic form for the establishment of democracy. Democracy and *demos* are mutually reinforcing concepts: Democracy delivers a common space within which accountability and community can develop, a *demos* in *statu nascendi* provides the basic elements of a public-interest orientation and solidarity.[72] The common space referred to is not necessarily that of a state; it has been noted that functional contexts can add to or even replace traditionally territorial contexts.[73] Nevertheless, many challenges remain for the establishment of democracy beyond the state in its known definition. It is this understanding of identity and democracy developed in Chapter 1.3 that is considered as one aspect informing the discussion of EU enlargement and the establishment of a constitution.

All equally common to both academic and public discussion of the European Union and its governance system, the three topoi sketched out above – the efficiency dilemma, the definition debate, and the identity question – each give a taste of the following chapters. At the same time, they reflect the main thrusts of Chapter 1, i.e., the normative, the com-

---

[...].« Note here too the subtle move from the normative to the empirical descriptive that can be found with many authors, as noted earlier.

71 Along similar lines Lodge specifically addresses government efficiency and how this »does not necessarily imply better or even good government« (1996: 205); it mainly and quite simply highlights the competition for restricted financial resources.

72 In the context of the European Union and European integration Offe speaks of political socialization. It is a necessary process for which he suggests five possible guiding images of Europe as 1) guarantor of peace, 2) bastion of freedom, 3) singular synthesis of political values and principles, 4) shared cultural space and way of life, and 5) economy of scale (2000: 80ff).

73 Peters seems to share the ideas of a European democracy beyond (territorial) state-like identity when she states that »democracy is an organizing principle which is not reserved for states, but which can be applied to all kinds of societal structures. We therefore do not need a *Staatsvolk* of a European state« (2003: 5).

parative descriptive, and the question of democracy (and political identity) beyond the nation-state. The order of the following chapters was chosen accordingly to reflect that of the democracy chapter in Part I. Chapter 4.1 picks up the normative debate of which the efficiency dilemma was exemplary. The alleged democratic deficit or deficits of the EU are placed and evaluated in the context of the normative framework developed in Chapter 1.1 with its basic principles and democratic cornerstones. As many of these challenges are related to the main EU institutions and their policy-making process the chapter includes an overview of these.

Just as the debate on a European democratic deficit is best put into perspective within the context of normative requirements, the consociational characteristics of governance prevailing in today's European Union are best understood through a comparative descriptive approach. The groundwork for this was laid earlier in Chapter 1.2. Following up on the definition debate, special attention is paid to the multi-level character of the EU system and the prevalence of networks within the policy process. In addition to the comparative analysis the findings of Chapter 4.2 are also scrutinized in the context of democratic norms to see whether the general shortcomings of consociational democracy identified in Part I are reproduced in the EU's consociational system of multi-level governance and policy networks.

The system of the European Union is in a constant process of development and redefinition either incrementally, e.g., through rulings by the European Court of Justice (ECJ), or in such large steps as the 2004 Eastern enlargement and the continuing process for the establishment of an EU constitution. Chapter 4.3 takes account of these recent challenges to democracy in the European Union with the identity question reappearing as one of several aspects.

4.1 The democratic deficit in perspective

The question of the democratic deficit of the European Union has acquired such a tradition that oftentimes specialists on Europe turn away in boredom. The dimensions of this deficit are well known to them and the debate on a »more or less« (e.g., of transparency), a »not yet or already partly« (e.g., established transnational party-system), or finally even a »possible or impossible« (e.g., transnational democracy) seems pointless to many. The phenomena have been described in detail, the arguments exhausted, and above all the actual development seems to take little notice of these normative questions. (Greven 2000b: 208, own translation)

If this were an exhaustive description of the debate, it would at this point suffice to simply refer the reader to those essays that seem to have been churned out at regular intervals when every new generation of European treaties provoked a public and academic debate on the democratic quality of the European Union (for a timeline see Zweifel 2002). However, the deficit debate is marked by a heterogeneity of argumentative structures, conceptual and normative reference points, and at times even a lack of methodological coherence, e.g., with unidentified shifts from normative to descriptive argumentation. The efficiency dilemma explored above was exemplary of a debate characterized by a confusing multiplicity of implicit assumptions, in its case a tacit abolishment of input legitimacy, i.e., democratic legitimacy, in favor of simple output legitimacy (among others see Costa et al. 2003, Olsen et al. 2000, Zweifel 2002). In addition, a first overview often leaves the reader with the impression that the debate is merely another playing-field for the opponents and supporters of the European project or a must on academic publication lists. Despite all this there are few definite answers to questions such as the following: Is there or isn't there a serious democratic deficit to the political system of the EU? What is the standard to which it is held and what are suggested measurement scales? And what are the possibilities for the EU of actually achieving a normative stretch-target?

This chapter analyzes the alleged democratic deficit by holding the European Union to the normative standard defined in Chapter 1.1 in the model of the four democratic cornerstones – equality of vote, equality of voice, authorization, and accountability. Since many items refer to specific EU institutions as well as to the current policy-making process, these are outlined in as far as they inform and clarify the analysis. The subsequent examination of possible solutions or at least an alleviation of a democratic deficit includes an overview of the different trends characterizing the debate, e.g., those that see no (serious) deficit, those that see in it a problem common to most western democracies, or those that see a deficit and no possibility of resolving it. One trend emphasizes the consociational character of the EU system and the trade-offs it demands within the framework of a normative standard. This school of thought is further explored in a comparative empirical examination in Chapter 4.2.

4.1.1 Challenges to the normative model

Following the structure of the four cornerstones the first question to ask the EU system is whether the *equality of vote* is ensured; are the individual citizens' votes of equal weight in the election of representatives to the European Parliament? The answer to this question is quite simply »no«. This is due to a system that systematically favors smaller member states. Schmitter calls this inequality of political weight one of the fundamental differences between national and EU-citizenship (1998: 18). At the heart of this small state overrepresentation and the disagreement it causes lie the conflicting ideas of the equality of states and the equality of citizens. In federal systems the idea of the equality of territorial units and the inherent overrepresentation of smaller units is taken into consideration through the establishment of a second legislative chamber, such as the German *Bundesrat*. In as far as a comparison is possible, this is the case in the Council where the distribution of votes assigns the largest member state, Germany, 0.3 Council votes per million citizens while Belgium as the tenth largest receives 1.2 votes per million citizens. However, overrepresentation in the first chamber, in federal parliament, seems unique to the EU system. Intergovernmentalism and with it the idea of member-state equality continue to dominate the EU. The Treaty of Nice and its post-enlargement distribution of Parliament seats grants Germany 1.2 seats, Belgium 2.1 seats, and Luxembourg 13.6 seats per million citizens (Bundeszentrale für politische Bildung 2002: 7).

Also to be considered here are the differences between the electoral systems used throughout the European Union for European Parliament elections. Up until the 1999 elections the main point of criticism was the multiplicity of electoral systems, i.e., the coexistence of both proportional and majority, winner-take-all systems in the member states. This strongly interfered with the equality of vote which guarantees each citizen the same weight of vote and possibility of success (Huber 1992: 363ff). With the introduction of a proportional system for the elections for European Parliament in Great Britain before the 1999 elections the most serious difference in electoral systems has disappeared – this includes the ten member states that joined in the 2004 enlargement (Nohlen 2004: 33). The remaining differences are mainly of a technical nature and hardly interfere with the equality of vote across EU borders.[74] However, the heterogeneity of electoral systems is seen as weakening the Parliament's representational powers; supposedly, the lack of a unitary system throughout the EU leads to a domination of national parties and interests in European Parliament elections (Benz 1998: 347f, Muntean 2000: 8).

Beyond the most common, most structured and therefore most easily evaluated channel of political participation, namely elections, how well is an equal chance for participation secured in the EU system? *Equality of voice*, the second cornerstone of the normative model, is not conveniently quantifiable, e.g., by measuring the weight and value of individual votes. Instead it calls for a more qualitative assessment of the citizen's possibilities of political participation and influence through a multiplicity of channels though mainly through interest groups and their participation, e.g., in non-elected bodies such as EU-level committees. In the EU much of the decision-making and policy process takes places within so-called policy networks. Their set-up and workings are explored in Chapter 4.2.1. At this point it is important to note that policy networks include both elected and non-elected decision-makers, governmental and non-governmental players and that their *modus operandi* is often as much informal as it is formal. It is in the »unequal and unfair access« (Weiler 1997: 512) to these policy networks that a certain inequality of voice manifests itself. A domination of business interests especially when it comes to the interaction with the most important formal bodies, the Commission and the committees instated by the Council under comitology, can be explained by a difference in resources and by the large role played by economic policies and regulations (Fouilleux et al. 2005: 616, Schmidt 1997: 128, Schmitter 1998: 20). A look at the main EU institutions and policy-making bodies later in this chapter reveals proportionality of interests or a certain lack thereof on the governmental side. The balance of interest group participation and influence recurs as a topic in Chapter 6.

»Most importantly, there is no way that individual citizens voting in free, equal, fair and competitive Euro-elections could influence the composition of Euro-authorities, much less bring about a rotation of those in office« (Schmitter 1998: 19). *Authorization* and *accountability* appear to be the two democratic cornerstones most strongly affected by the democratic

---

74 These differences include national age differences for EP candidates, the regulation of campaigning (advertising, finance, etc.), the organization of constituencies, the method of vote counting and the like (see Nohlen 2004: 31ff).

deficit. While the validity of the above quote may be carried by general argument, it is informative to examine the authorization and accountability or lack thereof for the individual institutions. From the point of view of the citizen, democratic authorization can generally be split into direct and indirect authorization such that one or several representative bodies are elected directly and in turn elect and instate further bodies. Accordingly, accountability is either direct electoral accountability or the accountability of non-elected bodies to those elected and thus directly accountable to the voters.[75] In the European Union this makes the Parliament the only EU institution directly authorized by and accountable to the electorate (Héritier 1999, Muntean 2000). It is, however, not responsible for the authorization of the Council and the Commission or only in a rather unsatisfactory manner.

The Commission is appointed by the member states, i.e., its President and other members are chosen by »»common accord« in the Council« (Wallace 2000b: 12) with the Parliament exercising (limited) powers of confirmation and dismissal. The 2004 confirmation process for the Barrosso Commission showed that the refusal of individual candidates for commissioner is indeed possible. However, the dismissal is restricted by the Commission's collegial responsibility allowing only for a dismissal of the whole body by a two-thirds vote in Parliament. While the 1999 Treaty of Amsterdam granted the power of confirmation as opposed to the former consultation, thus weakening former criticism that the Commission »lacks electorally based political legitimacy« (Schmidt 1997: 131f), parliamentary influence on the actual composition of the Commission continues to be slight (Decker 2002: 261).

Though some argue that the Commission receives its formal authorization through the Council, this chain of legitimation is mostly perceived as being too long and indirect to be of democratic quality especially when considering that the Commission has control over the legislative agenda (Höreth 1998: 12, Lord 1998: 26).Which brings us to the Council and its indirect authorization through the national governments. Similarly to the Commission the Council, as the second strong actor in EU legislation, is criticized for being too far removed from the electorate in the chain of

---

75 In a parliamentary system the legislative, i.e., the parliament receives the direct mandate from the voters and is responsible for the authorization of the executive and holds it accountable. In a presidential system legislative and executive are separately authorized and held accountable directly by the voters.

indirect authorization (Andersen et al. 1996d: 4, Decker 2002: 260f, Eichener 2000: 349).[76] The same can then be said about secondary institutions such as Council and Commission bureaucracy with its working groups and committees or the committees under comitology (Voelzkow 2000: 287).

The shortcomings in democratic authorization are magnified where it comes to the lack of accountability; it appears to stem mainly from three sources. The first lies in the intransparency and informality characteristic of the consociational, multi-level system. Secondly, a functioning system of EU-level accountability would have to rely on stronger intermediaries such as a European media and EU parties. Thirdly, the different EU institutions each have their own difficulties when it comes to democratic accountability; these are often inseparably linked with their lack of authorization as examined above.

As Lord remarks, »multi-level governance systems such as the EU will always produce distinctive problems of democratic control« (1998: 90) since responsibilities for policy decisions are hard to assign to a specific player and are instead lost between several levels of governance especially where this involves bureaucratic negotiations rather than those of more visible officials (Scharpf 1988: 249). While intransparent responsibilities may help pass unpopular decisions in a system of strongly segmented interests, they nevertheless foreclose the type of democratic control that can hold officials responsible for their policy decisions in cyclically recurring elections. This is also true for the intransparency and informality of negotiations on a single level which exclude the public and include non-elected players (Falkner 1994: 253, Eberlein et al. 2003: 442) and are so common to consociational systems of governance.

Even if better access to such information were possible in the consociational, multi-level system of the European Union, intermediary institutions that could aggregate, publicize, discuss, and explain the policy process and its results are more or less missing on the European level. Parties and the media are organized in the national context where European topics

---

76 In addition, some disapprove of the fact that the individual ministers are authorized by their respective countries alone and the Council is never authorized as a whole on the European level even though the interests represented are »more than the sum of their parts« (Beetham et al. 1998, see also Arnim 2000: 171). However, if the Council is regarded as one of two chambers in an EU legislative, i.e., the regional chamber in a federal system, then this appears as less of an issue.

play only a secondary role in public deliberation and democratic control.[77] Lack of such intermediary institutions heightens the accountability problems of the different EU institutions.

Since it is directly authorized by and accountable to the European electorate, accountability issues of the European Parliament are slight compared to those of the Commission or the Council. Nevertheless, its consensus mode of negotiating, bargaining, and decision-making often lacks sufficient formality and transparency to enable democratic control. As Lord puts it: »It [the EP] is more inclined to make issues complex through vote and veto trading than it is to simplify and differentiate political messages in preparation for the moment of electoral reckoning« (1998: 96). More important, however, regarding democratic accountability is the Parliament's weakness vis-à-vis the Commission. As was mentioned in the context of authorization, Parliament has little means of effective control since it is limited to a collective dismissal of the Commission. The risk of an institutional crisis makes the use of this method of censure rather unlikely as Parliament and Commission share a common interest in strengthening European integration, the EU system and its institutions (Lequesne et al. 2003: 698).[78]

Not only is the Commission unaccountable to the European people (Zweifel 2002: 818); second only to the Council, the Commission, its bureaucratic apparatus and committees, is a main site for the by now proverbial intransparency and informality counteracting usual mechanisms of democratic accountability. The faulty chain of accountability is extended by yet another link namely the fairly independent and non-hierarchical bureaucracy and its insufficient accountability vis-à-vis the however weakly authorized politicians, the Commissioners (Lord 1998: 81ff). Requirements, e.g., provision of information on the process, explanation of decisions, or openness to stakeholders, needed to satisfy accountability of dele

---

77 While this argument is well known and seems uncontested (e.g., Jachtenfuchs 1999: 271, Scharpf 1999: 167, Schmidt 2000a: 433), recent works have started to see a significant change in the European media landscape and their coverage of European politics (Trenz 2005).

78 For Lequesne et al. (2003) the establishment of Committees of Independent Experts by the European Parliament as a means of controlling and assessing the Commission, e.g., in the case of the investigation of the Santer Commission in the late 1990s, shows the weakness of parliamentary accountability that should be making use of such classical instruments as censure and Temporary Committees of Inquiry instead.

gated agents such as the committees under comitology are not sufficiently met (Magnette et al. 2003: 838, also Dehousse 2003).

But nowhere in the EU is lack of transparency as dominating a factor as it is in the Council and its processes. Where the Commission allows access to information – though knowledge of what to actually look for remains key – the Council practices what some call »transparency through communication« (Lord 1998: 87), others call it *Hofberichterstattung*, i.e., royal court reporting (Falkner 1994). The »secrecy« (Zweifel 2002) of Council proceedings makes what little accountability might be possible unactionable. In theory, electoral accountability is what the individual Council members are subjected to through their national parliaments and governments though as is the case with Council authorization the chain of accountability is too long and indirect to satisfy democratic standards.[79]

Table 15: The European Union's democratic deficit

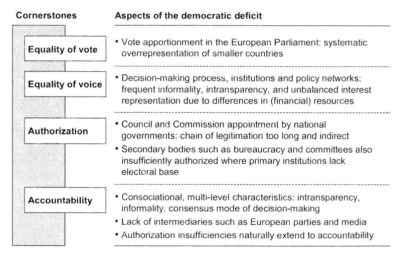

Cornerstones	Aspects of the democratic deficit
Equality of vote	• Vote apportionment in the European Parliament: systematic overrepresentation of smaller countries
Equality of voice	• Decision-making process, institutions and policy networks: frequent informality, intransparency, and unbalanced interest representation due to differences in (financial) resources
Authorization	• Council and Commission appointment by national governments: chain of legitimation too long and indirect • Secondary bodies such as bureaucracy and committees also insufficiently authorized where primary institutions lack electoral base
Accountability	• Consociational, multi-level characteristics: intransparency, informality, consensus mode of decision-making • Lack of intermediaries such as European parties and media • Authorization insufficiencies naturally extend to accountability

Source: Decker 2002, Dehousse 2003, Eberlein et al. 2003, Eichener 2000, Falkner 1994, Fouilleux et al. 2005, Héritier 1999, Höreth 1998, Jachtenfuchs 1999, Lequesne et al. 2003, Lord 1998, Magnette et al. 2003, Muntean 2000, Scharpf 1988, 1999, Schmidt 2000a, Schmidt 1997, Schmitter 1998, Voelzkow 2000, Weiler 1997, Zweifel 2002

---

79 This is also the case where softer methods such as best practice programs are initiated. The so-called open method of coordination which is being applied to an increasing number of policy fields has strengthened both the role of the Council and the Commission while at the same time passing over parliamentary involvement (see, e.g., Borrás et al. 2004, Kaiser et al. 2004).

Though general in its nature the following quote sums up the consociational, governance-inherent accountability problems and points to their institutional base as they were unfolded in the above:

The basic condition of representative democracy is, indeed, that at election time the citizens »can throw the scoundrels out« – that is, replace the government. This basic feature of representative democracy does not exist in the Community and Union. The form of European governance is – and will remain for a considerable time – such that there is no »government« to throw out [...] There is no civic act of the European citizen where he or she can influence directly the outcome of any policy choice facing the Community and Union [...]. Neither elections to the European Parliament nor elections to national parliaments fulfill this function in Europe. (Weiler 1997: 513)

With regard to the four democratic cornerstones this completes the inventory of the challenges facing the EU in form of the so-called democratic deficit. However, two strongly connected phenomena should be mentioned here. The first is the weak standing of EU elections, the second the debate on a European identity which many authors tie into their analysis of the democratic deficit. First pointed out by Reif et al. (1980), European elections for Parliament are generally understood as second-order elections dominated by national political agendas rather than European topics and have a continuously low electoral turnout (Decker 2002, Greven 2000a, Hix 2003). Blame for this is laid on the lack of intermediary institutions already mentioned in the context of the accountability process above. It is believed that only Europe-wide parties and media would be able to sufficiently inform and mobilize the European public that is seen as rather ignorant when it comes to European politics and in particular the activities of the European Parliament (Muntean 2000: 7).

If the lack of intermediaries is one factor generally considered as having a negative impact on the EU democratic system, another, in fact closely related one, is the claimed lack of a European public or, stronger yet, the lack of a European identity. Aspects summed up under the identity or *demos* label are prevalent in texts dealing with the European democratic deficit and are therefore mentioned here. The normative model proposed by this work does not include identity as a democratic cornerstone. It considers a homogenous identity – in the sense of a dominant culture and language – as neither a prerequisite nor a necessity of democracy. Instead a less homogeneous but nevertheless sustainable European identity is believed to be currently developing. However, it must be acknowledged that the identity aspects considered to be part of the democratic deficit by many authors form a significant factor in the challenge for further European integration. »A European people [...] a prepolitical »given«« (Greven 2000a: 37), »a collective subject in its own perception« (Jachtenfuchs 1999: 271, own translation), »a preexisting collective identity« (Scharpf 1999: 167, own translation) is what many demand of EU democracy. Others accept that an identity is something that may develop within a shared political system in a mutually reinforcing way and are less categorical about it as a prerequisite for democracy. However, they identify certain aspects which make such a development difficult and thus may negatively impact the democratic integration of Europe. Most important maybe is the multiplicity of languages that creates a large barrier for the development of a community of communication, a *Kommunikationsgemeinschaft* (Kielmansegg 2003: 58f). It is seen as one of the main reasons behind the missing intermediaries on the European level. The possibility of a general European public – informed and mobilized by European parties and media – is foreclosed by the lack of a common language; political communication remains the realm of elites comfortable communicating in English and French (Greven 2000b: 222f).[80]

4.1.2 Institutional backdrop and the EU policy process

Apart from the problems of intermediary institutions and of a missing common language there exist several other structural and institutional circumstances impacting EU democracy, which should be examined before returning to the deficit debate and an analysis of possible solutions. The above examination of the democratic quality of the EU system repeatedly made use of a differentiation between EU institutions – the Council, the Commission, the European Parliament, the committees, etc. To a large part the deficit seems to be a structural problem. So far mainly individual aspects of the EU policy process and its main official players have been mentioned; the following gives a coherent, concise overview. Though it

---

80 For one reason or the other the cases of other multilingual democracies such as Switzerland, Canada or India are dismissed as irrelevant for a comparison with the European Union (Decker 2002: 265). This dismissal should be reconsidered, a comparison possibly revealing feasible paths towards a common ground for political communication beyond the elite level.

has to be understood that there are many distinctions to be made between the skeleton that such an outline describes and the flesh and blood of EU decision-making (Van Schendelen 2002: 61ff),[81] it nevertheless informs both the deficit debate and the subsequent discussion of EU consociation-alism, multi-level governance, as well as the workings of interest represen-tation.

Exhaustive descriptions of the institutional setting including all minu-tiae of tasks, delegation, and interconnection within the policy process have been covered by many authors (among others Wallace et al. 2000: 9-28) and need not be reproduced here. Instead, those institutional characteristics that appear to have the strongest positive or negative effect on the democratic process, e.g., the scarce use of formal voting in the Council or the dominance of the Commission within comitology, are mag-nified within the context of a model policy process.

The model policy process is outlined in five consecutive phases while in practice, of course, the character of the process can be somewhat iterative and overlapping in its phases. These five phases are called drafting, con-sultation, decision, implementation, and enforcement (see among others Goodman 1997: 177, Van Schendelen 2002: 54). Each of these phases can be assigned key institutional actors and certain defining characteristics and particularities, which leads to the following abstract description of the policy process of the first pillar of the European Union.[82] To begin with, exclusive drafting competence lies with the European Commission. Usu-ally, one Directorate-General (DG) takes the lead and dominates the draft outcome though it will receive input from other Directorates-General concerned (Donnelly 1993: 79, Matláry 1998: 66ff). Resource limitations of the Commission and its DGs have lead to the establishment of a growing

---

81 Van Schendelen (2002) emphasizes the need to differentiate between formal power and actual influence that the individual institutions wield throughout the decision-making process.

82 A top-down look at the EU hierarchy shows a system of three pillars headed by the European Council, i.e., the heads of state, and below it the General Council, i.e., the ministers of foreign affairs. Pillars II and III (Common Foreign and Security Policy run by the ministers of foreign affairs and defense and Justice and Home Affairs run by the ministers of home affairs and justice) are dominated by the Council and its intergovernmental logic of negotiations and primary law, i.e., EU treaties. Pillar I, the European Community, is the setting of the policy process producing secondary and delegated law as described in this chapter.

number of so-called expert committees, which – while wielding no formal power – influence policy drafting in most fields.[83]

In the consultation phase three institutions are regularly consulted by the Commission or the Council: the European Parliament, the European Economic and Social Committee (ESC), and the Committee of the Regions (COR). The Parliament must be at least consulted though now it is in most cases more strongly involved through codecision (Van Schendelen et al. 2003: 6). Where specified by the treaties both the ESC and the COR have to be consulted; compared to other bodies they are, however, seen as marginal players (Neyer 2004). Besides this compulsory consultation there is both the possibility for optional consultation if the Parliament decides to solicit an opinion as well as the possibility for own initiative opinions by the ESC and the COR (Smismans 2000: 3).

The majority of secondary laws today are decided in the codecision procedure involving both the Council and the European Parliament (Rasmussen 2003: 3). This procedure can mean up to two readings and amendment phases in Parliament, its committees and intergroups, and up to two adoptions of a common position in Council or, where Parliament and Council cannot agree on this second common position, a conciliation phase with Parliament to find a final compromise (for an in-depth depiction see Burns 2004, Tsebelis et al. 1997). The legislative work in Council is divided between ten to fifteen specialized Councils under the lead of the respective ministers. The actual work, however, is handled by Coreper, the Committee of Permanent Representatives, and the Council working groups assembled from mainly national experts, both public and private. It is at this level that acceptability of legislation is checked, two-thirds of which then passes through the Council of ministers without further discussion. The wish to avoid the conciliation procedure has lead to a stronger involvement of Parliament committees and MEPs (Members of the European Parliament) in negotiations in the Council working groups, a sign for the process' overlapping character (Fouilleux et al. 2005: 617ff). The decision phase completes the process leading to secondary law, which makes up less than 20 percent of Pillar I legislation and »primarily settles only the

---

83 The *chef de dossier* acts as the interface between the DG and the expert committees concerned; often he or she is also the initiator of the expert committees. Sources quote approx. 1,000 registered expert committees with 50,000 or more persons involved as part-time experts and up to 1,000 more unregistered committees (Van Schendelen 2003b: 28f).

framework or the cadre for further common decision-making [...]. Then the Council decides to delegate the so-called implementation to a comitology committee, an agency or the member states« (Van Schendelen 2003b: 35).

In the implementation phase the majority of delegated law, constituting over 80 percent of EU legislation, is drafted under Commission DG lead with the comitology committees playing a similar role to that of the expert committees during drafting phase; again the *chef de dossier* functions as an interface between committees and the Commission.[84] Directives, regulations, and decrees are adopted in the implementation phase, the first of which require further steps of transposition into national law. While the Commission and the comitology committees are the key players where delegated law is concerned, Parliament can interfere in all cases where delegated law is based on secondary law established under codecision (Van Schendelen 2002: 56).

The European Court of Justice (ECJ), the European Court of Auditors (ECA), and national courts are all seen as actors in the enforcement of EU legislation (Goodman 1997: 177). EU law, primary, secondary, and delegated law, can be challenged through national and European courts. The power of ECJ rulings is astonishing given the fact that apart from some instances that allow the imposing of fines the Court wields no possibilities of sanctions (Wallace 2000b: 22f). Table 16 summarizes the overview of the five phases of the EU policy process and the key institutions and players involved.

Table 16 is a model overview of what van Schendelen (2002) would call the skeleton policy process, as opposed to the flesh and blood, but even here the true power allocation can be sensed. While the formal decision-making power lies with the Council and the Parliament, it is the Commission DGs and the various drafting committees that initiate and shape EU legislation.

---

84 The approximately 450 committees under comitology are divided into advisory, management, and regulatory committees with different levels of power over the Commission via the interference of the Council; they are established by the Council and are officially made up of member state representatives (see among others Dehousse 2003, Van Schendelen 2002).

Table 16: EU policy process for secondary and delegated law*

Drafting	Consultation	Decision**	Secondary law	Implementation	Delegated law	Enforcement
Main institutions/ players	• Commission – DGs – Expert commit-tees	• EP • ESC • COR	• Council – Coreper – Working groups • EP	• Commission – DGs • Comitology committees • EP • (Agencies; nat. legislative)		• ECJ • National courts
Particularities	Exclusive drafting competence	Possibility of own opinion initiative already during draft phase	Commission • Withdrawal rights • Gate-keeper vis-à-vis EP amendments • Mediator in conciliation	Commission dominance in comitology		

* Pillar I   ** Codecision in all fields but agriculture
Source: Dehousse 2003, Fouilleux et al. 2005, Rasmussen 2003, Smismans 2000, Van Schendelen 2002, 2003b, Van Schendelen et al. 2003, Wallace 2000

The Commission's role that is defined by the lead it takes in a) agenda-setting through the exclusive power of initiative, b) mediation between different institutions and interests in Council, Parliament, and committees, and c) securing the implementation and fulfillment of both the treaties as well as secondary and delegated law.[85] Lauresen (1996: 125) sums this up with a reference to Hallstein who described the Commission as motor, broker, and watchdog. However, Commission power can differ depending on the individual policy field or the politics of the policy initiative in question (Wallace 2000b: 12f). Also, it is restricted by the limited (personnel) resources at its disposal. The initiation and involvement of expert committees in the drafting phase is in part an attempt to overcome resource restrictions. The expert committees both strengthen and weaken the influence of the Commission; while their growing numbers give them an obvious omnipresence, they also allow the chefs de dossier to use their

---

85 An argument has arisen as to whether the Commission has lost, kept, or even gained influence in the wake of codecision. While some argue that through the rise of informal communication and coordination between Parliament and Council under codecision the Commission has lost ground to the European Parliament (Stacey 2003: 938), others prove through case studies that the Commission continues to shape legislative outcome more strongly than Parliament (Burns 2004: 10ff).

multiplicity (of interests) to formulate independent positions (Van Schendelen 2003b: 30), a phenomenon Grande calls the »paradox of weakness« (1996: 328ff). Similar things can be noted about the relationship between committees under comitology and the Commission. Though initiated by the Council to support the implementation of delegated law and to represent national interests, comitology committees are strongly influenced by their chairs, the Commission DGs (Dehousse 2003: 802).

The power of the Council and its individual members over the policy process has been seen as lying in the need for unanimity in Council voting and thus the need for consensus. Before the Single European Act (1986) qualified majority voting in the Council was made impossible by the so-called Luxembourg compromise. Since 1986 and especially with the Maastricht (1992) and Nice (2000) treaties qualified majority voting has been expanded into more and more areas of policy. Nevertheless, voting is seldom practiced and consensus decisions remain common (e.g., Hayes-Renshaw 1996: 157).With the alleged dominance of an intergovernmental logic it is often overlooked that most Council decisions, 85–90 percent (Wallace 2000b: 18), are reached in Coreper and the Council working groups. The relative permanence of these bodies has lead to less of an intergovernmental and more of a supranational, a »community method« (Lewis 1998: 12). Whether weakened or not by the decline of an intergovernmental logic of decision-making, Council has indisputably lost some of its power to the European Parliament in the wake of codecision.

With the exception of agriculture and new policy fields, »Council cannot overrule Parliament (not even unanimously, as under cooperation), or present it with take-it-or-leave-it proposals anymore. For the first time in EU history, Council and Parliament are equals« (Zweifel 2002: 823). Parliament is nowadays involved in the policy phases of decision and implementation to a similar extent as Council. While not sharing Zweifel's view of institutional equality between the two, the ever growing importance of Parliament is apparent, e.g., in the increasing role it has started to play for interest groups in EU lobbying (Lodge 1996). In addition and with direct implications for the policy process, Parliament has budgetary powers equal to those of the Council. In a procedure similar to that of codecision it is involved in the adoption or rejection of the budget and grants annual discharge to the Commission for its implementation (Laffan et al. 2000).

The policy process and the institutional set-up surrounding it display the same indecisiveness earlier revealed in the cornerstone-by-cornerstone examination of the so-called democratic deficit, the indecisiveness of a system searching for satisfactory trade-offs between democratic norms and system effectiveness. They continue a tale of insufficiently authorized and unaccountable institutions and players involved in all stages of policy-making and of inter-institutional and intra-institutional processes that lack transparency and often even formality.[86]

4.1.3 Alleviating the democratic deficit

Having examined the deficit debate and highlighted the challenges as they manifest« themselves in the policy process and its institutional setting, the final part of this chapter turns to possibilities of relieving the democratic deficit. At the outset it must be noted that there are several differing takes on the democratic deficit that by no means lead to a singular concept going forward. Some authors reject the notion of a democratic deficit to begin with, others see it as a more common problem of modern democracies, which possibly cannot be alleviated on the European level alone, yet others tackle the challenges to EU democracy, sometimes with individual measures and ideas, sometimes with encompassing concepts and visions.

As Majone (1998) points out, the deficit debate is taking place on two very different levels of abstraction: the first is the level of the European integration process and stems from different views on the different goals of integration and the respective systemic changes they demand; the second level deals more with the given state of institutional set-up and the possibilities of further democratization within. The first group mentioned above, those that see no democratic deficit in the European Union, are joining the debate on the level of the integration process and agree on something they call sufficient legitimation and accountability of the current system. In its verdict the German Constitutional Court (1993: 155-213) took a lead in this argument, which Gustavsson calls the »preservationist position« (1998: 63). It rests on the idea that the EU is a *Staatenverbund* and its democratic legitimation lies with the treaty members, the individual signatory nations (among others Moravcsik 2001). The legitimation granted the EU by its member states is believed to cover the different EU institu-

---

tions and the process of decision-making; it is further deepened by the direct election of the European Parliament (Schmidt 2000a: 425ff).

The polar-opposite of the preservationist position sees a major democratic deficit; it is rooted in the failure or refusal of the EU member states to relinquish their central position and instead shape a democracy on the supranational level (Kielmansegg 2003: 61f, Lodge 1996: 188). Authors arguing this point describe the EU democratic deficit as it was examined earlier in this chapter but see no possibilities of solution or alleviation under the given circumstances (Greven 2000a: 36); »the problems of democracy, legitimacy and effectiveness in the EU can never be solved within the present set of constraints placed upon it by the member states« (Andersen et al. 1996d: 10).

On a second level, removed from the immediate debate on more or less European integration, there is again no agreement on the actual existence of a democratic deficit. Costa et al. point out a group of authors claiming »that the EU is far from suffering from any democratic deficit but is rather inventing a new model of democracy, essentially founded on the diffuse mechanisms of control of the public authorities« (2003: 667). Andersen et al. might be counted to this group; while acknowledging challenges to democracy in modern societies, they see the EU system as a democratic system in development that has clear post-parliamentary governance characteristics, in which »the *democracy of organisations* tends to replace the democracy of citizens and their territorial representatives« (1996a: 230).

Among those that recognize a democratic deficit, there are some that wish to put it in perspective by pointing out that »the so-called democratic deficit is not a genuinely European, but a global problem« (Peters 2003: 12). While they might serve to soften criticism that moves from the democratic deficit directly to an all-out negation of the EU system, such statements can do little in terms of identifying possible development paths for the future if they are not followed up, e.g., with meaningful system comparisons (see for example Majone 1998, Zweifel 2002).[87] Yet, their proponents are right in as far as such phenomena as the lack of transparency and formality, the decline of public participation and accountability exist in most modern democracies, be they national or supranational.

---

87 Héritier (1999: 280) notes that in addition to a comparison with standards and developments in democratic nation-states it has been suggested to draw on intergovernmental organizations for a second take on the democratic qualities of the EU.

The following gives an overview of measures suggested to alleviate or solve the democratic deficit as it was depicted in Chapter 4.1.1, some of which are individual, stand-alone ideas, others are imbedded in larger concepts of where the EU should be headed in the near future. At the same time, trade-offs that such measures might demand are pointed out, e.g., the consociational process of decision-making, though not always democratic by the standards of the four cornerstones, may profit from a certain lack of transparency and formality.

The deficits concerning the equality of vote stem mostly from a systematic overrepresentation of smaller countries in form of a higher apportionment of votes in Council and seats in Parliament per individual citizen. To reach an equality of vote, overrepresentation especially in the European Parliament would need to be ended.[88] Furthermore, a uniform electoral system, i.e., the abolishment of the many (technical) differences between the national proportional systems for the elections for European Parliament, is regularly demanded (see Decker 2002, Føllesdal 1998: 43f). A possible secondary effect could be that such changes towards uniformity would »divest the European elections of their national character« (Decker 2002: 262). However, the elimination of small state overrepresentation would mean a trade-off, namely the loss of the effect that was its goal in the first place. It ensures that minority interests, in this case in the form of small states, are heard and secured within the heterogeneous union of the EU. Minimal representation for the smallest countries also enables a mirroring of national party pluralism in European elections (Nohlen 2004: 32). Last but not least, a forced uniformity of the interpretation of the proportional system would come at the cost of cultural political achievements and pluralism while doing little for the equality of vote. It should at most be a long-term goal of incremental change and adaptation.

Equality of voice in the EU, meaning mainly citizen participation and representation through interest groups, is infringed upon by a lack of transparency, formality, and equal possibility of access throughout the decision-making process, the institutions and policy networks involved

---

88 For two reasons an abolishment of small state overrepresentation in the Council seems less urgent. As mentioned earlier, state equality instead of citizen equality is the underlying idea of second chambers and other bodies representing the interest of regional units rather than of the citizen body as a whole. Secondly and despite qualified majority voting in many fields, unanimity still dominates decision-making in the Council, rendering the individual state allocation of votes insignificant.

therein. Deficits concerning transparency and access to information, also crucial to a functioning system of democratic accountability, are well-known and have been targeted by Commission, Council, and EP initiatives (for details see Héritier 2003). The EP even introduced the registration of MEP-lobbyist contacts and financial transactions. However, the different institutional approaches remain heterogeneous and leave lots of room for improvement. One point of criticism generally is that many mechanisms of access and involvement in the EU remain subject to the availability of resources thus privileging certain actors over others (Magnette et al. 2003: 839, Weiler 1997: 512). Where informality dominates, this will most certainly remain the case and leads to demands for participatory rights for all parties affected, e.g., by the work of comitology and expert committees (Dehousse 2003: 807). As the deficits connected to this cornerstone are central to the understanding of EU lobbying's achievements and short-comings, they are taken up in further detail in Chapter 6. Measures to be discussed at that point include such ideas as Weiler's *Lexcalibur* (Weiler 1997), an electronic public square benefiting all intermediaries, interest groups, the media, etc.

The insufficient authorization of the Commission, the Council, and their secondary bodies was discussed earlier as a third focal point of the EU's democratic deficit. The length and indirectness of the chain of legitimation is the obvious consequence of a system with strong intergovernmental characteristics designed to reserve a powerful and central role for the member states. Most measures suggested to alleviate the authorization deficit therefore call for a more supranational system in its own right with direct elections of all its main bodies and stronger powers of authorization for the directly elected bodies over indirectly authorized institutions. Institutionally speaking this leads up to two alternative models: a parliamentary or a presidential democracy (see among other Decker 2002, Lord 1998, Muntean 2000).

»According to the national blueprint, a European Union organized as a (strongly decentralized) federal state with a two-chamber system representing the European people and the member states is most desirable« (Höreth 1998: 19) – a parliamentary system, which for many seems more likely (e.g., Jachtenfuchs 1999, Muntean 2000), does not only mean an empowerment of Parliament, as first chamber legislator, vis-à-vis the Council. The EP would also become the main or even sole source of authorization for the Commission; this could include anything from the individual confirmation and dismissal of each individual commissioner (Williams 1991: 171) to the full-fledged election of the Commission from among the members of parliament (Zürn 1996: 43f). In addition to a strengthening of the EP there are suggestions to shorten the chain of legitimation for the Council through a direct election of the Council of Ministers by national constituencies (Arnim 2000: 284f, Zürn 2000: 104).

Other authors see the current system and its power relationship between the legislative (EP and Council) and the executive (Commission) as having a greater affinity to a presidential model (Decker 2002: 266) and assign such a system a better possibility of »differentiating the competition for power in the European and national arenas« (Lord 1998: 131). The core feature would be a direct election of the Commission president.[89] A popular election of the chief executive is desirable for such reasons as that it would turn EU elections into elections in their own right, no longer second-order national elections, and would strongly promote the EU-level development and organization of parties, a media, a European public (Decker 2002, Lord 1998).[90] However, such a presidential model seems less likely to develop in the near future as it would mean a bigger loss of power for the member states (Hix 2003: 176).

Both of these models would mean a radical shift away from the present system and its consociational and intergovernmental bargaining features. An improvement of the authorization of EU institutions and politics might also be achieved with less far-reaching reforms and additions to the present system, or so some authors ideas suggest.[91] The following gives a brief

---

89 For thoughts on the different electoral processes see Hix (2003: 175), e.g., a two-step procedure similar to the French presidential elections or a procedure involving an electoral college as in the U.S. presidential elections.

90 As an aside it can be noted that this argument provokes the same so-called chicken-and-egg problem (in German: *Henne-Ei-Problem*) known from the larger debate on a European *demos*. It evolves around the question whether a European-level media, public, etc. is needed as a system prerequisite or whether it might develop and later also change over time. For example Höreth (1998: 20) sees no possibility for substantial enhancement of legislative and executive authorization through one of the mentioned institutional reforms as long as there is no real European public to own such a system and its processes.

91 Some authors openly oppose the encouragement of a supranational parliamentary system, especially a unicameral one, on the grounds that »the EU lacks the political identity that is required for such a government« (Weale 1998: 50). Thus the discussion comes full circle and returns to one of EU democracy's possible waterloos, the identity question.

sketch of three such ideas: the substantial inclusion of national parliaments in the EU policy process, the implementation of the principle of subsidiarity, and the introduction of elements of direct democracy.

A rather preservationist possibility of securing greater authorization could be the tie-in of national parliaments or national parliamentarians into the EU legislative process. »Policy making in Europe is characterized by a heavy executive bias. In casting governments in the role of legislators, it alters the balance of power between governments and parliaments in member states« (Abromeit 1998a: 24). However, the national parliaments' loss of power over legislation is a common phenomenon in Western Europe – especially in parliamentary democracies (Decker 2002: 266) – and is merely underlined by the EU's dominance in certain policy fields. Also, as Eichener points out there is first the logistical problem of organizing such an enlarged process and second the inclusion could lead to just another level of parliamentary specialists »locked into iron triangles with bureaucracy and interest groups« (2000: 351) so that there is not much gained in terms of parliamentary control.

Rather preservationist as well but also driven by the desire for more participation is the suggestion of increasing subsidiarity, i.e., decentralizing as much of the decision-making process as possible and bringing it closer to those affected by it. The main model based on this principle is that of a »Europe of the regions« (Jachtenfuchs 1997), but subsidiarity benefits both the national and the regional decision-makers. This is why Matláry calls it »the fashionable remedy […] a strategy to weaken inter alia the EP« (1995: 115) and points out that it can cancel out the advantages of EU-wide policies, e.g., in the environmental field. Also, the supposition that the regions form the base for European civil society (Benz 1998: 348) remains to be confirmed.

A third concept follows in logical progression from the two preceding – the Europe of the nations and the Europe of the regions – and that is the Europe of the citizens. The introduction of elements of direct democracy, i.e., referenda and public initiatives, is widely proposed as a solution to the EU's legitimation problems in the areas of authorization and accountability (Abromeit 1998a, Arnim 2000, Benz 1998, Grande 2000b, Hix 2003, Nentwich 1998). Such elements could bring with it further advantages such as increased public deliberation, mobilization of EU civil society, and might generally enhance integration and European identity (Papadopoulos

2005: 457ff, Weiler 1997: 513f, Zürn 2000: 105f).[92] However, there exists the possibility of failure such as might be perceived in current EU elections: first, such referenda could become mere second-order national elections failing to mobilize a European public (versus a national public); second, they could meet with a general disinterest in European topics (Hix 2003: 174).[93]

Institutional reform towards a supranational parliamentary or presidential democracy, a Europe of the nations, a Europe of the regions, a Europe of the citizens – all of these concepts have been developed with an aim, among others, of enhancing the democratic authorization of EU decision-makers and the decision-making process (or at least trying to create a substitute legitimacy for decisions made). As a result of regular re-authorization such an enhancement would also positively affect democratic accountability. Yet, accountability is more than simple cyclical authorization. Accountability demands informed and effective authorization. First, this demands a process in which the citizens and their representatives are given the possibilities to access information – directly or through intermediary bodies such as the media, parties, interest groups – about the policy process, its development, the decision-makers involved, and those supporting and influencing their work. Second, to make effective use of this information the accountability process must enable the citizens to indeed reach all those involved in the EU policy process and hold them accountable for their actions and decisions.[94]

It has been suggested that the effectiveness of the accountability process could be heightened by refining the Parliament's censure mechanisms vis-á-vis the Commission. One step could mean ending collegial responsi-

---

92 See Abromeit (1998a: 95ff) for a detailed proposal on the different types of referenda and initiatives to be introduced, their areas of application, details of the actual process, and possible scenarios to be expected.

93 On a more general note, Schneider reiterates one well-known criticism of plebiscitary instruments, especially in complex and functionally differentiated societies, namely the risk of »trivializing politics« (2000: 263).

94 Similarly, the Commission recognized these demands in its White Paper on governance which »promotes greater openness, accountability and responsibility for all those involved [in the policy process]« (European Commission 2001: 3). The individual action points suggested in this context focus less on overly formalized, legal procedures and more on such instruments as standards, guidelines, and codes of conduct. Furthermore, the importance of European parties and the media as intermediaries within a process of accountability and participation has also been officially recognized (e.g., Committee of the Regions 2001).

bility and instead making each commissioner the individual subject of accountability, e.g., through the President who is again accountable to the EP – a suggestion triggered also by the 1999 censure vote of Parliament and the resignation of the entire Commission after the investigation of some of its members (Muntean 2000). For those secondary bodies, such as committees and agencies, only indirectly accountable through the Commission control mechanisms would include:

clear statutory objectives, oversight by specialized legislative committees, strict procedural requirements, judicial review, appointments of key personnel, budgetary controls, reorganization, professionalism, public participation, monitoring by interest groups, even inter-agency rivalry. (Majone 1998: 27)

With such mechanisms not fully in place in the EU today Magnette et al. (2003) is prompted to speak of the »pathologies of delegation«. To include the EP on a level beyond that of controlling the Commission would mean taking into account the network-character of the EU policy process especially in its committees and equipping the EP with instruments to monitor its multi-level proceedings (Dehousse 2003: 804f). Apart from possible logistical challenges there are no obvious down-sides to the above suggestions except for those that wish to argue in favor of a collegial accountability of the Commission securing a unified approach, positive support, and consensus oriented problem-solving.

The multi-level policy process is characterized by a lack of transparency and formality, its usual consensus mode of decision-making further obscuring responsibilities. The lack of intermediaries on the European scene does nothing to facilitate electoral control. On the one hand, the natural reaction to these observations is the widely stated demand for more transparency and formality and a support for the development of EU-level media, parties, and interest groups. Intransparency and informality, on the other hand, are said to have positive effects on producing actionable outputs in the consociational reality of the EU policy process; the one sure result of formalizing would thus be bureaucratization (Schneider 2000: 262). This brings the argument back to the so-called efficiency dilemma.

Table 17: Measures towards alleviating the EU's democratic deficit

Cornerstones	Suggested measures
Equality of vote	• Abolish systematic overrepresentation of smaller countries in Parliament (and Council) • Standardize electoral system throughout member states
Equality of voice	• Throughout decision-making process: Ensure transparency and access to information, formalize interest group participation, provide for equal access possibility
Authorization	• Fundamental supranational reform: Parliamentary or presidential system (i.e., parliamentary authorization of Commission or popular authorization of its President) **OR** • Incremental reform as substitute for popular authorization of EU bodies, e.g., EU of nations, EU of regions, EU of citizens
Accountability	• Profit from measures enhancing authorization and further sharpen parliamentary or electoral accountability of Commission and electoral accountability of the Council • Heighten policy process transparency and formality • Support the development of EU intermediaries

Source: Abromeit 1998a, Benz 1998, Decker 2002, Dehousse 2003, Eichener 2000, Føllesdal 1998, Héritier 2003, Hix 2003, Höreth 1998, Huber 1992, Jachtenfuchs 1997, 1999, Lord 1998, Magnette et al. 2003, Majone 1998, Muntean 2000, Weiler 1997, Williams 1991, Zürn 1996, 2000

All of the characteristics of the democratic deficit as examined in Chapter 4.1.1 and the measures suggested to alleviate it in Chapter 4.1.3 as well as many characteristics of the EU policy process described in Chapter 4.1.2 bear a strong resemblance to the democratic challenges identified for a consociational democracy in Part 1 of this work. Its contrasting of the comparative empirical concept with the normative model yielded a dilemma between the satisfaction of democratic standards and the practicability and effectiveness of a political system encompassing several heterogeneous segments – in the case of the EU: member nation-states – none of which represent a coherent majority. Some have gone so far as to declare consociationalism to be the answer – »not anti-democratic, but just a particular form of democracy« (Peters 2003: 10) – to various democratic challenges found in the EU, e.g., in the absence of a European *demos* it becomes the only source of legitimacy (see Zürn 2000: 96) and its multi-leveled nature even functions as a »double guarantee« (Beetham et al. 1998: 30) for the protection of citizen rights. Lord (1998: 129) gives us a taste of the two-sidedness of its nature that seems to lie at the center of the EU's democratic shortcomings when he says:

The very strength of the Union as an elite-level consensus democracy is an important cause of its defects as a mass democracy. It is the elaborate arrangements that are made to involve all kinds of elites in consultation and decision-making that make it so very difficult to introduce an element of contestation to the system, or to allow publics the opportunity to throw one set of decision-makers out and replace it with another.

Chapter 4.1 has merely made brief mention of these consociational patterns for understanding the functioning of the EU and its policy process; they are therefore examined in depth in the following chapter.

4.2 The consociational system

This chapter takes a closer look at the European Union's consociational system – such as it has been identified by a majority of authors (among others Hrbek 1981, Lijphart 1999, Lord 1998, Peters 2003, Schmidt 2000a, 2000b, Wessels 1996).[95] In a first step the examination considers existing consociational characteristics and EU-specific deviations from the pure comparative-descriptive model. A second step analyzes the effects of consociationalism on EU democracy in general and its implications for EU lobbying in particular.

While partly risking a repetition of the discussion in Part I, it is necessary at this point to be explicit about the value-added of using an empirical model in addition to the normative one. By no means is it the goal of this chapter to weaken the normative model and introduce a degree of relativism to the democratic standards it proclaims. Instead, the descriptive frame offered by the concept of consociationalism functions as a means of structuring an understanding of the EU system and its challenges to democracy – further heightened by the lobbying system in place – while at the same time checking for possible practical solutions found in the political reality of other consociational democracies. The fact that some may recognize consociationalism as a source of political stability and efficiency, a source of output legitimacy (see Lord 1998: 48, Muntean 2000: 2) is thus simply acknowledged without substituting the normative model with the

---

95 For a dissenting view see Scharpf (2000: 8): »Certainly, the European Union is not a majoritarian or a consociational democracy [...]. Instead, I suggest, that we should work with a plurality of lower-level and simpler concepts [...].«

descriptive, consociational one.[96] In this context it is should also be noted that Schmidt makes an effort to differentiate between consociationalism in general and consociational democracy (2000b: 34), actually characterizing the EU as a system of bureaucratic rather than democratic consociationalism due to the lack of a European people (2000b: 43ff).

In *Patterns of Democracy* (1999), which categorizes and compares 36 modern democracies, Lijphart includes a subchapter on the European Union. His analysis is structured along ten variables that most clearly differentiate majoritarian from consociational democracies; these variables are again clustered into two dimensions. As a »relatively pure case[s] of consensus democracy« (Lijphart 1999: 7) the European Union conforms to the consensus characteristics both in the executive-parties and in the federal-unitary dimension (for the EU analysis: 42-47).[97] Its executive body, the Commission, is characterized by broad power-sharing in coalitions as well as a power balance in its relationship with the legislative, the Council and Parliament. A multiparty system and relative proportional representation characterize the legislative. In the fifth variable of the executive-parties dimension Lijphart sees the EU leaning towards a corporatist rather than a pluralist system of interest intermediation. The five variables of the federal-unitary dimension confirm the consociational character: federal, decentralized government, strong legislative bicameralism, constitutional rigidity based on the treaties, institutionalized judicial review, and central bank independence. Lijphart's analysis is a comprehensive starting point for an overview of supporting, complementary, or contrary observations.

The consociational system of the EU is both explicitly named – synonyms such as concordance system included (Hrbek 1981, Wessels 1996) – or implicitly circumscribed when consociational characteristics are enumerated such as the elite-level policy process embedded in a consensus culture

---

96 Schneider launches an attack on what he calls empirical democracy theories, explicitly naming the concept of consociational democracy as one. »The unrealistic liberal democracy theory is thus confronted with a »realistic« or »empirical« democracy theory that seemingly pronounces the factual as the democratic norm. […] The relativization of modern democracy has been observed in many variations since the 1970s which in general lead to an »erosion of the liberal democratic ideal« (O'Brien 1972, Schneider 1985). Since then consociational and bargaining democracies have become increasingly important« (2000: 261).

97 While the terminology and its choice of the word consociationalism over other synonyms is continued from Chapter 1.2, it should be noted that in *Patterns of Democracy* (1999) Lijphart choses to use the terms consensus model of democracy and consensus democracy instead of consociational democracy.

(Elgström et al. 2000a: 688, Wallace 2000c: 63, Wallace 2000d: 533). Most of Lijphart's variables can be found in other authors descriptions; both Lord's (1998: 46ff) and Schmidt's (2000a: 428ff, 2000b: 42) summaries of EU consociationalism list shared decision-making in community matters including a large number of veto positions, large autonomy in non-community matters, as well as (relative) proportionality in political representation, administrative appointments, etc. A systematic comparison of the EU with this work's consociational model suggested in Chapter 1.2 might help to further clarify its consociational character.

The comparative empirical model defines the following consociational characteristics: shared decision-making in matters of common concern, autonomous decision-making on all other issues, proportionality of political representation, of civil service appointments, and of allocation of public funds, a minority veto for the protection of minority interests, all-party coalitions in government, and proportional access to public mass media. These can all be found in the EU as defining system characteristics though some exceptions must be made with regard to proportionality. As described in Chapter 4.1.1 there is a systematic overrepresentation of smaller countries; this, however, may be seen as securing minority vetoes and rights. Also, the allocation of funds is driven rather by economic considerations than by proportionality.

The model in Chapter 1.2 further quoted factors seen as facilitating the development and stability of consociationalism: the absence of a majority segment, the absence of large socioeconomic inequalities, segments of similar size, small population, foreign threats (though this factor is rather strongly debated), loyalties spanning all segments, and consensus traditions of elite cooperation. The EU lacks most of these criteria for consociational stability: the 2004 enlargement especially introduced large socioeconomic inequalities between individual segments; the EU has neither a small population nor are its segments, i.e., the different nation-states, of an even roughly similar size; loyalties such as a European identity are still questioned in the context of the EU so far.[98] This leaves two stabilizing factors: the consensus tradition of EU elites, which also exhibit European loyalties spanning national interests, and the absence of a majority segment. Also,

---

98 Though Peters (2003: 9) argues that there are strong transnational membership overlaps and cross-cutting cleavages (Eder et al. (1998: 325) call this the development of public *issue orientation*), national affiliations still largely define the dominant segmentation within the EU's general, non-elite public.

the existence of a possible threat, namely that of another European war, was one of the forces that encouraged the European founders in the post-World War II period.

One variable suggested by Lijphart (1999), which he introduced in earlier works on consociational democracy (see Lijphart et al. 1991, Crepaz et al. 1995), is obviously absent from other authors' characterizations and was likewise dismissed by the model developed in Chapter 1.2. In his examination of the EU's system of interest intermediation, the fifth variable of the executive-parties dimension, Lijphart detects a clear tendency towards corporatism, which he deems the interest group system typical of consociational democracy. This alleged relationship between corporatism and consociationalism was discussed earlier in this work in the context of the comparative empirical model with the conclusion that no fixed assumptions can be made about the system of interest intermediation favored by consociational structures. While there are shared characteristics between the two such as elite cooperation, societal segmentation, and a bargaining and consensus tradition, they also show opposing preferences, e.g., consociationalism favoring central governments with more market allocation and less redistributive policies, while corporatism favors left governments with government allocation and redistribution policies (for details see Chapter 1.2.1). The EU's system of interest intermediation is featured more prominently in Chapter 5; nevertheless, a quick examination is fitting at this point.

Lijphart's main argument in favor of categorizing EU interest intermediation as developing towards corporatism is that the Commission showed a strong preference for corporatist, trilateral negotiations in the 1970s, a preference which is said to have persisted up until today. The Economic and Social Committee is seen as further structural evidence (1999: 44f).[99] Preemptively, Lijphart also picks up the so-called debate on the decline of corporatism and tries to show that this decline is more often just a matter of degree or of a possible transposition of corporatism from its traditional, industrial areas such as employment and labor to postindustrial issues in education, health, etc (1999: 173ff). In his categorization of EU interest intermediation he is joined by other authors who recognize »patterns of corporatist decision-making« (Falkner 2000: 289) or »eurocorporatism«

---

[99] However, it important to note that the ESC's creation dates back to 1958 and its present role in interest intermediation is marginal compared to the role of the numerous Commission and Council committees involved in the policy process.

(Jachtenfuchs et al. 2003: 31). According to them, corporatism in the EU still manifests itself most clearly in the interactions of the social partners, i.e., the traditional playing field of capital and labor. Falkner examines the Commission's ongoing interest in a social dialog between the umbrella organizations of capital and labor on the European level that was finally institutionalized in the Maastricht treaty. Since Maastricht collective agreements between employer and labor interests can be transformed into law by the Council. The threat of decision-making without the social partners functions as an incentive for serious corporatist involvement (for details see Falkner 2000: 286ff). However, corporatist methods seem limited to their traditional field of the so-called social partners, and the term corporatist policy community is suggested to differentiate from full-blown corporatism (Falkner 2000: 289, Jachtenfuchs et al. 2003: 31).

Besides those that see – or wish to see[100] – corporatist interest intermediation evolving in the European Union, there are those authors who recognize clear evidence of a pluralist system developing, culminating in *lobbyism* as its purest embodiment (Aleman 2000), as well as a third group that believes that a new concept is needed to grasp the developing form of EU interest intermediation in a multi-level system. Belonging to the latter is Grande (1996) who suggests a concept he calls joint public decision-making. His main argument is that, though the EU shows all the typical patterns of pluralism in interest intermediation, official bodies such as the Commission play a much more active role in interest intermediation than a true pluralist system would permit. Grande's approach accounts for the multi level, interdependent policy process in the EU and the effects this has on the role and influence of interest groups, in particular the paradox of weakness.[101]

Those authors arguing that the EU is a pluralist system and unlikely to develop towards corporatism make use of these same structural arguments, i.e., the multi-level, fragmented nature of EU governance and policy-making, to explain dominant EU interest intermediation (Kohler-Koch 1998:

---

100 Compare for example Schulten's examination of Eurooptimists and Europessimists (1998: 155ff); he himself sees little reason to share the optimists' view that transnational corporatism is developing on the EU-level.
101 Grande describes this effect as follows: »Public actors purposefully use the »internal« ties and commitments produced by joint decision-making to strengthen their bargaining position *vis-à-vis* »external« (private) actors and interest groups. This logic of »self-commitment« (Schelling 1960: 27) is well known in theories of international negotiations and I would like to call it the »paradox of weakness«« (1996: 328).

132). In addition, they may also take a closer look at the structure of the interest group system, e.g., Greenwood et al. (2000) who come to the conclusion that the ability of EU business associations to be regular governance partners for EU institutions is rather questionable and it is not appropriate to speak of EU corporatism even on a sectoral basis. It will have become obvious by now that it is not possible to categorize EU interest intermediation as a corporatist system following the common understanding of corporatism as a highly institutionalized system of interest groups and interest intermediation, a limited number of hierarchically organized, functionally differentiated, and officially recognized interests taking part in a state-moderated, even state-initiated (trilateral) process. Whether the EU system can be simply grouped with other pluralist systems or whether new concepts such as joint decision-making or policy networks are needed to fully account for its workings is further explored in Chapters 4.2.1 and 5.

Returning to the current chapter's main subject, EU consociationalism, it can be stated in summary that the EU shows nearly all the characteristics typical of a consociational system as defined by authors such as Lijphart and by the model suggested in Chapter 1.2. And though it lacks many of the factors conducive to the development and stability of a consociational system, the European Union has exhibited growing stability, a stability that is to a large part both a positive and negative result of the consociational structures. The consociational advantages and disadvantages identified in Chapter 1.2 seem to apply to the transnational, multi-level system of the EU just as they apply to nation-state consociationalism. On the one hand, political stability is achieved through the accommodation of heterogeneous societal segments, including minorities, via consensual problem-solving, proportional representation, and segment autonomy. On the other hand, the EU is seen by some as exhibiting a stability that borders on immobilism and a status quo bias and which is gained through elite domination as well as intransparency and informality throughout the political process, possibly leading to the frustration and alienation of its citizens.

The EU's transnational, multi-level character can lead to an interpretation of the consociational structures uncommon in the national context. Lord examines these EU specific ramifications in the context of what he calls consociational representation (1998: 46ff). He acknowledges that consensus decision-making leads to an alignment with the needs and values of the greatest number (of interests). Several factors, however, undermine this alignment all of which stem from the system's multi-level character. Consociational decision-makers rely on fairly strict societal segmentation which in most cases means a segmentation mainly along the territorial dimension; in Lord's opinion this disallows cross-cutting boundaries, i.e., by integrating the functional dimension through other actors such as transnational interest groups, parties, etc.[102] Instead, the aggregation of interests across several levels can mean losing sight of the greatest number of interests and the oligarchic tendencies in consociational elite domination can mean collusion between governments on the EU level. Checks and balances then are displaced by national executives acting as EU-level legislators. While all of these are problems inherent in consociationalism – and lead Lord to conclude that consociationalism in its pure form is inappropriate for the EU -, they are heightened by the peculiarities of transnational, multi-level governance. As such they resurface in the examination of the EU's multi-level system and policy networks in Chapter 4.2.1.

The consociational character of the EU with its preference for consensus and unanimity, intransparency and informality can be seen as a source for many of the democratic deficits discussed in Chapter 4.1, in particular those affecting the so-called democratic cornerstones of authorization and accountability. Its advantages, the stability and accommodation discussed above, have EU-specific ramifications as well. These especially concern the development of democracy beyond the nation-state. Chapter 1.3 developed three paths towards a trans or postnational democracy and *demos*: unification, activation, and accommodation (see Table 6). The instruments identified to achieve the positive effects of accommodation are the consociational ones of subsidiarity and consensus decision-making. The latter has been given many different, sometimes conflicting names and interpretations and therefore demands closer examination to ensure common understanding of what is meant by consensus decision-making throughout this work.

---

102 There seems to be strong disagreement about the depth and dimensions of societal segmentation in the EU. While some speak of especially strong and exclusive national segmentation (Schmidt 2000b: 42), others claim additional dimensions such as functional segmentation that cross national boundaries and can even weaken these (Lord 1998, Peters 2003: 9).

Table 18: EU consociationalism

Characteristics	Effects
• Shared decision-making in community matters • Segment/national autonomy in non-community matters • Consensual decision-making • Proportionality in political representation; overrepresentation of small countries securing minority rights • Proportionality of access to public functions and media **Supporting factors** • Elite consensus tradition • Absence of majority segment	+ Political stability + Accommodation of heterogeneity (also conducive to democracy beyond nation-state) - Possible status-quo bias - Elite domination, oligarchic tendencies - Intransparency, informality, accountability problems

Source: Lijphart 1999, Lord 1998, Schmidt 2000a,b (among others)

EU decision-making or rather its decision-making style has been termed bargaining, arguing, negotiating, problem-solving, sounding-out and the like. Term definition is often unclear so that at times bargaining appears as a simple synonym of the rather neutral negotiating (Héritier 2003), then again as a more confrontational concept as opposed to a consensus-oriented problem-solving or arguing (Benz 2003b, Elgström et al. 2000a, Neyer 2004, Staeck 1997), or again as a style distinct from both problem-solving and confrontation (Scharpf 1988). This work has tended to use bargaining as synonym for negotiating; the latter is clearly a very broad term covering »almost everything that goes on in the EU« (Elgström et al. 2000b: 673). However, at this point where a characterization of decision-making style as either confrontational or consensual is called for, this work adopts the differentiation most common in the relevant literature between bargaining as self-interested and often conflictual, on the one hand, and problem-solving as cooperative and common interest oriented, on the other.

Some authors have characterized the dominant EU decision-making style as bargaining; i.e., bargaining in the sense of self-interested log-rolling, pork barrel buffets or ineffective joint-decision traps. Most prominent among these is Scharpf who has blamed the combination of unanimity rule and bargaining style in the EU for »not simply a prevalence of distributive conflicts complicating all substantive decisions, but a systematic tendency towards sub-optimal substantive solutions« (1988: 265). More recently Abromeit has criticized the EU for shortcomings common to bargaining systems: inefficiency, expensiveness, and lack of accountability (1998b: 116). These views of self-interested seeking of relative, short-term advantages are further informed by such phenomena as the exchange of political influence between different sectors analyzed by Pappi et al., among others this is used to explain the inefficiency of EU agricultural policies (2003: 305). Within the overall bargaining system such influence exchange entails that »every player has an incentive to trade votes in political dimensions of little interest to them for votes in dimensions of greater interest« (Pappi et al. 2003: 298, own translation).[103]

This picture painted of an ineffective and inefficient bargaining system is, however, too one-sided and undifferentiated. Many policy fields such as environment or consumer rights, in which negotiations take place on an EU level and for which competences no longer lie with the individual member states, are marked by effective problem-solving well above the smallest common denominator (Benz 2003b: 328f).[104] Many authors also point to the fact that time plays a crucial role in determining the style of negotiations and decision-making. Thus the past and the future figure into the present of EU »permanent negotiation« (Elgström et al. 2000a: 687, see also Elgström et al. 2000b: 676) leading to cooperation or as some call it »deliberative« problem-solving or bargaining (Héritier 2003: 817, Neyer 2004: 35) that takes other players' interests into account with the goal of long-term benefits.[105] Elgström et al. examine further contextual factors apart from time that have lead to empirical results that show that »day-to-day negotiations in the EU are clearly to a large extent problem-solving exercises« (2000a: 689). Their examination shows that, while the decision-making rule does not preclude the negotiation style, the level of politicization and the type of policy, the stage in the decision-making process, and the characteristics of the players and networks may very well affect the

---

103 However, Wallace points out that cross-sectoral trade-offs are far less common than claimed or implied, intra-sectoral trade-offs being much more common (2000a: 76).

104 For another positive assessment of the EU's effectiveness and efficiency based on a deliberative problem-solving style of decision-making see Neyer (2004).

105 This basic principle of cooperation was identified and termed »the shadow of the future« by Axelrod in his *The Evolution of Cooperation* (1984).

decision-making style.[106] With a majority of the EU's day-to-day negotiations taking place on a permanent, institutionalized, non-politicized basis, concerning distributive and regulative issues, involving knowledge-based networks mainly during early stages and for implementation, this explains a certain predominance of problem-solving and consensus-seeking in the EU's consociational decision-making.

As has been continuously implied the EU's consociational problem-solving and the search for consensus is strongly determined by the system's vertical and horizontal, institutional and functional, formal and informal multi-level governance and policy-networks to be examined in the following.

4.2.1 Multi-level governance and policy networks

The most prominent and suitable concept with which to structure an understanding of EU governance beyond the more general concept of consociationalism is that of multi-level governance (first mentioned in Jachtenfuchs et al. 1996, Marks 1993, Marks et al. 1996) – further enriched by the complexity of policy networks. Why suggest a new term in the EU context when every federal system is a multi-level system? Does the EU deviate from the common understanding of federalism and if so how? Does this produce its own specific advantages and disadvantages to the democratic process?

Hooghe et al. (2001) examine two distinct but not exclusive ideal-types of multi-level systems concluding that the EU seems to combine features of both. Type I, broadly termed federalism, has at its core a limited number of multi-task, territorially exclusive jurisdictions and of jurisdictional levels little open to jurisdictional reform. This type is echoed by what Grande (2000a) calls the institutional understanding of the EU multi-level system identifying several permanent, territorially defined and separated levels (Europe, nation-states, regions, local/municipal) or by Ast's (1999) similarly described vertical view. Type II, by contrast, is characterized by a large number of functional, task-specific, territorially overlapping jurisdictions and jurisdictional levels, flexible rather than permanent in their organiza-

---

106 This contradicts Scharpf who sees a better chance for problem-solving in a majoritarian environment (1988: 272), an environment which tends to produce a more conflictual climate according to Elgström et al. (2000a: 691).

tion. It compares with a functional (Grande 2000a) or horizontal (Ast 1999) view of the multi-level EU. The term of multi-level governance in the EU context underscores the system's departure from a classical federal understanding due to an adoption of variable, functional, non-hierarchical structures in addition to the existing permanent, territorial ones. This adoption is visible in the involvement and interdependence of all vertical (territorial) as well as horizontal (functional, public/private) levels throughout the policy process, the separation of pillars, the number of independent agencies, etc. (Ast 1999: 32f, Grande 2000a: 16f, Hooghe et al. 2001: 9f, Wessels 2003: 354).

The multi-level character has developed to accommodate EU requirements but has in turn also caused specific complications for the democratic process. Generally stated, the main argument in favor of multi-level governance is that it internalizes externalities; it can reflect heterogeneous preferences and project higher credibility – particularly valuable in a consociational system – as wells as open up jurisdictional competition and innovation (Hooghe et al. 2001: 4). Studies indicate that the multi-level character enhances problem-solving capacities and efficiency (Benz 2003a: 101, Grande 2000a: 24).[107] Other effects demand trade-offs or show both positive and negative variations. In many cases, for example, the higher costs of coordination can be seen as the trade-off between higher up front decision-making costs and lower implementation costs thanks to functional specialization and compartmentalization – a logic known to students of consociational systems in general. Interaction between different levels also brings with it the possibility for blocking and vetoing decisions but it may just as well produce knowledge transfer and positive competition (Grande 2000a: 21f).

Multi-level governance, however, also creates problems pertaining to democratic norms, problems the reader has encountered in the chapters on the EU's democratic deficit and consociationalism. First, there is the everpresent lack of accountability caused by long, complex decision-making chains, a growing amount of informal institutional interactions, and by the formal and informal involvement of non-institutional players (Benz 2003a: 101f, Grande 2000a: 22, 2000b: 125f). In the context of a possible loss of legitimacy some bemoan the shifting of directional authority within the

---

107 Yet, there are claims to the opposite, i.e., that the multi-level system causes decision-making ability to be lost somewhere between the member state and the EU level (Teuber 2001: 29).

multi-level system away from the democratically more legitimate member states (Teuber 2001: 29). There are also interest group and lobbying-specific aspects of the multi-level system that appear problematic. The large number of formal and informal access channels on all levels generally means an increased openness to interest groups. However, the effectiveness of their lobbying is strongly determined by asymmetrical amounts of lobbying resources available to cover all relevant access points.

Summing up the above, the EU's multi-level governance can hardly be understood as a static, fully institutionalized system but is instead characterized by a multi-level diffusion of decision-making powers and by actors participating on multiple levels in varying roles and in changing degrees of formality or informality (Costa et al. 2003: 668f, Imig et al. 2003: 129f). To more deeply understand the multiplicity of players and their modes of interaction it is helpful to see them as part of so-called policy networks, which became a focal point in European integration literature in the 1990s.

Policy networks are a key organizing principle of EU policy-making; some even claim they are »the real core of the political system« (Andersen et al. 1996a: 232). Looking back at the linear version of the EU policy process and its institutional framework examined in Chapter 4.1.2, these might be surprising statements. Yet, the institutional setting and the policy networks, which seem to fill the policy process with much of its life, are not mutually exclusive; rather, they are two different ways of approaching the same process. The institutional approach focuses on the, more or less, official players as part of a quasi-formalized process that has a defined beginning and end. But as was already obvious in Chapter 4.2.1 this understanding is only the tip of the iceberg and fuzzy around the edges where the policy process starts to include unregistered committees, informal meetings, etc. The activities of the policy networks help describe the workings behind the formalized view and also extend an understanding of the processes beyond the idea of closure in terms of players involved, institutional and formal structures, or timeframe.

Commonly, definitions of policy networks include both public and private players (see Andersen et al. 1996a, Cooke 1996, Marin et al. 1991), which in the multi-level system of the EU can mean anything from a DG official to an association of regional producers. While they appear to develop in response to systemic needs, especially a need for additional resources, caused by changes such as »societal differentiation, sectoralization and policy growth« (Kenis et al. 1991: 36), networks supplement but do not replace formal institutions. In the context of the EU most of them appear to be fairly stable, organized around continuous policy debates, though they remain structurally variable and permeable for players both vertically and horizontally and are generally of a decentralized, informal, non-hierarchical nature (for more general network definitions see Cooke 1996: 64f, Marin et al. 1991: 16).

As interorganizational networks are composed of autonomous, but interdependent actors who have different, but mutually contingent interests, the most likely candidate for a specific network logic appears to be bargaining and exchange, in contrast to the market logic of competition and the logic of authority and obedience typical of hierarchies. (Mayntz 1991: 13)

Much of the vocabulary encountered in the context of policy networks as well as the interaction it describes is reminiscent of both consociationalism and interest intermediation. The above quote exemplifies the typical characterization of network negotiation style and outcome as cooperation, consensus, compromise, or exchange (see also Cooke 1996, Mayntz 1991, Staeck 1997). As with most consensus oriented negotiations, this implies high upfront costs while implementation costs are minimized. Though they join in order to influence the policy process according to their individual agenda, most network players come or are asked to the table as information and communication brokers expected to mobilize additional resources (Ast 1999: 45, Kenis et al. 1991: 41, Staeck 1997: 68f).

The impression so far may be that all policy networks resemble each other. However, depending on such factors as the policy type, e.g., regulative or distributive, the policy field, or the phase within the policy process, networks can differ strongly. In general, network typologies agree on the significance of the following characteristics: number of players/members, membership type/structure, interdependencies, power/resource distribution, underlying strategies/values (Ast 1999: 47ff, Grote 1998: 66, Peterson 1995: 77, Staeck 1997: 67ff).[108] While the earlier characterization of networks described an intermediate type most common to the EU policy process, typologies arrange all possible types along a continuum with polar opposites at its ends. One end of this continuum recognizes so-called policy communities with a small or at least limited number of members within a stable structure and with strong interdependencies, often marked by fairly

---

108 Most typologies refer back to one or several of the following authors and their typologies: Atkinson et al. (1989), Heclo (1978), and Rhodes (1990).

balanced resources and similar values or attitudes. The other end is formed by so-called issue networks with large, fluid membership based on weak interdependencies, unbalanced resources, and divergent underlying values. Of course intermediate types occur in political practice, i.e., in the reality of the European Union.

In the EU the occurrence of policy communities or issue networks, or the predominance of certain of their characteristics, varies according to context. This context can refer to the type of policy, the policy field, the phase within the policy process, or the territorial context (in cases where networks have strong regional or national components). Depending on the general policy type, networks exhibit more or less structural and membership stability. Unchanged, continuous policy communities seem to dominate distributive politics whilst more instable and open issue networks can be found in regulative politics (Heinelt 1996: 26, Staeck 1997: 74). It can also be along the lines of individual policy fields that networks differ; in the field of environmental and consumer policies, for example, networks are characterized by a large number of changing members with large resource imbalances and divergent attitudes/values – a clear tendency towards issue networks (Peterson 1995: 77). Within the individual policy field different types of networks can also control different phases of the policy process and their differences will then often be due to their function. Decision-making, implementation, and development networks tend to be policy communities working in fairly stable structures providing the necessary environment of trust and consensus whilst information networks have the large and fluid membership of issue networks (Ast 1999: 50ff, Heinelt 1996: 25). Finally, where there is a strong focus beyond the EU-level, e.g., in implementation networks, regional or national differences can have an effect on the development of these networks (Grote 1998, Waarden 1993).

Just as the form of interaction of policy networks is reminiscent of consociationalism and interest intermediation so is the debate about their legitimacy when held to democratic standards. Advocates of governance through policy networks emphasize the legitimation gained through broad participation, expertise, and effectiveness (Jachtenfuchs 1997: 10, Peterson 1995: 88); some even speak of accountability through networks as »pareto superior« to accountability through hierarchies (Lord 1998: 102). Networks are also said to have the advantage of protecting small-scale identities in a pluralist sense and of opening new opportunities for interests so far ignored in national contexts (Jachtenfuchs 1997, Peterson 1995). However, where networks become closed and their dealings intransparent and informal, the accountability problem reappears together with the possibilities of collusion and insulation, i.e., the freezing out of other, new players (Lord 1998: 104f, Peterson 1995: 87). All of these arguments have by now become reoccurring themes.

Table 19: EU multi-level system and policy networks

Multi-level system	Effects
• Territorial, institutional, vertical (federalism) • Functional, horizontal	+ Internalization of externalities + Accommodation of heterogeneous interests and broad participation + Knowledge transfer, competition, innovation + Better problem-solving and efficiency + Lower costs of implementation
Policy networks • Public and private players • Stable but structurally variable and permeable • Decentralized, non-hierarchical, informal • Predominantly policy communities; but also issue networks	- Possible blocking, vetoing - Accountability problems (intransparency, informality, lack of authorization) - Possible collusion, insulation - Lobbying asymmetries - Higher costs of coordination

Source: Andersen et al. 1996a, Asl 1999, Benz 2003a, Cooke 1996, Grande 2000a,b, Hooghe et al. 2001, Jachtenfuchs 1997, Marin et al. 1991, Mayntz 1991, Peterson 1995, Staeck 1997, Wessels, 2003

So finally, the examination of EU policy networks leads back to the earlier debate on interest intermediation and its legitimacy within democratic governance. Policy networks can be seen both as a willingness to integrate and cooperate with diverse interests, including those of regional and local levels, as well as a sign of the weakness of the state (Ebner 2000: 164f). Again the question as to the dominant system of interest intermediation must be asked. Do the policy networks in the consociational context of EU multi-level governance bear witness to a pluralist or to a corporatist system of interest intermediation, to Lijphart's »competitive and uncoordinated pluralism« or his »coordinated and compromise-oriented system of corporatism« (1999: 171)? The network model could quite possibly become a third model that replaces the two present ones as it best incorporates the dissolving boundaries between the public and private sectors (Staeck 1997: 65, 71). While policy networks are characterized by their openness to a multiplicity of players and by no means exhibit the characteristics of closure known from the examination of corporatist systems, the prevalence in the EU of policy communities and their relative stability does not allow us to speak of a simple pluralist system either. For now the picture of EU interest intermediation remains a mixed one with further examination in Chapter 5 pending.

The comparative descriptive approach of Chapter 4.2 developed an understanding of today's EU governance system beginning, top-down, with an analysis and evaluation of its apparent consociationalism, moving down through its structuring as a multi-level system into the workings of networks on the level of policy- and decision-making. The continuous modification of known structures and processes has to be factored into an understanding of the EU's political system and what holds true today is open to change tomorrow. Therefore, the seemingly static understanding given in Chapters 4.1 and 4.2 is rounded off in the following chapter with a look at two larger recent and current events that might have significant influence both on the normative and the descriptive view of the European Union.

4.3 New challenges

The previous discussion of democracy in the European Union, both from a normative and from a comparative empirical point of view, focused almost exclusively on the EU-level situation and developments. In the subsequent discussion of the May 2004 enlargement and of the process surrounding the *Treaty Establishing a Constitution for Europe* the member states regain center stage. These recent developments remind us that the sustainability of the political and the economic integration in Europe is continuously being tested. The criticism with which both the enlargement and the process of constitutionalization have been met stems from similar questions, dissatisfaction, and fears; it must be taken into account in a concept of future EU democracy.

4.3.1 May 2004 enlargement and beyond

The integration project's larger goal of securing a peaceful and prosperous Europe with the principles of liberal democracy and market economy at its core also became the goal of Eastern enlargement in the wake of the 1989 events (Martens 2004: 3, Sedelmeier et al. 2000: 432). The May 2004 accession of ten countries to the EU, the eight central and eastern European countries of Poland, Czech Republic, Hungary, Slovakia, Lithuania, Latvia, Slovenia, Estonia as well as Cyprus and Malta, and the pending accession of Rumania and Bulgaria do not represent the conclusion of this goal but are instead major steps in an ongoing process. The unfolding of this process between the late 1980s and 2004 – from support to association to accession – has been sufficiently covered (Jetzelsperger et al. 1999, Rothacher 2004, Schimmelfennig 2003, Sedelmeier et al. 2000). This chapter therefore focuses on problems and uncertainties that surfaced throughout this process and continue to challenge the integration project in such areas as identity, political institutions, and democracy.

The effects of the enlargement process have to be considered in at least two directions, that of the new member states and that of the EU. Ambitious but necessary demands were made of the accession candidates both in the political and the economic dimensions as laid out in principle at the Copenhagen European Council in 1993: stable institutions guaranteeing human rights, democracy, and the rule of law; functioning market economy in the face of EU competition; acceptance of and ability to adopt the *acquis communautaire*. The basic institutionalization and acceptance of democratic principles and processes seems achieved though problems such as corruption within the institutions and lack of political participation through parties and organizations, or indicated in low election turnouts are ongoing challenges (Ismayr 2004: 13f). Much can be said in this context about the missing link between the people and the (new) political and economic elites; the latter are seen by many as not trustworthy or even corrupt, as betraying values they once proclaimed, and are held responsible for the negative effects of the economic transformation (Bozóki 2004: 3, Fehr 2004: 53f, Ismayr 2004: 14). In the central and eastern European countries strong economic hopes were and are connected to the association with and accession to the EU. However, financial transfers through pre accession programmes such as PHARE (Poland-Hungary: Assistance to Economic Restructuring; extended to other Central and Eastern European Countries) and then through CAP (the Common Agricultural Policy) and the Structural Funds may have a negative impact where they either lead to higher national debt due to cofinancing requirements or where political energy is spent on obtaining higher funding while neglecting necessary reforms (Rothacher 2004: 26ff). The adoption of the *acquis communautaire* forms a major part of these reforms and, as in the other two dimensions of accession criteria, its timeline can strongly differ between the candidates.

The lack of political participation and the distrust of political elites mentioned above may in part indicate a lack of popular identification in the countries of central and eastern Europe with the system of the EU, a phenomenon which Bozóki calls »membership without belonging« (2004). This is the recurring theme of the so-called identity question and its effect on democratic legitimacy. So while the alleviation of many of the democratic deficits identified in Chapter 4.1 relies on further steps of integration, the sustainability of political integration is questioned. In addition, the limiting of national sovereignty that the EU integration project entails is expected to provoke an opposition to further steps of integration by the new member states who have only recently gained national self-determination (Rothacher 2004: 25f).

In the context of enlargement the identity question surfaces not only with the new member states. Allegedly, enlargement has lead to an alienation of the EU citizens from the idea of a European identity and has at the same time drained the idea of any meaning (see Rothacher 2004, notes 75 and 76). Whether these are measurable and enduring effects remains to be seen. Other effects of the Eastern enlargement on the system of the EU have obviously come to pass. Negotiations concerning the EU budget, agricultural and structural funds, and institutional changes have long been shaped by the pending accession and the social and economic disparities that the EU would have to face. The latter have been mentioned before as problematic in the context of a consociational system that relies on the cooperation of the political elites; whether such cooperation can succeed in the face of such strong disparities has to be questioned (Martens 2004: 4). On the other hand, the political systems of the new member states, encouraged by the accession process, have developed the institutional requirements that enable cooperative and democratic negotiating on the EU level.

The support of democratic institutional development in the new member states, the substantial geographical expansion of such policy fields as energy, infrastructure, and environment as well as the expansion of the single market belong to the many positive effects that are easily forgotten by those that simply speak of a problem of »widening versus deepening« in the context of EU enlargement (Laursen 1996: 141, Schmuck 1993: 14). Instead of being in stark contradiction, widening and deepening are the double challenge for an enlarged union and point a spotlight at the task of ensuring equal representation and participation in EU governance as well as democratic authorization and accountability thereof.[109]

4.3.2 Establishing a constitution for Europe

A political union, a »deepening« of political integration, would need a constitution and not just institutions; and constitutions, if they are to function successfully, need to be founded on some set of shared values and to express commitment to some form of collective identity. (Wallace 1993: 101)

The theme of a deepening political union and its link to the identity question has been carried on and evolved from the 1990s through the enlargement process and along with the drafting and ratification process of an EU constitution. A European identity continues to be seen by many as a prerequisite for further integration and in particular for the adoption of a constitution, the latter, it is believed, cannot function in reverse as a bedrock of EU identity (Abromeit 1998a: 97ff, Decker 2002: 270, Schieder 2004: 14f). At the same time the creation of the Constitutional Convent in December 2001 and its draft of a constitution for the EU completed in June 2003 were prompted by the need for a reform of the existing treaties in view of pending enlargement and by the wish to heighten democratic legitimation, political effectiveness and social integration through the vehicle of a European constitution (Grimm 07.01.2004, Sterzing 12.07.2003).[110] Again it is a well-known dilemma that many instruments that could support an environment conducive to the development of a common identity seem to require such an identity to start with. This also recalls questions posed in Chapter 1.3 – in that case concerning democracy and *demos* be-

---

109 The interpretation as a combined challenge was similarly chosen by Jetzelsperger et al. (1999).

110 Similarly, earlier reforms of the different treaties had the enhancement of problem-solving capacities and the alleviation of democratic deficits as two of their main goals (Jachtenfuchs et al. 2003: 27).

yond the nation-state – e.g., if a constitution indeed requires a common identity, how unified and homogenous must this identity be?

As Auer (2005: 419) rightly remarks, constitutions can be understood both as basic legal concepts and as ideologies. While some might use the terms constitution and constitutional contract synonymously in the EU context – the text itself carries the title *Treaty Establishing a Constitution for Europe* –, the choice of naming it a constitution was deliberate and for many carries the symbolism of a supranational state extending well beyond intergovernmental treaty agreements (Schieder 2004: 15, Verhofstadt 25.11.2003). How much of the change, which a ratification of the constitution would bring, would be legal and how much of it would be symbolic? On the one hand, the EU has always been considered as having a constitutional base made up of the treaties and continues to rest on it legally with the ratification of the constitution presently pending indefinitely. On the other hand, even in the case of ratification the constitution is said to remain in many ways a contract, an intergovernmental treaty in which the member state governments and not the European people continue to function as decision-making parties (Grimm 07.01.2004: 15, Schieder 2004).[111] Though perhaps lacking the full-blown constitutional character, the EU constitution, its naming and drafting have, nevertheless, brought to attention the steady evolution of the union towards »a multinational federal state construction« (Auer 2005: 428). Some of the main changes sought by the constitution and examined in the following have underlined the steady development of state-like characteristics.[112]

Unless amended or repeated by it, all earlier treaties are repealed by »this Treaty establishing a Constitution for Europe« (Art. IV-437), the three pillar structure disappears, and the EU receives legal personality (Art

---

111 The 1963 ECJ ruling considered the Treaty of Rome as having created a constitutional regime, a ruling which has not met with unanimous approval, see, e.g., the 1993 ruling of the German Constitutional Court (Bundesverfassungsgericht 1993: 155-213, Goodman 1997: 184). Altogether an EU constitution has been expected to be developed through an explicit process of constitutionalization rather than through judicial procedure (Schmitter 1998: 23).

112 In his top-down, comparative approach Auer (2005) recognizes three characteristics of federal constitutions all of which can be found in the EU: a definition of the constituent units, a distribution of powers between the federal and the constituent units, and a (judicial) scheme for the resolution of conflicts between these levels. Similarly, Follesdal (2005) identifies and analyzes federal features central to the proposed constitution.

I-7).[113] The text is divided into four parts plus the preamble: Part II incorporates the Charter of Fundamental Rights of the European Union originally decided in 2000; Part III, The Policies and Functioning of the Union, contains the former Community policies; Part IV states the General and Final Provisions. The constitution then concludes with 36 additional protocols and 50 explanations to various articles. The majority of changes and new sections can be found in Part I of the constitution. It is these changes that the following paragraphs wish to concentrate on without rendering a complete overview of Part I.

Concerning power relations between the EU and the member states Articles I-11 through 18 include an explicit delineation of categories of competence which is new to EU treaties. The union receives exclusive and shared competences and areas of coordinated action are defined while member-state competence remains as default where not further specified.[114] Furthermore, the section dealing with union membership now contains provisions for the voluntary withdrawal of member states from the EU (Art. I-60).

Considerable changes are made to the main EU institutions and their roles in the decision-making process. In the interest of effectiveness and efficiency the areas of qualified majority voting (QMV) in the Council are extended significantly. In addition, the Council President is elected for a term of two and a half years, limited to two terms (Art. I-22). The position of the European Parliament is strengthened: legislative codecision of Council and Parliament becomes the rule (Art. I-34) and the Commission President is to be elected by a majority of EP members (Art. I-20 and 27). In an effort to strengthen the EU's foreign affairs profile a Minister of Foreign Affairs, in the double role as head of the Foreign Affairs Council and as a Vice-President of the Commission, is appointed by a qualified majority of the heads of state (Art. I-28).

Articles I-45 through 52 are concerned with the democratic life of the union. The democratic equality of EU citizens is declared – however, citizen representation in Parliament follows the principle of digressive pro-

---

113 All versions of the text being equal (Art. IV-448) an English and a German version are used for reference here (Treaty Establishing a Constitution for Europe 2005, Vertrag über eine Verfassung für Europa 2005).

114 The principles of subsidiarity and proportionality are defined in the second of the attached protocols and compliance to these principles is to be ensured by the national governments (Art. I-11).

portionality (Art. I-20) and »direct universal suffrage in a free and secret ballot« is ensured though not the equality of vote (Art. I-20 and II-99). The principle of participatory democracy (Art. I-47) is new to EU treaty texts and is of special interest here because it encompasses both the individual citizen and interest organizations. Among other things it provides for »an open, transparent and regular dialogue with representative associations and civil society«, »broad consultations with parties concerned«, as well as a European citizens' initiative.

Many of the changes sought in the constitution mean a step both in the direction of system effectiveness and efficiency and towards enhanced democratic legitimation.[115] Why then has the adoption process repeatedly stalled and might have possibly even found a premature end with the constitution's rejection in the French and Dutch referenda in May/June 2005?[116] Prior to the *non* of the French people this chapter could have chosen to simply explore the democratic implications of changes envisaged by the constitution in comparison to the earlier treaties. Instead it now seems appropriate to ask about the state of the EU and EU democracy in the face of public opposition to an EU constitution and the deepened integration it implies.

The long list of reasons for the public opposition to the constitution – some of which clearly have to be seen in a national context, e.g., the dissatisfaction of the French people with government under prime-minister Raffarin – was predicted and best captured in the print-media. Spanning national borders the European public seems to share a disappointment with EU political elites and bureaucracy, an aversion to EU-level decisions at the cost of subsidiarity, and a fear of losing national sovereignty, identity, and democratic accomplishments (Beste et al. 06.06.2005, Pinzler 14.04.2005, Rothacher 2004: 34). These reasons are joined by more country-specific disappointments and fears vis-à-vis European integration in general and shortcomings of the proposed EU constitution in particular.

---

115 This assessment is not shared by everyone, e.g., Abromeit et al. see the Constitution as contributing little to an enhanced legitimacy of the European Union. In particular, they criticize that the text is as complicated and inaccessible to the general public as its predecessors, it does little to heighten governance accountability, it is biased in favor of the Union securing its rights vis-à-vis the member states, and it does not concern itself much with effective citizen participation (Abromeit et al. 2005: 17).

116 Due to an initial lack of support by the heads of the member states during the Brussels conference in December 2003 the draft wasn't approved until June 2004 and signed until October 2004.

There is the mistaken devaluation of the Dutch currency at the introduction of the Euro and Dutch opposition to a Turkish EU accession, the unfulfilled Polish wish for a mention of God or Christianity in the constitution's preamble, and the British EU-skepticism and a fear of too much integration in areas such as social politics. On the other hand, a lack of social standards and an EU driven by neoliberal globalization are lamented, especially by the French, and seen as predetermined by the emphasis on economic integration in earlier EU treaties (Cassen 11.07.2003, Greffrath 02.07.2003, Pinzler 14.04.2005).[117]

Thus runs the multifaceted argument of public rejection rounded off by the criticism of the process of drafting and negotiating the constitution, a process dominated by political elites rather than by the people, and by a proclaimed lack of a constitutional occasion which could have prompted public enthusiasm (Darnstädt et al. 06.06.2005, Grimm 07.01.2004, Walther 06.05.2004). The outcome of the French and Dutch referendum was answered by the decision of the political leaders to halt the ratification process for the time being and has raised questions about the possibilities of continuing, adjusting and improving, or reversing the process of European integration. The fear of political paralysis is reminiscent of reactions to the initial public opposition to Maastricht in several countries and is at the same time put into perspective by such experiences (compare Gustavsson 1996); to speak of the end of the EU integration project therefore appears rather premature. Suggestions for an incremental adoption of changes outlined in the constitution seem to be as much a possibility as a reversion back to a Europe of state leaders with a majority of decisions again being made by the European Council (Fritz-Vanahme 28.04.2005). The member states presently dominate the scene while the supranational, federal aspects have been pushed to the background. A stabilization of the current situation is unsatisfactory considering the democratic deficit and instruments identified for its alleviation most of which are part of a reform process as envisaged by the constitution and beyond. It has been suggested that a compensation of EU heterogeneity with the help of territorial and functional subsidiarity and the granting of veto rights to national parliaments and to the citizens in the form of referenda could improve the con-

---

117 The French public disapproval of the constitution due to a lack of social goals and standards mentioned was known long in advance and EU-wide campaigns promoting the social aspects of the constitution were prevalent (see among others the initiative of the majors of seven European cities Delanoë et al. 13.10.2004).

stitutional draft and further EU integration; such steps are deemed more promising than efforts of homogenization and supranational reform (Hurrelmann 2005: 230ff + 273ff). However, the best chance for a democratic EU and the alleviation of its deficits seems to lie in the three-pronged approach developed in Chapter 1.3 combining efforts of unification, activation and accommodation in measures of constitutionalization, of direct democracy, and of consociational democracy and subsidiarity.[118]

A short recap of the analyses and findings concludes Chapter 4 before proceeding into the realm of EU lobbying in Chapter 5 and its specific challenges to democracy in Chapter 6. Chapter 4.1 held EU democracy to the normative standards of equality of vote and voice, authorization, and accountability and tried to appreciate the EU-specific aspects through an in-depth understanding of the policy process. The chapter went on to develop measures towards an alleviation of the identified democratic deficits in all four areas. The normative approach was complemented by the descriptive approach of Chapter 4.2 and its examination of the positive and negative effects of EU consociationalism on democracy. These were explored further through the system of multi-level governance and the complexity of its policy networks. Among other things, this recognized recurring themes such as the tendency towards stability and problem-solving effectiveness at the cost of transparency, formality, and participation. Chapter 4.3 dealt with the continuous political and economic integration and its sustainability in light of enlargement and the proposed EU constitution. Integration seems challenged by a popular distrust of elites, a lack of citizen identification with the EU, a wish to secure national sovereignty, and the strains on the social systems attributed to ambitious economic reforms.

---

118 The suggested paths of unification, activation, and accommodation are in parts comparable with Hurrelmann's models of homogenization and compensation of heterogeneity.

5. EU lobbying

With enlargement, lobbyists will have to work in an EU that is becoming even
more complex. [...] Organised interests and their capacity to plan and execute
campaigns will probably become more manifest, as has already been recognized by
EU bodies, particularly the Commission, by increasing the consideration given to
improving consultation and the dialogue with civil society. It is all the more important that competition among lobbying groups remains open for newcomers,
thus assuring that European interest representation does not develop into a closed
shop system. (Directorate-General for Research 2003: 54)

Taken from a working paper on the current situation of lobbying in the
EU produced by the EU Directorate-General for Research at the request
of the European Parliament, this quote addresses several of the topics that
should feature prominently in an examination of EU lobbying, also and
especially in the light of its democratic sustainability. Such topics are,
among others: the continuously changing political and institutional environment in which European interest representation operates; the competition for attention between different and differing interests, some well-or-
ganized and others less so; the role of the EU institutions as addressees of
lobbying efforts; the need to ensure that the EU remains equally open to
all interests.[119] Further topics include those deferred earlier in Chapter 4
for more in-depth examination in the current chapter, e.g., the nascent
system of interest intermediation.

Chapter 5.1 examines the organization of interests in the European
Union from its historical development and today's statistics to a classification of EU lobbying groups and an analysis of present power structures
between them to a tentative naming of the unique system of interest intermediation in place. The corresponding examination of the addresses
within the EU institutional system, their importance to different types of

---

119 The Directorate-General for Research (2003) also mentions the effects of enlargement
on lobbying; this topic is taken up in Chapter 6.2.

lobbying efforts and their accessibility follows in Chapter 5.2. An analysis of the EU-specific lobbying process, of methods and resources employed, and an assessment of the heterogeneous regulatory environment in Chapters 5.3 and 5.4 round off the picture of EU lobbying.

It should be briefly mentioned here that many topics in the current chapter will reference back to earlier chapters, especially Chapter 2.3 with its development of interest group terminology and systematics. Suffice it at this point to recall the broad use of the terms interest group, interest representation and intermediation in this work. In the context of the EU these will be used synonymously with the terms lobby groups, lobbies, and lobbying, a context in which the latter terms have lost the negative connotation known from national contexts (Claeys et al. 1998b: 420).[120]

5.1 Interest organization in Brussels

The presence of interest groups in Brussels and on the political playing-field of the European project dates back to the late 1950s. Of the large European umbrella organizations, the European federations of national associations, most were founded within the first two decades of the European Union, then still the European Economic Community (plus the European Coal and Steel Community and the European Atomic Energy Community, joined together in the European Community in 1965). The first to enter the European stage were employers, industry and commerce, and farmers: UNICE (Union of Industrial and Employers' Confederations of Europe, 1958), CEEP (Centre of Enterprises with Public Participation and of Enterprises of General Economic Interest, 1961), Eurochambres (Association of European Chambers of Commerce and Industry, 1958),

---

120 The rather inclusive definition of these terms is in line with an approach that treats all group interests equally in terms of their legitimacy and uses classification only to examine differences in lobbying methods and resources. In contrast to this, some authors wishing to grant certain groups and their activities more legitimacy refuse the use of the term lobbying and lobbyists in connection with these interests, e.g., labor unions (Gobin 1998: 110f). Also, works examining the how-to of EU lobbying often differentiate between insourced and outsourced interest representatives, calling only the latter lobbyists (Buholzer 1998: 11, Lahusen et al. 2001: 52), or allow the use of the term lobbying only for unorthodox ways of influence, »falling outside the standard patterns of permitted or invited behaviour« (Van Schendelen 2002: 205).

and COPA (Committee of Professional Agricultural Organisations, 1958). Some of the interests termed general got off to comparatively early starts with umbrella organizations such as BEUC (European Consumers' Organization, 1962) and EEB (European Environmental Bureau, 1974). Interestingly, labor unions did not organize on a European level until 1973 (ETUC – European Trade Union Confederation); the inward orientation of the national members that is a main reason for this late start continues to impede effective EU interest representation and is explored later on.[121]

The actual boom of lobbying in the EU began with the Single European Act (SEA) in 1986. The endorsement of the single market, the introduction of qualified majority voting for most measures concerning it, and the establishment of the so-called 1992 programme to complete single market legislation by 1992 triggered interest group lobbying of a new quality and quantity (for a detailed overview see Young et al. 2000: 51f, also Andersen et al. 1996c). Interest lobbies that had so far only organized nationally made the move to Brussels at this point (Abromeit 1998a: 34) as did professional lobbyists and consultants (Mazey et al. 1993b: 8). The majority of regional and local government representative offices arrived shortly after, in the wake of the Maastricht Treaty (1992), its endorsement of the principle of subsidiarity, the creation of the COR, and in the wake of general federalization tendencies in several member states (Badiello 1998, also Gray 1998: 288). Even lobbies that had established themselves before the boom years showed a rise in Brussels spending, mainly in the form of an increased number of personnel (Mazey et al. 1993b: 8).

The expansion of lobbying seems to have plateaued with the completion of the single market. However, a quantitative proof of this common assessment by both EU institutions and Brussels lobbyists isn't easy since individual statistics from the early 1990s can strongly vary. In addition, many authors still compare today's more established figures with very widely quoted figures approximated by the Commission in 1992 – the Commission then spoke of 3.000 Brussels based interest groups employing some 10.000 people – which have since been recognized as »somewhat exaggerated and based on rough and ready assumptions« (Directorate-General for Research 2003: 3). In any case, the lobbying landscape has expanded only gradually over the past years as a look at the annually published *European Public Affairs Directory* reveals. In the following, the 2004

---

121 For details on the above mentioned European federations, their development and membership structures, see, among others, Eising (2001) and Teuber (2001: 88-93).

directory figures are compared to those of the 1996 directory as quoted in Buholzer (1998: 365). The 2004 figures are subsequently used as a base for the classification of EU interest groups and an understanding of the distribution of power.

Table 20: Development of Brussels representative offices (1/2)

| | Number of offices, 1996 |
| | Number of offices, 2004 |

* Bilateral and trilateral
Source: Buholzer 1998 (based on European Public Affairs Directory 1996), European Public Affairs Directory 2004

In 2004 the *European Public Affairs Directory* registers 2.081 representative offices. This number is up 13 percent from 1.834 in 1996. However, not all thirteen categories of offices listed grew in proportion to this 13 percent rise. Only the largest category, European trade and professional associations, which accounts for one third of all offices, paralleled the average growth rate with 12 percent, its numbers rising to 695 offices. The number of major corporations with representative offices in Brussels remained more or less stable at 315. The smaller categories of business interests paint a very mixed picture. The number of national trade and professional associations dropped by 81 percent to a total of 21 offices, hinting at a trend favoring Europe-wide associations to be discussed later. The number of bilateral and trilateral Chambers of Commerce also shows a downward trend, totaling 31 in 2004, while national associations of Chambers of Commerce grew by 25 percent to a total of 15 representative offices. In the area of employers and labor interest representation there is a clear trend towards a heightened presence in Brussels. However, the number of national employers' federations has grown faster at 50 percent in eight years to 33 offices while in comparison European labor unions numbers have grown by 15 percent to 23. Labor unions make up 1 percent of all Brussels representative offices in 2004, a third of them representing civil services employees.

Table 21: Development of Brussels representative offices (2/2)

* Municipal, local, and regional authorities
Source: Buholzer 1998 (based on European Public Affairs Directory 1996), European Public Affairs Directory 2004

With 319 offices non-profit organizations account for 15 percent of all representative offices, a number achieved with the help of a 71 percent growth rate over eight years.[122] Infranational government authorities, i.e., regional, local, and municipal representative offices, seem to have similarly discovered the EU as a place for interest representation growing by 81 percent to 194 offices. The directory further lists 115 offices of international organizations including UN organizations, development banks, and the International Committee of the Red Cross. Listings of such organizations went up 34 percent between 1996 and 2004; however, a closer look reveals that a sizeable number of offices listed under this

---

122 In the *European Public Affairs Directory* these groups are simply categorized as »interest groups« (2004: 4). In the following they are mostly referred to as NGOs.

category are located not in Brussels but in Geneva, London, New York, and Paris.

Finally the *European Public Affairs Directory* lists three categories of professional services with offices in Brussels: law firms, consultancies (political, economic, and public relations), as well as think tanks and training institutions. All three categories considered together, the presence of professional services has remained stabled between 1996 and 2004 making up 15 percent of all representative offices, i.e., 320 offices in 2004. The number of specialized law firms has, however, gone back 25 percent to 120 offices while think tank and training institution figures almost tripled, going up to 53 offices. The number of consultancies remained more or less stable with 147 offices.

None of the larger trends that can be observed in the changing lobbying landscape are especially surprising. The trend favoring a presence in Brussels and European-level association is a clear sign interests have understood that both are necessary prerequisites for a meaningful participation in the EU policy process, a process that decides an increasingly large number of policies implemented in the member states – the often quoted 80 percent of economic policies and 50 percent of all other plocies having become common knowledge. Especially NGOs and regional authorities are making up for a time-lag which identifies them as fairly late adopters to the Brussels scene of interest representation. The rising number of European business associations might be more astonishing considering the weakness European associations have been accused of in the past. As umbrella organizations for national associations they have been at the same time rather under-resourced and overwhelmed with the task of coordinating interests, which often leads to so-called lowest denominator interests being articulated (Grant 1993: 31, Greenwood et al. 2000: 1, Knill 2001: 229). While the EU institutions do value aggregated interests and an EU-wide perspective, European associations have often proven to be of little help. A reform of membership structure has brought many European associations, some of them newly founded for this purpose, back towards center-stage by allowing membership not only of national associations but also direct membership of individual companies (Knill 2001: 230). European associations are now dominated by multi-national companies opting for dual-track lobbying through both associations and individual representative offices (Eising 2001: 461, Greenwood et al. 2000: 2ff); this dominance has in many cases done away with lengthy processes of interest coordination. Altogether, these developments may also explain the dramatic reduction of the number of national associations present in Brussels.

Several related topics have been touched by the discussion of EU lobby group statistics and their recent development, e.g., the perspective of the EU institutions and what they look for in interest representatives, or the question of lobbying success as related to what has been called the power structure between interest groups, between associations and their individual members, between business and non-profit interests, etc. The following classification functions as an analytical structure with which to answer these and similar questions.

The system of interest group classification developed in Chapter 2.3.2 suggests a two-by-two matrix based on the type of interest represented by a group. Its first dimension differentiates between public and private interests, its second between national or unilateral and international or multilateral interests. These dimensions seem appropriate in the context of EU lobby groups for several reasons. First, the groups encountered in the above examination of the EU lobbying landscape all differ from each other to a certain degree in these dimensions which therefore allow for a meaningful separation of group interests. Second, as discussed in Chapter 2.3.2, the public-private dimension can in most cases be a helpful pointer as to the resources available to an interest group and the influence these resources can help generate. Third, the public-private dimension represents the most widely used categories of differentiation between interest groups in Brussels.[123] The terms may differ but the separation of business interests from other interests in their definition is consistent. In its communication on the consultation of interested parties (European Commission 2002a) the Commission defines civil society organizations as including a variety of interests but clearly excluding business interests. Similarly, the Directorate-General for Research, while avoiding the use of the public-private dichotomy, does opt for close synonyms, »civic interests« and »producer interests« (2003: 6 and 11). The analysis of lobbying addressees in Chapter 5.2 reveals a variation in access granted to different interest groups by different EU institutions that can be explained in parts with the help of the public-

---

123 While the following examples focus on the EU institutions and their categorization of interests, it should be noted that the public-private dimension also dominates academic discussion of EU lobbying groups (among others, Claeys et al. 1998b: 419, Eising 2001: 456f, Pollack 1997: 572f).

private dimension. Fourth and along similar lines, the national/unilateral-international/multilateral dimension, which functions as a proxy for the degree of interest aggregation within the group and its European-level perspective, helps differentiate between probabilities of institutional access granted, access being essential to effective lobbying.

Table 22: Brussels representative offices 2004 – distribution of interest

100%* (2.081 representative offices)

Catering mainly to business interests

Major corporations

15% (315)

European trade and professional associations

33% (695)

Independent professional services 15% (320)

15% (319)

Non-profit organizations

9% (194)

Regional and local authorities

6%

2% 3%
1%

National associations**
Chambers of Commerce (bilateral)
European labor unions
International organizations

* Percentage values do not add up to 100% due to rounding errors
** This includes national trade and professional associations, national associations of Chambers of Commerce, and national employers' federations
Source: Own clustering based on European Public Affairs Directory 2004

Table 22 recapitulates the earlier discussion of number and type of representative offices and serves as a starting point for the classification of the lobby groups.[124]

---

124 According to several authors this visualization of Brussels lobby groups leaves out one type of lobby group, namely the EU institutions themselves and their officials. Depending on their position at different times throughout the policy process, the Commission, the European Parliament, national governments, and their respective bureaucratic substructures are seen by some as acting as lobby groups vis-à-vis each other (Earnshaw et al. 2003: 67f, Eichener 2000: 267f, Van Schendelen 2002: 204). This is a debate that can be referred to the systematics of lobbies and addressees developed in Chapter 2.3.3 and adapted to the EU in Chapter 5.2. Suffice it here to restate that government bodies are strictly addressees, while part of their tasks, of course, includes interacting and influencing each other and the decisions being made. An exception is the government official with additional sources of income (e.g., as board member of a

As indicated in the table, roughly two-thirds of all listed offices represent business and economic interest. This is obvious for individual corporations, for the trade and professional associations, and for the different types of Chambers of Commerce present in Brussels. By degrees these lobby groups all qualify as so-called private interests in this work's classification framework. The interest orientation of the employers' and labor groups has been widely debated and, though they have been relatively unsuccessful in being recognized as public or general interest groups (Claeys et al. 1998b), the Commission includes the so-called social partners in their definition of civil society organizations (2002a). Professional lobbies such as consultants, law firms or PR agencies are included here in the block of business interest oriented lobbies by the virtue of the clients they service. Such services are often costly and present a (supplementary) lobbying route mainly to the well-resourced interests. Studies show that individual companies and trade associations make up the bulk of the professionals' clients, though NGOs are occasionally serviced by some (Lahusen 2002: 707ff).

The public interest orientation of NGOs was debated in Chapter 2.3.2 with the conclusion that NGOs can be classified as public interest groups in the sense of a non-profit, ideal interest orientation. This is underlined by the status granted or definition used by many governments or international organizations. The definition in place in the Commission confirms this:

NGOs are not self-serving in aims and related values. Their aim is to act in the public arena at large, on concerns and issues related to the well being of people, specific groups of people or society as a whole. They are not pursuing the commercial or professional interests of their members. (2000: 4)

Most international organizations listed in the European Public Affairs Directory match a non-profit, public interest definition though, different from NGOs, these organizations have strong government ties, their membership generally consisting of states. Some of them, e.g., those pursuing standardization in fields such as telecommunications and technology, could also prove to have special industry ties.

Moving on to the second dimension of the classification matrix, it is easy to identify those categories of lobby groups with a national or unilateral focus. National associations, Chambers of commerce, and national

corporation) who could potentially act as lobbyist for the interests (the corporation) behind these sources.

employers' federations belong to them, with possible international interests they have being expressed by their European-level umbrella organizations such as UNICE for the national employers' associations. As representatives of their clients, professional lobbyists in a sense pursue unilateral interests, though of course these can become more multilateral or international depending on the type of client. Infranational government authorities naturally have a focus that is even narrower than national. However, cross-border regional cooperation is becoming more common (Smets 1998) even to the point where shared representative offices are established in Brussels as in the case of the Liaison Office Trentino/Tirol/South Tirol joining Austrian and Italian border regions.[125]

A national or unilateral focus is already less clear-cut with corporations present in Brussels most of which are multinationals, so-called MNCs. Similarly, NGOs can generally be split along the national-international line; yet, a closer look at the directory listings reveals fewer than ten explicitly national organizations. Clearly of an international and multilateral focus are the European trade and professional associations, the European labor unions, and the international organizations. A visualization of the classification argument is presented in Table 23.

What does this classification tell us about the influence wielded by different types of lobby groups within the EU system? As van Schendelen (2002: 110f, 2003a: 304ff) points out, interest representation in the EU today has moved beyond national coordination, i.e., the influencing of EU policies via national associations and governments, to a self-reliance of lobby interests and their professional, collective organization on the EU level. Factors of successful influencing are thus the ability to organize, to aggregate interests to a European perspective, joining with others and altogether professionalizing one's approach and methods. Additional success factors are linked to the size and resources of an organization, the type of interest represented, group reputation and the like. Most of these are discussed in the next chapters. Chapter 5.2 deals with the addressees of the EU systems and the so-called access goods they favor, which include the type of interest (public-private) and focus (national-international or

---

125 Over 300 such Euro-regions are said to have already existed by the early 1990s (Goodman 1997: 188) – the »Four Motors« association between Catalonia, Lombardy, Baden-Würtemberg, and Rhône-Alpes and the »Motor Industry Cities and Regions« being among the more broadly known – many of which have not established a separate Brussels presence in addition to traditional regional representative offices.

unilateral-multilateral) represented. Chapter 5.3 concentrates on the lobbying process, how it is interwoven with the EU policy process, and the methods and resources it demands. However, before moving to a greater level of detail, the following serves as a quick-guide to the distribution of influence between Brussels lobbies, roughly generalized by group type.

Table 23: Classification of EU lobbying groups

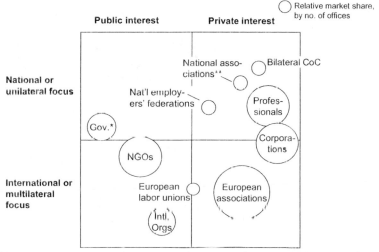

* Regional, local, and municipal government authorities   ** Including national associations of CoC
Source: Own framework

Some believe that the EU's focus on economic policies and deregulation issues favors business interests to begin with (Lahusen et al. 2001: 64, Pollack 1997). Yet, even if this is the case, there are significant differences in lobbying success between the various types of business interests. The multinational companies are unanimously hailed as the most professional and successful in lobbying Brussels institutions (e.g., Directorate-General for Research 2003: 13f, Van Schendelen 2002: 193, 197). In addition to the advantages of their international company structure and experience they profit from the weakness of the European and national associations presenting similar business interests. In comparison to these associations, MNCs seem better equipped for the issue specialization they encounter in the EU institutions and are less hindered by the need to aggregate member interests. This leads to assessments like the following:

As to the specificity of lobbying efforts coming from European associations, officials sometimes deplore bland consensus statements, e.g., from UNICE, which fail to address the specifics of proposed legislation. Rich firm clubs, i.e., small and sometimes temporary coalitions of large companies, enjoy a better reputation with European legislators. (Directorate-General for Research 2003: 14)

The weakness of European associations in Brussels has been mentioned here more than once; Pijnenburg (1998: 304) conveniently summarizes the main reasons for this weakness: insufficient resources, lack of internal hierarchy and discipline, country-related differences, too much distance between individual companies and their European association, and an ambiguous attitude of EU institutions towards European associations. While the idea of weak European associations still prevails, some authors detect changes brought about by shifts in organizational structure (Knill 2001: 230) and by the need of individual companies to cope with a large number of legislative issues and limited lobbying budgets (Coen 1997: 97).[126] The steady rise in the number of European association offices hints at the role they continue to play in representing their members' interests. By comparison, national association offices have all but disappeared.

The problems of European business and employers' associations are mirrored by their counterparts in organized labor. European labor associations are weakened by internal competition, caused by a continued national orientation of their members wishing to preserve national power centers while at the same time trying to exploit the dual track approach (Eising 2001: 464, Grant 1993: 41f, Wendon 1994). It remains to be seen whether such instruments as the social dialogue will in fact strengthen European-level labor organization (Falkner 2000).

Most public interest NGOs arrived late on the Brussels scene and are therefore still underrepresented compared to private interests; this gives evidence of the EU timeline and the relatively late point at which public interest issues appeared on the agenda of European institutions (Alhadeff et al. 2002, Eising 2001: 466). Many of these interests, especially social interests, suffer from an inability to organize and to acquire funds – this, of course, refers back to the earlier discussion of Olson and his *Logic of Collective Action* (Olson 1965). There is a certain weakness in their ability to follow an issue through the policy process (Directorate-General for Re-

---

126 However, this revival of interest representation through European associations clearly differs from earlier associational representation – MNCs now dominate the organization and the process (Eising 2001: 461, Knill 2001: 231).

search 2003: 7), which is strongly determined by the lobbying resources available to cover all relevant access points (Grande 2000a: 21, Jachten-fuchs et al. 2003: 25). At the same time, NGOs profit from the fact that they rarely compete amongst one another but either join in like-minded coalitions or divide topics amongst each other. Also, their issues often necessitate a cross-border perspective, which is clearly welcomed by Euro-pean officials.

The second group of late-comers to EU interest lobbying are the re-gional and other infranational government authorities. Seen in the exami-nation of interest group statistics, this group's presence has been growing rapidly and its members »have asserted themselves as relatively autono-mous and flexible players in Europe« (Directorate-General for Research 2003: 9). Though national governments question the influence of regional representations in Brussels, the regional offices themselves as well as third parties identify specific strengths, especially in their ability for tapping EU funds (Allen 2000: 259, Smets 1998).

The ever growing number of interest groups on the EU level and the limited number of seats at the table emphasize the importance of the lob-bying success factors of organization and professionalization quoted ear-lier. Along similar lines, Lahusen et al. detect two parallel processes, on the one hand, an opening and »pluralization« of the lobbying landscape, and, on the other hand, a growing closure and exclusiveness of power networks and elites (Lahusen et al. 2001: 194).[127] This obviously brings us back to the question as to which system of interest intermediation is developing in the EU – the question of opening or closure, of pluralism or corporatism (or yet a third, new »-ism«) – and the implications this has for both the organization of interests and for the democratic policy process in general. An attempt at a more definite answer to this question is made here.

Abstractly speaking, the system of interest intermediation describes the way in which contacts between lobby groups and government officials and decision-making institutions are structured. So far, academic literature

---

127 In its lobbying study the Directorate-General for Research makes a similar observation: »As a consequence of the ever-increasing number of lobbyists active in Brussels, the Commission also sought to use its resources more effectively and attempted to focus on a stronger »inner core« of interest groups. Its effect has been to privilege a small number of better established groups at the expense of a larger number of smaller, newer and/or less institutionalized groups. There is therefore a rise of »secondary lobbying« – whereby the latter groups lobby others that they believe to have the ear of the Commission« (2003: 39).

provides two main labels – corporatism and pluralism – which function for the most part as general points of orientation while the reality of interest intermediation in most modern systems lies somewhere in between. However, considerable efforts are often made to match existing structures with one of the two labels. In the case of the European Union this has lead to antithetical labeling. As was shown Chapter 4.2, some see a corporatist system in place in the EU (Buholzer 1998, Jachtenfuchs et al. 2003) or at the least the beginnings of such a system (Falkner 2000, Marques-Pereira 1998, Obradovic 1995) and seemingly dismiss EU characteristics that oppose a corporatist labeling.[128] Others, emphasizing pluralist characteristics while ignoring others, define the EU system with variations on the pluralist label as »lobbyism« (Aleman 2000), »pluralist Eurolobbyism« (Lahusen et al. 2001: 22), or »elite pluralism« (Coen 1997: 98, 106).

It appears that an ambivalent mix of what have been termed corporatist and pluralist characteristics disallows a simple »either-or« labeling of the EU system of interest intermediation. Instead, it is helpful to look at some of the EU-specific features of interest intermediation. Given the multi-level character and network organization of European governance as well as the technocratic nature of the main lobbying addressee, i.e., the Commission and its DGs, it is no surprise that terms such as fragmentation, specialization, and sectoral networks dominate descriptions of EU interest intermediation (Andersen et al. 1998: 179, Buholzer 1998: 155, Mazey et al. 1993a: 256). Continuing a line of thought developed in Chapter 4.2.1, which suggested the possibility of a network model of interest intermediation, this work contradicts Kohler-Koch's statement that »no uniform European system of interest intermediation will develop« (1998: 131). A network model indeed already seems to be in place in the EU responding to sectoral, technocratic needs with flexible constellations of players while at the same time providing a structure for continuous relationships between interest groups and EU institutions. Such a model is better equipped to describe the EU reality than either corporatism or pluralism. Finally, it matches the observation made by Lahusen et al. (2001: 194) about the coexistence of opening and closure in EU interest intermediation quoted above and is further corroborated in Chapter 5.2, which examines the EU

---

128 The list of authors who oppose the idea of EU corporatism, not even as »islands of (sectoral) corporatism« (Greenwood et al. 2000: 13), and base this on the evidence of such non-corporatist characteristics is long (compare Zweifel 2002).

lobbying addressees and the institutional setting with which lobbying and interest intermediation are faced.

5.2 EU institutions as lobbying addressees

In accordance with the definition of addressees developed in Chapter 2.3.3, which differentiates between addressees (i.e., the decision-makers in the executive, legislative, and judicial branches), intermediaries, interest lobbying groups, and the original interests, this chapter examines the four main institutional addressees of lobbying efforts in the European Union – the Commission, the European Parliament, the Council, and the ECJ.[129] In addition, the ambiguous role of the ESC and the COR is briefly considered.

Its agenda-setting power and leading role throughout the policy process, described in Chapter 4.1.2, makes the Commission the single most important addressee of EU lobbying efforts (e.g., Andersen et al. 1996c: 46, Buholzer 1998: 260ff, Peterson 1995: 85, Teuber 2001. 124f). At the same time, the Commission is also the institution most open to interest groups, to the point of actively seeking contact or even supporting group development so as to receive a broad picture of interests from which to develop its own position (Eising 2001: 454). The willingness to involve lobbying groups in the policy process is rooted in the Commission's need for additional resources and the awareness of its lack of legitimacy, two goods it hopes to be provided with by the interest groups (Eichener 2000: 270ff, Laursen 1996: 138). Of the various lobbying resources described in Chapter 2.3.4 information, both expert and more general information on policy implications, is clearly the most important and is sought for not only by the Commission but also by the EP and the Council. As a lobbying resource legitimacy through the inclusion of interests appeals mainly to the Commission though the Parliament, too, is interested in a certain type of legitimacy which public interests with large constituencies might offer.[130]

---

129 See Table 10 for a quick overview of the different types of players involved in a model lobbying process.

130 In the context of the EP Kohler-Koch (1998: 140) remarks: »Although being very close to an interest group is not considered to be acceptable when the external partner is an

Of course, the Commission as an institution cannot be an actual addressee for most types of lobbying efforts. Instead, interest groups have to decide which officials to approach to achieve a positive outcome in their interest. In the case of the Commission the most important official is the *chef de dossier* who remains responsible for the respective policy throughout the whole process and who is especially important during the drafting phase (Hull 1993: 83, 85, Mazey et al. 1993b: 10), drafting being the phase during which lobbying has the best chance of creating a sustainable impact. Beyond the *chefs de dossier* – and thinking back to the model policy process depicted earlier (compare Table 16) – there are other important addressees at the working level of the Commission, e.g., officials from other DGs involved, chairmen and other important figures in the Commission's expert committees.

Considering the nature of the work done by these addressees and especially during the drafting phase, it is not surprising that Bouwen, in his empirical studies of access goods sought for by the different EU institutions, has discovered a strong bias in the Commission towards expert technical knowledge (Bouwen 2002b: 379f). Also, in the institution's search for further legitimation, information on what Bouwen terms »European encompassing interests« is also highly valued. These preferences favor certain interest groups in their access to the Commission. Examining the different types of business interests Bouwen observes that the highest degree of access is granted to European associations and individual large corporations while national associations seem unable to provide the access goods of interest to the Commission (Bouwen 2002a: 24ff, 2002b: 379f). The preference for aggregated interests would seem to imply a similar openness towards European NGOs; however, with its focus on economic topics and its specialized structure the Commission is judged less suited for approaches from public or »diffuse« interests (Eising 2001: 468, Pollack 1997: 579f) – with the exception of DGs V, XI, and XXIV.[131]

Lobbyists judge the EP to be similarly open to interest representation as the Commission (Directorate-General for Research 2003: 35). With the expansion of codecision the EP has gained considerably in importance as addressee of lobbying efforts and is now approached by all types of groups

---

industry representative, being connected to a social movement with broad public support gives weight to the rapporteur's position.«
131 DG V: Employment, industrial relations and social affairs, DG XI: Environment, DG XXIV: Consumer Affairs and Health Protection

after traditionally being a minor access point considered by weaker, under-resourced interests, i.e. mainly NGOs (Mazey et al. 1993b: 12). In addition to becoming a primary addressee, the EP continuous to be targeted as an intermediary by lobbyists wanting to increase pressure on the Commission or the Council (Eichener 2000: 267f, Kohler-Koch 1998: 136f).

Within the EP structure the most important bodies from the point of view of a lobbyist are the specialized committees where the largest part of legislative work is done and which normally meet in public. Though the individual MEP can table amendments during committee meetings – as opposed to during plenary sessions where thresholds exist – the committee chairs and *rapporteurs* are key, the latter being responsible for preparing a report and proposing amendments for plenary decision (Eising 2001: 454, Kohler-Koch 1998: 147, Pollack 1997: 581). Bouwen (2003: 6) also mentions the committee administrators as possible access points for lobbying groups since they remain in their positions for longer periods of time and acquire an interesting position as experts vis-à-vis the MEPs. The MEPs are, however, by far the most important targets within the EP structure for lobbyists – a study done in 2000 reveals that 50 percent of MEPs have weekly contacts with interest groups, one third has weekly contacts with lobbyists (quoted in Earnshaw et al. 2003: 62).[132]

The information and type of interests the EP and its officials seem most interested in can be described as encompassing and aggregated public perspectives provided by interest groups with a large base and differing strongly in character from the rather specialized, technical policy proposals produced by the Commission (Bouwen 2003: 4, Kohler-Koch 1998: 153, Lord 1998: 72). This is where NGOs can play on their strengths and mobilize public opinion to influence the EP. It should also be mentioned that so-called diffuse or public interests can be at an advantage in the less specialized structures of the EP where committees cover broader topics than is the case in the Commission (Eising 2001: 468). The EP's preference to talk to broader, more representative interests is corroborated in Bouwen's empirical studies of business interest access to the institutions. In addition to a European perspective provided by European associations, MEPs may,

---

132 Another interesting figure are the estimated 75 to 80 percent of amendments tabled by MEPs in committees that have been drafted by interest representatives (Earnshaw et al. 2003: 64).

in the interest of reelection, also seek national perspectives (Bouwen 2002a, 2002b, 2003).[133]

Compared to the Commission and the EP the Council is fairly closed to direct access. It is lobbied indirectly via national channels, i.e., national government officials in the capitals but also in Brussels (Andersen et al. 1996c: 52, Directorate-General for Research 2003: 42, Teuber 2001: 125f). Interests lobbying the Council wish to either amend or, more often than not, block legislative proposals coming from the Commission. In order to block a policy it formerly sufficed to convince one member state – even though the unconstructive nature of such demands has never made them widely appreciated. However, the gradual shift of the dominant decision-making rule in the Council from unanimity to QMV has made lobbying more complex and costly. QMV has created the need to influence more than one member state and monitor the process closely to minimize the chance of last minute compromising behind closed doors (Directorate-General for Research 2003: 42, Eichener 2000: 265ff). Complexity can also be amplified by high political turnover in the Council and the Coreper caused by national elections and the frequent replacement of ministers (Buholzer 1998: 264).

The rule stating that effective lobbying targets officials on the working level also holds for the Council. Apart from the structures in the member state capitals, the national officials to best approach in Brussels are those involved in the Council's working groups or, on the next higher level, the members of Coreper (Eichener 2000: 267, Hull 1993: 85). They all show a strong interest in information on domestic encompassing interests which favors access for national associations but also for large national companies, so-called national champions (Bouwen 2002a: 26ff, 2002b: 379f). Information with a European perspective coming from European business associations is also valued by the more permanent bodies in Brussels where a certain supranational community-method, geared towards problem-solving and compromise, has developed (Lewis 1998). Yet, interestingly, Coun-

---

133 Other studies, however, find no substantial link between national interests and MEP voting behavior, the latter instead reflecting an orientation along ideological lines (Wallace 2003: 275). Yet, this may not be a contradiction since constituency interests and national interests do not necessarily correspond.

cil's responsiveness to public interests of a European perspective varies strongly between member states (Pollack 1997: 577).[134]

Access to the fourth institutional addressee of EU lobbying, the European Court of Justice, differs strongly from what has been said so far about the other institutions. Lobbying the ECJ is a lobbying through cases. Its main goal is to enforce the implementation of EU policies delayed or left incomplete in the member states – Pollack calls such lobbying efforts »appeals for the nationally disenfranchised« (1997: 581f, see also Eising 2001: 455). Literature quotes a number of mostly public interest regulations, environmental and gender issues, the implementation but also interpretation of which was advance via the ECJ (Directorate-General for Research 2003: 42f, Eichener 2000: 269f, Mazey et al. 1993b: 15). According to some authors, lobbying efforts vis-à-vis the ECJ can even go beyond the more prominent lobbying through cases with some interest groups trying to install themselves in legal expert groups connected to the Court (Staeck 1997: 50f). Furthermore, lobbyists may also target officials on the lower levels, advocates-general and referendaries, which are believed to strongly impact Court decisions (Van Schendelen 2002: 96).

This rounds off the examination of the main lobbying addressees in the European Union, though one question remains as to the special role of the Economic and Social Council and the Committee of the Regions in the EU lobbying landscape. Should these bodies – institutionalized by the EU and made up of representatives from groups regarded as interest lobbies – be considered addressees, intermediaries, or lobby groups in their own right? According to the systematics developed in Chapter 2.3.3, the ESC and COR cannot be considered addressees since they are not counted among the EU's decision-making institutions but rather carry out consultative functions (Lahusen et al. 2001: 47, Wallace 2000b: 25f). The Commission defines them as intermediaries between European institutions and civil society or regional bodies respectively, »established especially to assist the Commission, the Parliament and the Council« (European Commission 2002a, see also European Commission 2001: 15). From the

---

134 Business interests proved their superior strength in influencing the Council via national channels in 2003 when during EU negotiations on chemical policy the industry lobby convinced national governments of threats posed to jobs by demands from the environmental lobby. Negotiations were subsequently shifted from the ministers of the environment to the ministers of the economy, much to the advantage of the industry lobby (for more detail see Bolesch et al. 09.12.2003).

point of view of lobbying groups the role of intermediaries, e.g., the media, is simply to channel interests and build up pressure on the addressees. The ESC and COR's activities clearly extend beyond this since, not unlike European associations, they also bring together interest groups for debate and aggregation of interests. However, in the eyes of EU interest groups they play an altogether very minor role in the lobbying process since groups prefer a direct approach of the primary addressees to using the ESC and COR as access points (Linsenmann 2002: 363, Wallace 2000b: 25, 2003: 276).

The EU policy process and institutions place high demands on the interests lobbying them. Without wanting to sound too much like a lobbying manual, these demands result in the following summary: Successful interest groups lobby early and continuously, they lobby the working levels, and they are aware of their strengths, i.e. the access goods they have to offer. This turns EU lobbying into a complex process of balancing and reconciling issues, timeframes, addressees, methods, and resources, which is more closely examined in Chapter 5.3.

5.3 Lobbying process

The EU lobbying process, much like the EU policy process, is a continuous, often iterative process that can at the most be subdivided in terms of the individual policies it shadows, from drafting to implementation. Yet, lobbying begins well before the drafting of the individual policy, even before its originating thought in the mind of a government official or an interest lobbyist; the lobbying process begins instead with the internal preparation of the interest group. Van Schendelen tags the necessary internal variables as cohesion, knowledge, resources/skills, and image (Van Schendelen 2002: 168ff). What this entails, in short, is the decision on and coordination of a group's position and its activities on an issue, the timely organization of knowledge, skills and resources, and the awareness of its image, both general and as a reliable supplier of relevant goods to lobbying addressees. Following this internal analysis and management, external analysis and management forms the second part of a well managed lobbying process. Analysis of the lobbying environment has to take account, first, of the stakeholders and their agendas, especially the institutional addressees and other lobbying interests, second, the issues related to a policy proposal, also those that may lie just outside its boundaries, and, last but not least, the timeframe of a given policy (for details see Van Schendelen 2002: 137ff). Managing this environment to achieve the desired outcomes then is a question of applying the appropriate lobbying methods and the relevant resources.

This chapter does not intend to supply a detailed list and explanation of lobbying methods for the EU arena, which can be found in the various handbooks and how-to guides on lobbying the European Union. Instead, the top-down examination of lobbying activities intends to create a better understanding of how interest groups influence the policy-making process, an understanding which can serve as part of the basis for the evaluation of lobbying's effects on EU democracy in Chapter 6.1. The reader might also notice that since lobby groups and their representatives form part of the EU policy networks, which are at the core of the policy process, part of what is said here also refers back to observations made in Chapter 4.[135]

Lobbying in the EU is still very much in development and differs greatly between the various categories of interest groups as wells as between individual groups. This has a lot to do with their level of organization in Brussels, i.e., the size of the representative office, the level of independence granted by the organization's headquarters, the amount of resources not only available but then also devoted to lobbying in Brussels (versus lobbying nationally), etc. The most common example quoted is the choice of direct or indirect lobbying, i.e., individual lobbying or lobbying through associations, between different types of business interests. In his study Bennett (1999) shows that only large companies take the route of direct lobbying, playing on their economic and political importance and prestige, which is also influenced by the weight of the industry sector they belong to. Size and prestige are factors small companies cannot match

---

135 Though not impossible, it is at least very hard to quantify the involvement of lobby groups in the committees surrounding the Commission and other institutions. Some quote »75 consultative committees with a mixed membership of Commission officials, national civil servants and private-interest representation« (Lord 1998), others speak of the existence of over 1.000 such committees (Teuber 2001: 82), or yet, of 1.000 registered and 1.000 unregistered expert committees (Van Schendelen 2003b: 28f), the membership structure of which is not quite clear. Whether they are directly involved in the multitude of committees or indirectly influencing them through support and lobbying from the outside, EU lobby groups play an important role in the policy networks influencing the outcome of EU decision-making.

instead opting for the indirect route of lobbying through associations. In terms of resources, Coen's survey (1997: 99ff) sees companies shifting their allocation of funds for the lobbying of EU issues towards Brussels and away from national routes. This heightens the importance of Brussels representative offices and provides them with more resources to broaden and deepen their lobbying approach. However, there are still large differences within the group of business interests with some sectors still concentrated mainly on lobbying on the national level. In the case of the Common Fisheries Policy (CFP) this means that fishermen make little direct appearance in Brussels while the environmental NGOs working on the same issues concentrate their efforts on EU institutions and policies (Lequesne 2000: 369).

After deciding on a direct or indirect approach, i.e., on direct or indirect methods of communication (the association becoming a sort of intermediary in the latter case), the basics of these methods would seem to compare to the known options introduced in Chapter 2.3.4 such as convincing through personal contacts, participation in formal and informal hearings, committees, etc., and the general provision of relevant information. A second look at the EU lobbying environment, however, reveals a complexity that demands more than the simple application of traditional lobbying methods. The sheer amount of access points in the EU's multi-level system including the necessity of lobbying the working levels and the large number of lobby groups seeking access is paradoxically joined with the limited institutional attention given the individual interest representative. This and resource restrictions necessitate coalition-building and interest aggregation among lobby groups as well as a high degree of specialization and professionalization (Lahusen et al. 2001: 105f, Van Schendelen 2003a: 304ff). None of these strategies as such are closed to the individual lobby group. But the breadth and depth to which a group can extend its own lobbying process becomes largely a matter of the adequate resources.

Information in the form of expert knowledge or as information on broad political implications and interests is a lobbying resource or, more precisely, a bargaining resource and access good as they were described in Chapters 2.3.4 and 5.2.[136] Access goods can be financial (donations and

---

136 The generic term information used here covers anything from a particular piece of expert knowledge to a complete policy draft. A Commission official is quoted as saying: »Commission officials advance their careers through policy proposals. Some of them are

other contributions, personnel loans) or non-financial (information, support, legitimacy). A few of these goods can be intrinsic qualities of the type of interest group in question, e.g., technical knowledge at the disposal of a company. Most access goods are, however, a function of other resources available to a lobby group, i.e., personnel, organizational structures, and cash flow. Altogether resources decide whether at any given time throughout the policy process all addressees can be covered and supplied with the right information, and whether this can be flanked with other measures, e.g., public relations work. Though differences between individual groups in the different categories of lobby groups exist, the rule of thumb that private interests outweigh public interest groups when it comes to lobbying resources is confirmed by most (Eising 2001: 459, Eising et al. 1994: 191f, Fouilleux et al. 2005: 616, Grande 2000a: 21, Commission official in Bolesch et al. 09.12.2003). The less well resourced have to focus their efforts on fewer addressees, on certain phases of the policy process, or on a selection of issues.[137]

An unlevel playing field, as van Schendelen (2002) calls the inequalities of access and influence between interests, can result from resource inequality, different levels of professionalization, contact selection by addressees (Coen 1997: 105, 1999: 30) and the like. One remedy to this and other challenges posed by interest lobbying that is often suggested is the possibility of lobbying regulation. The following chapter examines the beginnings of such regulation on the EU level and assesses the potential of regulation for actually balancing interests and curbing unwanted effects of lobbying on EU democracy.

5.4 Regulatory environment

There is a long-standing belief that lobbying regulation through such instruments as rules of procedure and codes of conduct plays an important part in bringing informal, intransparent und unbalanced cases of interest

---

happy to receive a draft from the industry lobby which they can in parts adopt without changes« (Pfister 05.12.2002: own translation).

137 For example, of the offices representing infranational authorities only the largest go beyond the Commission to lobby the EP, the Council, or to attend the COR (Badiello 1998: 332).

group lobbying out in the open and under the scrutiny of the public. Its ultimate goal is to ensure the democratic accountability of the institutions addressed by lobbyists and make the playing field more level in terms of equality of voice. Though the idea is not new, lobbying regulation is in place in very few countries and even in these countries critics are dissatisfied with the outcome and demand further regulation.

The US *Federal Regulation of Lobbying Act* was first introduced in 1946. Based on the principle of disclosure it obliged those lobbying Congress to register individually and state the name of their employer, of their client, the period of employment, their salary and the expenses to be refunded (Lane 1964: 7ff, Saipa 1971: 81ff). Before its replacement in 1995, criticism of the 1946 act focused on two points. Firstly, the information disclosed was declared insufficient and meaningless because it didn't create transparency as to the interests behind the lobbyists and the actual resources channeled to individual issues. Also, the information was merely collected but no process was in place to ensure the analysis of the data. Secondly, registration and disclosure rules didn't extend beyond Congress, leaving the lobbying of the Administration, its ministries and bureaucracy unchecked. The *Lobbying Disclosure Act* of 1995, also called the *Public Disclosure Act*, acted on this second point of criticism (Graziano 1998: 41f). However, while disclosure has been extended to lobbying contacts with the US Administration, the question of the usefulness of the disclosed information remains.

In addition to the disclosure demanded from lobbyists, the 1978 *Ethics in Government Act* and the 1989 *Ethics Reform Act* deal with aspects of government officials conduct (for details see Thunert 2003: 327ff). The first lists restrictions of lobbying activities by former government officials and politicians. This mainly means a waiting period of one year before having any direct lobbying contact with government bodies; however, former officials and politicians are not restricted from working for a lobbying consultancy or public affairs firm in the meantime. Also, the lobbying of government bodies that are directly connected to the official's area of earlier government occupation is prohibited for an unlimited period of time. The second act restricts the gifts, meals, invitations, etc. that can be received by members of Congress and their employees as well as additional remunerated activities on their part. While these acts might prevent blatant bribery and corruption, they have not, e.g., had an effect on the proportion of former administration officials taking up jobs with lobbying firms and companies – figures quote more than 50 percent of former staff making this transfer (Thunert 2003).

In Germany an official register of lobby groups exists for the *Bundestag* but no list is available of the some 4500 lobbyists that have been issued individual passes by the parliament (Hildebrandt 15.02.2006). Here demands are more extensive asking for a two-way regulation to include transparency on parliamentarians and their contacts to lobby groups that also covers the disclosure of all paid or unpaid employment of officials (Frankfurter Rundschau 07.01.2005, Kröter 25.11.2005). These examples can put into perspective the examination of the current regulation of lobbying practiced in the EU and a general assessment of the possibilities and limits of lobbying regulation in the following.

There is no single standard for regulation of lobbying in the EU institutions. Of the four main lobbying addressees only two, the Commission and the EP, have taken up the question of regulation at all while the Council simply states that »all contact with lobbyists and NGOs is handled by the European Commission« (Council secretariat quoted in Directorate-General for Research 2003: 42) and the ECJ, too, has no explicit rules governing interactions with lobby groups.

In accordance with its strong interest in good relations with interest groups the Commission relies on the self-regulation of these groups rather than on rules and regulations (Buholzer 1998: 19ff, Teuber 2001: 122). The principles of participation, openness, accountability, effectiveness, and coherence promoted in the Commission white paper on European governance (European Commission 2001) are emphasized in the Commission's communications on the consultation of interested parties and the collection and use of expertise (European Commission 2002a, 2002b).[138] The Commission is well aware of the scrutiny under which its contacts to lobby groups are placed; it underlines that »the guiding principle for the Commission is therefore to give interested parties a voice, not a vote« (2002a). Also, interested parties must »be ready to provide the Commission and the public at large with the information [on interest represented and inclusiveness of representation] described above« (European Commission 2002a). However, disclosure is not enforced and the responsibility of ensuring that the principles of good governance are applied to the consultation of inter-

---

138 These communications had a predecessor in 1992, the Commission communication called *An Open and Structured Dialogue Between the Commission and the Special Interest Groups* (for details compare Preston 1998).

ests and experts lies with the Commission officials (Aleman 2000, Claeys et al. 1998b: 422).[139] Finally, two official reasons are given for the Commission's lack of lobbying rules or regulation: first, the wish to differentiate between Commission consultations and the decision-making process prescribed in the Treaties and, second, the wish to avoid later court challenges of decisions on the basis of procedural arguments concerning interest consultation (European Commission 2002a).

In the wake of wider debate in the 1990s, stimulated in parts by the EP's efforts between 1989 and 1996 to agree on a regulation of lobbying (Earnshaw et al. 2003: 76, Schaber 1998), and prompted by the Commission's emphasis on self-regulation several associations of lobbyists have established professional codes of conduct. However, these codes are judged to be rather high-level and do not include any form of sanctions; also, only a very small number of lobbyists active in Brussels has subsequently signed (Lahusen et al. 2001: 135f, Preston 1998: 225).

The European Parliament's handling of the issue contrasts strongly with the Commission's principle of lobby self-regulation. Rule 9 of the Parliament's *Rules of Procedure*, titled »Members' financial interests, standards of conduct and access to Parliament«, undertakes a two-way regulation that includes both the interest lobbyists and the MEPs and their assistants in its provisions.[140] In accordance with Rule 9(4) lobbyists are issued specially marked passes, which are subject to annual renewal. In turn, they are obliged to register with the EP and respect the code of conduct published in Annex IX(3) of the *Rules of Procedure*. The code demands the clear statement of interests represented by the lobbyist in all contacts to the EP. Lobbyists should not claim any formal relationship to the EP, nor should they distribute for profit any documents obtained from the EP and, furthermore, they should ensure that any assistance given to MEPs, financial or in the form of staff and material, is duly registered. A breach of the code is sanctioned with the withdrawal of the access pass.

Rule 9(1) and Annex I provide for the transparency of MEPs' financial interests. On an annual basis MEPs have to declare their professional ac-

---

139 Buholzer also mentions measures securing the independence of Commissioners; they are forbidden to hold any additional paid or unpaid position for the time of their commissionership (1998: 149).

140 All references made to the *Rules of Procedure of the European Parliament* (European Parliament 2006) are based on its 16th edition published in February 2006, available on the EP's homepage.

tivities and all other remunerated functions and activities and register any support received additional to that provided by the EP.[141] Also, any direct financial interest in a meeting's subject is to be disclosed orally before the respective meeting. In kind, unofficial groupings of MEPs, intergroups and the like, must declare any support received. In line with the transparency of MEPs' financial interests, Annex IX(2) requires all registered assistants to declare their professional activities and all other remunerated functions and activities. Both the lobby register and the register disclosing the MEPs' remunerated functions and activities as well as any support received are available to the public. The upkeep of the different registers is the responsibility of the quaestors of the EP.

While the European Parliament's provisions take a large step in the direction of two-way lobbying regulation, especially compared to the self-regulation principle pursued by the Commission, both the EP's and the Commission's approach to the regulation of lobbying are called minimal and inconsequential, neither having a real effect on the lobbying landscape and on lobbyists' behavior (Buholzer 1998: 21, Claeys et al. 1998b: 421f, Eising 2001: 456). The lack of compliance control criticized in the US is also a shortcoming of the EU system(s): The quaestors are accused of lenient implementation of the Parliament's *Rules of Procedure* (Bouwen 2003: 8) and it lies in the nature of self-regulation that no process overseeing its effectiveness in the context of the Commission is in place. Yet, both the Commission and Parliament go further than might be expected in the sense that they include their officials in their approach, the Commission by providing them with guidelines and minimal standards of interaction with interest parties, the EP by creating transparency of possible financial interests of MEPs and their assistants. This is unusual since, as Lane (1964: 182) rightly remarks, there in general is a certain unwillingness of politicians to regulate themselves through codes of conduct and disclosure.

It does not seem realistic to expect much more from lobbying regulation than what can be accomplished through disclosure rules, codes of conduct, and an effective process monitoring the compliance of the players on both sides. While it is only fair to demand regulations that manage to balance the access and influence of interests (Schaber 1998: 220), feasible suggestions have yet to be made that do not infringe on the democratic right of interests to organize and represent themselves. As was described in

---

141 The President can suspend MEPs that repeatedly fail to declare their financial interests.

Chapter 3, measures to curb the negative effects of lobbying have to extend well beyond simple regulation. They are often part of the institutional logic or are anchored in the basic principles of the policy process (see Table 13 for details). By contrast, rules and regulations will always depend strongly on extensive monitoring; or as an expert of US lobbying regulation puts it: »In a sense no less real for being inadvertent, these laws can put a central aspect of the democratic thesis to the test: Do citizens in a democracy care enough about »the facts« to seek them out and use them well?« (Lane 1964: 16f).

Chapter 5 aimed at providing a comprehensive picture of EU lobbying covering the lobby groups, their addressees, the process, methods and resources of lobbying, and the EU approach(es) to lobbying regulation. The discussion in Chapter 5.1 of the development and current state of the organization of lobby groups in the EU and Brussels included an analysis of group statistics and a group classification. Both indicated a power distribution in the current EU lobbying landscape in favor of (large) business interests. Chapter 5.1 also examined the network logic of EU interest intermediation which follows neither a corporatist nor a clear pluralist pattern. The different institutional addressees, their most relevant (working level) access points for lobbyists, and their varying willingness to interact with different types of interests were analyzed in Chapter 5.2. The examination of Chapter 5.3 found the complexity of the EU policy process reflected in the lobbying process. The latter extends well beyond the individual methods of direct and indirect communication and is characterized by a continuous need for specialization and professionalization. The access goods and other lobbying resources available throughout this process play a large part in determining the influence of individual interest lobbies. Finally, Chapter 5.4 addressed the two opposing principles present in EU lobbying regulation; on the one side the self-regulation of groups as demanded by the Commission, on the other side the two-way disclosure and regulation practiced by the European Parliament. In combination with the findings of Chapter 5, Chapter 5 forms the basis for Chapter 6 with its analysis of the impact of lobbying on EU democracy, an outlook on probable future developments, and recommendations for institutional, procedural, and regulatory approaches to a more democratic lobbying in the EU.

6. Reconciling EU democracy and lobbying – opportunities and limits

The examination of the European Union, of both its governance system and its lobbying, performed in the first two chapters of Part II is combined in the present chapter with the findings of the theoretical concept in Part I in order to understand if and how lobbying can be reconciled with democratic governance in the EU. For this purpose, Chapter 6.1 investigates the impact of EU lobbying on the policy process and on basic aspects of democracy. In a second step, it illustrates how the effects of lobbying mingle with those of the democratic deficit and of EU consociationalism and where these intertwined effects may mutually reinforce each other. Chapter 6.2 considers developments to be expected in EU lobbying in the near future such as changes provoked by the events of the 2004 enlargement or a possible ratification of the EU constitution; also, it explores the possibility of EU lobbying developing in a direction similar to that of another prominent lobbying system, i.e., that of the USA. Finally, opportunities and areas of measures suitable to reconciling EU lobbying impact with democratic governance are examined in Chapter 6.3 together with the limits to such a reconciliation dictated by the broader aspects of EU governance.

6.1 Lobbying impact on EU democracy

Having understood, in Chapter 5, the large role interest groups and lobbies play in the policy process not only as providers of information from the earliest phases of agenda-setting to implementation but allegedly also as providers of legitimacy and enablers of participation and having seen, in Chapter 4, how they are implicated in the shortcomings of EU democracy, the so-called democratic deficit, caused by intransparency, informality, and lack of accountability, it is now important to examine the actual effect lobbying has on EU democracy. What are the positive and negative impacts of EU lobbying and are they in line with the effects anticipated by the theoretical concept in Part I? Also, apart from the more general impact on democracy, does lobbying reinforce the effects of the consociational system with its multi-level, network logic as suggested in Chapter 3?

The anticipated positive impact of lobby groups on democracy concerns the policy process, the institutions, and the two principles of self-determination and political equality. The following gives a short overview of the argument made in Chapter 3, which structures the subsequent examination of lobbying impact in the EU. Especially in view of limited government resources, lobby groups can support an effective and efficient policy process throughout its different phases by acting as agenda setters, by facilitating the formulation of and deliberation on issues, and, finally, by assisting and monitoring policy implementation. The positive effects this has on the output and the involvement of a broader public may enhance the legitimacy of government and its institutions. The link that lobby groups form to the citizens through the provision of information and transparency on the decision-making process and through the possibilities of participation and interest representation can strengthen the democratic principle of self-determination and is even seen as emphasizing political equality if all interests are given equal weight throughout the process.

The positive assessment of EU lobby groups concentrates on their role in the policy process. They are seen as contributing strongly to both its effectiveness and efficiency (Andersen et al. 1996c: 55, Eberlein et al. 2003: 438ff, Grant 1993: 28, Knill 2001: 242). This concerns not only those groups present in Brussels but also those that monitor the implementation of EU policies in the member states, a phase in which EU institutions are in a rather weak position vis-à-vis national and regional government bureaucracies. In addition, the EU institutions are considered as profiting from the output enhancement through a gain in legitimacy (Andersen et al. 1996c: 55). However, the contribution of interest groups to the EU policy process and to alleged institutional legitimacy seems to come at a price. This was addressed, in a different context, in Chapter 4 as the efficiency dilemma, i.e., democratic principles such as equality of voice and accountability are traded in for government efficiency and effectiveness. This will be more closely examined as the negative impact of EU lobbying is assessed.

Though interest lobbying in the EU appears to have little noticeable positive impact on citizens' self-determination, some voices do speak of interest groups as likely providers of transparency on committee processes (Dehousse 2003: 810) or even speak of their involvement in the EU policy process as an involvement of civil society (Bieling et al. 2003: 520) implying that interest groups in Brussels constitute a functioning link between citizens and EU governance that enhances participation.[142] While this already seems hard to accomplish considering the degree of separation between the individual citizen and public interest lobbies in Brussels, the idea of individual self-determination becomes even more questionable in the light of the group statistics and influence distribution examined in Chapter 5 indicating the disproportionate weight of business interests, i.e., large companies and EU-level business associations. Instead this suggests that citizen participation through interest groups, or rather lack thereof, will appear among the negative effects of EU lobbying. However, van Schendelen makes a less ambitious point in favor of lobby groups; theirs is a more general role in the area of citizen integration, not one enabling participation but a role enabling integration through »representation and acculturation« (Van Schendelen 2003a: 318).

The anticipated negative impact of lobby groups on EU democracy is the flipside to the possible positive impact and accordingly concerns the policy process, institutional legitimacy, and the two principles of self-determination and political equality. A disturbance of the policy process by the lobbying of interest groups can happen for two different reasons. First, imbalances between interests due to resource, influence, or organizational inequalities can lead to a manipulation of the process and can hamper a balanced, effective outcome. Second, the sheer number of lobbies targeting the policy process can lead to a breakdown of process efficiency and an explosion of complexity and bargaining costs. If the lobbies appear to dominate the policy process, this may in addition threaten government and institutional legitimacy. Finally, imbalances of interest representation and a missing link back to the citizens providing transparency, information, and the possibility of participation threaten self-determination and political equality.

---

142 Greven makes the interesting observation that academic literature, in an attempt to rationalize EU democracy, conveniently reworks its formerly more critical assessment of lobbying (2000b: 223); defining lobby groups, experts, think tanks and the like as the beginnings of EU civil society could be seen as part of this attempt.

That the EU policy process or, more precisely, its involvement of interest lobbies is impacted by resource and influence inequalities has been discussed in Chapter 5. The dominance of well-resourced, mainly business interests (Schmidt 1997: 134) is no positive indication of a balanced policy process.[143] Also, some interests, e.g., social and community interests, appear to lack the ability to organize effectively (Directorate-General for Research 2003). Some would argue that EU institutions and officials do a good job of balancing interests, especially when faced with a large number of interested parties (the paradox of weakness). Whether this is the case or whether the large number of groups rather leads to a heightened complexity and the loss of efficiency is debatable. The Commission appears to have reacted to the overload of interests by focusing on established core groups (Directorate-General for Research 2003: 39), a discrimination that can lead to further interest imbalances.

Equally great is the more general threat to self-determination and political equality posed by the intransparency and informality of the lobbying process:

> The unorthodox ways and means of lobbying bring them [the interest groups] the closest possible to those being finally in charge of making the decision. [...] Especially the lobby element of informality can create a relationship of trust, necessary for mutual listening and agreeing. (Van Schendelen 2003a: 306)

While van Schendelen points to a possibly more positive effect of lobbying's preference for informality, the negative effect on the equality of voice also comes to mind as does the obstruction of democratic accountability. Informal networks, which play an important part in the EU policy process, cannot be democratically controlled and again privilege stronger interests (Eberlein et al. 2003: 442), while intransparency is a threat not only to democratic accountability but also to any legitimacy possibly gained through the involvement of interest groups (Bieling et al. 2003: 525). In addition, and even if transparency and formality were introduced, the variety and layers of non-elected decision-makers in the EU governance system can render any accountability process meaningless. The process is further removed from the citizen by its technocratic, bureaucratic nature. Some see

---

143 The dominance of business interests is, however, not the only interest imbalance detected. For example within the group of regional representations size and resources also play an important role in deciding the breadth and depth of a lobbying approach, to the point where many regions have no Brussels representation at all (Badiello 1998: 334, 338).

this policy style as opposing more common forms of citizen participation, e.g., public protest, and as crippling the approach taken by public interest representations in favor of the informal routes chosen by private interests (Gobin 1998: 118f, Gobin et al. 1998: 26ff).

Table 24: Lobbying impact on democracy in the European Union

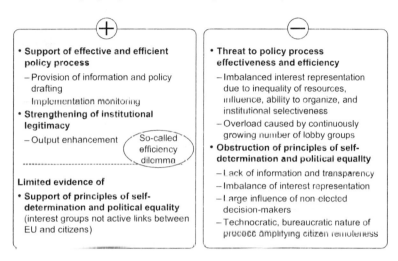

$\oplus$	$\ominus$
• **Support of effective and efficient policy process** – Provision of information and policy drafting Implementation monitoring • **Strengthening of institutional legitimacy** – Output enhancement *So-called efficiency dilemma* **Limited evidence of** • **Support of principles of self-determination and political equality** (interest groups not active links between EU and citizens)	• **Threat to policy process effectiveness and efficiency** – Imbalanced interest representation due to inequality of resources, influence, ability to organize, and institutional selectiveness – Overload caused by continuously growing number of lobby groups • **Obstruction of principles of self-determination and political equality** – Lack of information and transparency – Imbalance of interest representation – Large influence of non-elected decision-makers – Technocratic, bureaucratic nature of process amplifying citizen remoteness

Source: Own analysis; parts compiled from Andersen et al. 1996c, Badiello 1998, Bieling et al. 2003, Directorate General for Research 2003, Eberlein et al. 2003, Grant 1993, Knill 2001, Schmidt 1997

The impact of lobbying is not isolated from other circumstances effecting democracy in the European Union. Due to the in-depth examination of EU democracy, its multi-level, consociational characteristics and policy networks much of what is said here has already been mentioned in some form earlier on. Yet, in order to round off the analysis, a final, lobby-centric look is taken at the following questions. Bearing in mind the examination in Chapter 4, where does the lobbying impact mingle with the larger democratic deficit? Also, where do the effects of EU lobbying and EU consociationalism reinforce each other?

The intransparency and informality characteristic of the EU policy process, of its institutional procedures, of the policy committees and networks are put to good use by the interest lobbies. Lobbyists' preference for personal communication and informal interactions reinforces these characteristics and worsens their consequences, stimulating their tendency to enable unbalanced interest representation and, thus, an inequality of voice.

At the same time a meaningful realization of accountability, which relies on information on the decision-making process and those involved, is obstructed. Intransparency and lack of information are heightened by the absence of EU intermediaries such as a European media or European parties. As Aleman (2000) puts it, bureaucracy and lobbying take over and fill out the vacuum left by the absent EU intermediaries and the missing accountability process. More likely than not, they profit from the freedom this gives them and at least the stronger, already privileged interest lobbies can have no interest in solving these shortcomings of EU democracy. Beyond the problems of intransparency and informality, some might say that the involvement of interest lobbies helps alleviate the EU's legitimacy problem, especially the lack of authorization of the Commission and its overstretched chain of legitimation. However, the earlier discussion of the so-called efficiency dilemma and its reoccurrence in the above analysis of the impact of EU lobbying come to the conclusion that output legitimacy – in this case the policy output enhanced by interest participation – remains an illusion as long as it is lacking its companion piece, i.e., input legitimacy and democracy.

Chapter 3 addressed the possibility that lobbying reinforces both the positive and the negative effects of consociationalism on democracy. The examinations of EU consociationalism and of EU lobbying identify such patterns of reinforcement, confirming the earlier theoretical reasoning. The preference for consensus and proportionality central to EU consociationalism is matched by the logic of EU lobbying. As van Schendelen describes it, lobby groups will seek to dominate the policy and lobbying process and to gain a desired outcome in its entirety. However, faced with a multitude of competing interest lobbies and with EU officials under pressure to reach a balanced position, »compromise, respect and backing might be seen as second-class prizes to win, but are in reality frequently valued as the highest attainable and thus as satisfying ones« (Van Schendelen 2002: 91). Hence, lobby groups choose proportionality and consensus over the possibility of loosing out altogether. Though van Schendelen's description may turn out to include a slightly idealized idea of balancing and self-control mechanisms in the lobbying process, EU lobbying does generally follow and support the consociational logic of decision-making thereby reinforcing its positive effects. Similarly, the EU system of interest representation, as long as it remains open to new interest groups, reinforces the accommodation of heterogeneous interests which is another positive outcome achieved by the multi-level system of EU governance.

As concerns the reinforcement of less positive characteristics, EU consociationalism and lobbying both have a preference for and foster intransparency, informality, and the involvement of non-elected decision-makers in the policy process. This is a fact that has been sufficiently examined and needs no further elaboration at this point. Finally, elite domination, i.e., the lack of citizen participation and the missing connection between them and the political leaders and decision-makers, is a fault both EU consociationalism and EU lobbying have been accused of and which they mutually reinforce in each other.

Is the picture that has been painted so far of EU lobbying in general and its impact on EU democracy in particular that of a stable, matured system or are there indications of change and future developments to be anticipated? If change is indeed to be expected, where is the system of EU lobbying headed? What are the possibilities of directing it towards democratic sustainability with the help of suitable measures in institutional and procedural design or in lobby regulation? These are questions tackled in the following two chapters.

6.2 Expected developments in EU lobbying

Brussels has established itself as a worldwide center of lobbying second only to Washington, D.C. in the number and diversity of lobby groups it attracts; and these numbers continue to rise. »More like Washington as a setting for lobbying than any European capital« (Grant 1993: 34), it is not surprising that EU lobbying is most frequently compared to US lobbying and the question whether the European Union is headed towards a US-style of lobbying is regularly asked.

Many similarities can be detected between the two systems and their lobbying styles. Both have strong pluralist features with an open and diverse landscape of interests represented and a considerable proportion of professional lobbying services in place as well (Grant 1993: 34). Both systems tend towards issue-specific lobbying processes where policies are formulated with the help of frequent and strong interactions between officials and interest lobbies (Coen 1999: 27f, Schmidt 1997: 134). Some of this resemblance might have been driven by the large presence of US business lobbies in Brussels in the 1980s when they took the direct route to European legislation while their European counterparts still opted in favor of lobbying national governments. This presence remained substantial beyond the 1980s with US firms accounting for 37 percent of all Brussels representative offices in 1997 (Coen 1999: 35ff).

However, closer analyses comparing the EU and US lobbying systems and styles find that the differences outnumber the similarities. Though it shows a great heterogeneity of lobbying styles and methods (Lahusen et al. 2001: 153), the EU system is generally seen as more subtle and less noisy than US lobbying, EU interest representation being embedded in the policy process to a much larger extent rather than lobbying from the outside (Coen 1999: 41, Van Schendelen 2002: 228).[144] This has to do with the addressees of lobbying in the EU that are more frequently bureaucrats than politicians. The type of addressees favorably affects the development of long-term relationships between lobbyists and addressees and makes informality more prevalent in EU lobbying. In addition, the emphasis on working-level addressees demands a more technocratic approach and style of interaction; this gives rise to the relative sophistication of lobbying in the EU (Coen 1999: 31, Lahusen et al. 2001: 150ff). The low degree of concentration within the professional services is an indication of this need for specialized niche players (Lahusen et al. 2001: 153f).[145] At the same time, pluralist features are less dominant in EU lobbying. In comparison to US lobbying, it is less competitive or confrontational and, like the political process in general, more oriented towards consensus. Some even speak of a statist process in the sense that the process lies mainly in the hands of the EU officials (Schmidt 1997: 134).

While the differences to US lobbying give a clue as to where the EU system of lobbying is not headed, it says little more about possible developments than what could be discerned from earlier observations. However, several sources of possible change come to mind that could have an impact on lobbying, one of which is the 2004 enlargement. Whereas its

---

144 By contrast, outside lobbying constitutes a rather big part of US lobbying efforts; it includes the influencing of opinion makers in the media, the sciences, in think tanks and the activation of public opinion via so-called grass-roots lobbying (Thunert 2003: 322).

145 By contrast, Washington shows a strong concentration in professional services. For example, this means that the top five lobbying firms boast an annual turnover of over $20 million while the economic figures of all other firms follow with a substantial gap (Thunert 2003: 323).

impact is still to be seen and though a rise in absolute numbers of lobbying groups is certain, many predict a proportional shrinking of the lobbying scene compared to the size of the new EU. This is said to be due to an underdevelopment of group interest representation in the new member states (e.g., Lahusen et al. 2001: 139). However, it is probable that enlargement heightens political and lobbying complexity as an effect of large differences between political cultures (Directorate-General for Research 2003: 54).

A second source of certain change would be the adoption of the European Constitution, its many modifications to EU decision-making and the policy process naturally impacting the lobbying process. In particular, the proposed extension of QMV in the Council and the establishment of co-decision more or less as default procedure would lead to shifts in lobbying styles in many policy areas. It would also be interesting to see what effects, if any, the explicit mention in the Constitution of regular dialogues with representative associations and civil society and of broad consultations of parties concerned would have on the interaction between EU institutions and lobby groups. Yet, at this point in time thoughts about such changes remain speculative pending a decision on a continuation of the ratification process.

Developments in the lobbying landscape and changes in the lobbying system and style are likely to continue to occur on an incremental level, EU interest lobbying settling into a pattern close to what has been observed in this work. More substantial changes depend on the larger developments of the EU. In the past, the transfer of new policy areas and governance responsibilities to Brussels has always brought with it a growth of and change in the lobbying landscape; developments outside EU lobbying itself continue to carry this potential.

6.3 Institutional, procedural, and regulatory opportunities

As EU lobbying appears to be settling into the patterns explored in Chapter 5 and in Chapter 6 so far, what possibilities are there to curb or prevent its negative impact on the policy process and on EU democracy in general? What specific measures promise prompt and meaningful effects and what more ambitious ideas have been offered? Also, what are the limiting factors to a reconciliation of lobbying and democracy in the European Union? The areas of institutional, procedural, and regulatory measures identified by the analysis in Chapter 3 suggest a useful structure for the exploration of the opportunities and limits of the EU system.

»Hence, to reconcile group process with democratic theory it must be demonstrated that the system of group intervention in politics is impartial among the interests present or potential in the community« (Anderson 1979: 279) – the first area of possible measures concerns the strengthening of underrepresented and unrepresented interests and, more generally, the balancing of the diverse interests impacting the EU policy process. Only a well-rounded picture of the many interests concerned with an issue under debate provides the decision-makers with a sound basis for impartial and effective policy decisions. It seems that measures in this area can be divided into three main thrusts. One group of measures aims directly at strengthening weaker interest lobbies. For example, both the Commission and the European Parliament are already involved in financially strengthening public interest NGOs. Approximately 60 percent of these groups in Brussels receive either core funding covering organizational costs or project-specific funding as part of EU programs (Directorate-General for Research 2003: 10, Eising 2001: 469). In the year 2000 funding coming directly from the Commission and going to several hundred NGOs in the development, social, educational, and environmental sectors amounted to over € 1 billion (European Commission 2000: 2).[146] Measures creating a political environment favorable to interest articulation and organization could also indirectly strengthen weak interests and stimulate a higher degree of organization; e.g., in the US a significantly higher proportion of non-economic interest groups can be found in states that allow for popular initiatives (Thunert 2003: 333). Others believe that a strengthening is already taking place without any outside support as interest lobbies, driven by self-interest and competition, are activating, establishing, and professionalizing themselves on the EU level (Van Schendelen 2002: 304f).

A second group of measures aimed at balancing interests proposes what could be called an institutionalization of balancing efforts. Hart (2003: 79) suggests transferring decisions on policies and regulations to

---

146 However, many NGOs decline any funding by EU institutions in order to ensure the independence of their political work. Often it is part of their founding principles or mission statement not to accept donations from government bodies, the industry, or political parties (for Greenpeace see Wallmeyer 2004).

larger bodies concerned with a broad range of issues so that both the size and the breadth of these bodies makes them less prone to influences from special interests and their decisions more representative; the introduction of requirements for larger majorities is expected to have similar effects. The possibility of sunset legislation also belongs in this group of measures.

The third group of measures in this area considers balancing interests by involving the broader public in the policy process and making citizens' input available to decision-makers. Some authors speak rather broadly of using known instruments of direct democracy (Arnim 2000: 293) while others develop specific ideas tailored to the special characteristics of the European Union. Nentwich (1998: 135) adapts the idea of deliberative opinion polls to the EU. Though his idea of organizing such polls in all member states on the same day and on the same issues – and subsequently publishing summaries throughout Europe is aimed primarily at enhancing citizen participation, the results of such deliberative opinion polls could also inform policy decisions on the deliberated issues. Similarly ambitious is the idea of using the possibilities of e-governance and e-democracy to inform and involve citizens and allow them to directly submit input on the policy process and policy drafts. Weiler calls his project »Lexcalibur – the European public square« (1997: 514f); it reappears in this chapter in the context of both institutionalization measures and transparency measures. One last, rather complex idea should be repeated here even though it does not consider the particulars of the European context. With the help of an interest tax and voucher system Schmitter (1994) suggests to balance interests through public involvement, allowing citizens to indicate and support interests that are of special importance to them. This measure, of course, brings with it a direct strengthening of interests through financial support and recalls other forms of tax benefits already employed in some member states to strengthen public interest groups, e.g., tax exempted donations to common interest and charitable groups in Germany.

The second area of possible measures aimed at preventing negative lobbying impact was already hinted at in the idea of institutionalizing the balancing of interests. Measures directed at more generally institutionalizing and formalizing the lobbying process are broadly debated in academic literature and are also regularly voiced by weaker interest lobbies. Institutionalization measures would have to be implemented by the EU institutions involved in the policy process and could include anything from the creation of lists mapping all interest lobbies active in a certain policy area, to a standardized access to all relevant documents, to a formal notification and consultation process (Lahusen et al. 2001: 207, Nentwich 1998: 135). An institutionalized information and consultation process, which could make use of the instruments and possibilities of e-governance and e-democracy (Weiler 1997: 515), would not only allow the weaker interest to get involved on time but would also reduce the informality of the lobbying process. However, such measures are criticized for the possibility that more formal processes of consultation and representation could provoke a rise in the number of lobbies wanting in on the process thus leading not to participation but to paralysis (Telò 1998: 162). Critics of institutionalization measures also fear that the introduction of formal procedures invites legal disputes over procedural issues the primary goal of which can, however, simply be an intentional blocking and delaying of decisions (Dehousse 2003: 809).

The third area covers a variety of transparency measures from information, to registration, to disclosure. Within this area a first group of measures aims its suggestions at an enhanced process for the information of the public at large that would strengthen democratic accountability processes and could even stimulate more active citizen participation. Disseminated via European mass media and the internet information would include details and timetables of policy processes encompassing all levels of decision-making down to the committees, lists of the parties involved and their positions, and information on the implications of policy proposals (Hart 2003: 81ff, Nentwich 1998: 134f, Schneider 2000 264, Weiler 1997: 514).

A second group of transparency measures more specifically addresses the activities of lobby groups and the interactions between lobbyists and officials. Lobbying regulation could demand the registration of lobby groups as well as the disclosure of information on the interests represented and the financial resources dedicated to the respective activities. Regulation could also introduce a code of conduct and measures sanctioning its violation. While some of these instruments are already in use in the EP and to a far lesser extent in the Commission, the EU could profit from a single standard of lobbying regulation maximizing the possibilities of transparency. In a next step, two-way regulation could create transparency on and disclosure of the ties between EU officials and lobby interests.[147] Whereas

---

147 Normally this means disclosure of all remunerated, but often also unpaid activities. In addition, Hart (2003: 81f) suggests creating transparency on the actual voting behavior of parliamentarians.

the common demand for transparency on the ties of elected parliamentarians and their employees (Eigen 2003: 109, Schneider 2000: 264) appears, at least theoretically, to have been satisfied with the EP *Rules of Procedure*, the larger part of EU decision-makers, especially in the Commission bureaucracy, remain a black box as far as their ties and personal interests are concerned. However, no example exists for disclosure rules covering non-elected officials.[148]

The fourth area of measures suggests a strengthening of the independence of officials with measures that go beyond a simple creation of transparency. Due to resource limitations officials depend on information and other resources offered by lobby groups. Providing officials with sufficient financial and personnel resources and with independent services for research and information would go a long way in securing a larger independence of their decisions (Neunreither 2003: 57f). The independence of parliamentarians and other officials could also be enforced through regulations prohibiting any other (remunerated) activities during their time with the EP and the Commission   as is already the case for Commissioners – and demanding waiting periods following their time of employment and before taking up positions with lobby interests (for examples see Schindler 25.02.2006, Thunert 2003).

The fifth and last area of measures comprises not so much individual measures but rather a general enabling of self-correction mechanisms, which van Schendelen identifies as being inherent in the EU lobbying system. Ideally, these mechanisms mean that the self-interest of all players involved in the policy and lobbying process leads them to monitor each other and curb or sanction any excessive behavior. The environment enabling such self-correction needs only ensure an open entry for and fair competition between all interests (Van Schendelen 2002: 308). Parallels to the suggestions made by Madison in *The Federalist Papers* on how to cope with the dangers of factions by encouraging an even larger number of factions are obvious -- »a pluralist remedy to the ills of a plural society« (Graziano 1998: 49). While this possibly enables a form of self-correction, the danger of complexity and intransparency also again grows with the number of lobby groups involved (Lahusen et al. 2001: 208).

---

148 Instead the various US acts on ethics in government come to mind and suggest at least a minimal code of conduct covering non-elected officials.

Table 25: Institutional, procedural and regulatory opportunities to prevent negative lobbying impact

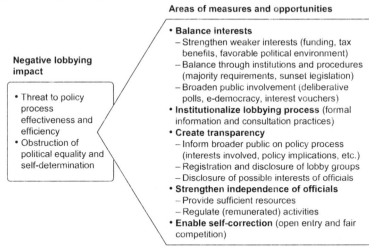

Source: Own analysis; parts compiled from DG Research 2003, Eising 2001, European Commission 2000, Hart 2003, Lahusen et al. 2001, Nentwich 1998, Neunreither 2003, Schmitter 1994, Schneider 2000, Van Schendelen 2002, Weiler 1997

To complete the direct analysis of measures and opportunities that could help prevent the negative impact of lobbying it should be mentioned that one area of measures suggested in Chapter 3 was not taken up and analyzed in the EU context. These measures concern requirements of internal democracy for lobby groups. The earlier examination concluded that since these requirements would not apply equally to all groups, e.g., not to corporate lobbies, and other mechanisms for the sanctioning of unpopular, self-interested group leadership exist such as the withdrawal of membership or financial support, it would be unnecessary to require internal democracy from some organizations hampering their processes and putting them at a disadvantage. Based on this conclusion the area of measures was omitted here.[149]

Of the measures analyzed and listed here clearly not all are equally easily implemented and not all have the same degree of effect on curbing any negative lobbying impact. Most easy to realize are measures that do not require larger financial investments or major institutional and procedural

---

149 However, minimal requirements play a role where it comes to funding and tax benefits for interest organizations; in those cases groups and their activities have to fulfill certain requirements though internal democracy need not be one of them.

reforms. This could mean starting by broadening and deepening already existing approaches such as the lobbying regulations practiced by the institutions or the Commission guidelines for the consultation of interested parties and the incorporation of expert input. However, in the long run measures directly concerning lobby groups have to be supplemented with institutional and procedural changes such as the introduction of sunset regulation in strongly debated policy areas as well as with larger approaches involving the general public. At the same time, measures will become more effective when embedded in a larger process aimed at alleviating the EU's democratic deficit of which the negative aspects of lobbying represent only one of many components. Negative lobbying impact would certainly be reduced if processes in the EU were to be generally laid in the hands of truly authorized and accountable decision-makers and if the many loopholes left by a complex, informal and intransparent policy process were to be steadily identified and closed.

This work set out to explore the legitimacy and boundaries of interest lobbying in a system of representative democracy, in particular that of the European Union. The theoretical concept in Part I concluded, on the one hand, that while interest lobbying is a defining part of democracy, its logic, which seeks to create an unlevel playing field and satisfy a special interest regardless of other interests or a common good, will always necessitate an institutional and regulatory environment that safeguards democratic principles. On the other hand, the comparative empirical model of consociational democracy – introduced to the concept in order to supplement the normative model with a practical perspective and enable a more realistic assessment of the opportunities for and limits to a reconciliation of lobbying and democracy – illustrated the compromises that are continuously being made between normative democratic standards and a functioning, stable system of governance. In light of such a system's imperfect implementation of institutional checks and balances and its shortcomings in authorization and accountability, interest groups have the opportunity to shine in a more positive role, e.g., by creating transparency and holding decision-makers accountable or by enhancing citizen participation.

An optimum integration of lobbying in EU democracy would have to demonstrate a balance of interests informed by the principle of political equality, a transparency of the policy and lobbying processes that activates mechanisms of accountability, and a relative independence of decision-makers reflected in their policy decisions. However, as Part II depicted, the European Union faces a double challenge; not only is it confronted with the paradoxes of lobbying, its positive and negative impact on democracy, but – on a much broader front – the EU has to concern itself with a system of governance that is strongly criticized for its democratic shortcomings. Many of these deficits are closely related to the consociational features of the EU's multi-level system that have developed or have been adopted with the purpose of creating political stability in a heterogeneous polity, accommodating societal segments and minorities through proportionality and autonomy. The price paid for the EU's political stability and a functioning representative system are its proverbial intransparency and informality and an elite domination of decision-making processes that entails citizen passivity. The impact of interest group lobbying joins forces with both the more positive and the negative aspects of EU consociationalism and democracy in general. Efforts aimed at promoting the positive effects of lobbying and finding a sustainable solution that curbs the negative ones will, in the long run, also have to address the broader issues of EU democracy.

Bibliography

Abromeit, Heidrun (1993). Interessenvermittlung zwischen Konkurrenz und Konkordanz: Studienbuch zur Vergleichenden Lehre politischer Systeme. Opladen: Leske + Budrich.
– (1998a). Democracy in Europe: Legitimising Politics in a Non-State Polity. New York: Berghahn Books.
– (1998b). »How to Democratise a Multi-Level, Multi-Dimensional Polity«. In: Albert Weale & Michael Nentwich, eds., Political Theory and the European Union: Legitimacy, Constitutional Choice and Citizenship (112–124). London: Routledge.
– (2002). Wozu braucht man Demokratie? Postnationale Herausforderung der Demokratietheorie. Opladen: Leske + Budrich.
Abromeit, Heidrun & Sebastian Wolf (2005). »Will the Constitutional Treaty Contribute to the Legitimacy of the European Union?« In: European Integration online Papers 9/11; http://eiop.or.au/eiop/texte/2005-011a.htm.
Albert, Mathias (1998). »Entgrenzung und Formierug neuer politischer Räume«. In: Beate Kohler-Koch, ed., Regieren in entgrenzten Räumen (49–75). Opladen: Westdeutscher Verlag.
Aleman, Ulrich von (2000). »Vom Korporatismus zum Lobbyismus? Die Zukunft der Verbände zwischen Globalisierung, Europäisierung und Berlinisierung«. In: Aus Politik und Zeitgeschichte 26–27 (n.a., online edition).
Alhadeff, Giampiero & Simon Wilson (2002). European Civil Society Coming of Age.
Allen, David (2000). »Cohesion and Structural Funds: Transfers and Trade-Offs«. In: Helen Wallace & William Wallace, eds., Policy-Making in the European Union (243–265). Oxford: Oxford University Press.
Almond, Gabriel A. (1983). »Corporatism, Pluralism, and Professional Memory«. In: World Politics 35/2 (245–260).
Almond, Gabriel A. & G. Bingham Powell, Jr. (1966). Comparative Politics: A Developmental Approach. Boston: Little, Brown.
Almond, Gabriel A., et al., eds. (2004). Comparative Politics Today: A World View. New York: Longman.
Andersen, Svein S. & Tom R. Burns (1996a). »The European Union and the Erosion of Parliamentary Democracy: A Study of Post-parliamentary Govern-

ance«. In: Svein S. Andersen & Kjell A. Eliassen, eds., The European Union: How Democratic Is It? (227–251). London: Sage.

Andersen, Svein S. & Kjell A. Eliassen (1996b). »Democracy: Traditional Concerns in New Institutional Settings«. In: Svein S. Andersen & Kjell A. Eliassen, eds., The European Union: How Democratic Is It? (253–267). London: Sage.

– (1996c). »EU-Lobbying: Between Representativity and Effectiveness«. In: Svein S. Andersen & Kjell A. Eliassen, eds., The European Union: How Democratic Is It? (41–55). London: Sage.

– (1996d). »Introduction: Dilemmas, Contradictions and the Future of European Democracy«. In: Svein S. Andersen & Kjell A. Eliassen, eds., The European Union: How Democratic Is It? (1–11). London: Sage.

– (1998). »EU Lobbying – Towards Political Segmentation in the European Union?«. In: Paul-H. Claeys, et al., eds., Lobbyisme, pluralisme et intégration européenne (167–182). Bruxelles: PIE.

Anderson, Charles W. (1979). »Political Design and Representation of Interests«. In: Philippe C. Schmitter & Gerhard Lehmbruch, eds., Trends Towards Corporatist Intermediation (271–297). Beverly Hills: Sage.

Anderson, Liam (2001). »The Implications of Institutional Design for Macroeconomic Performance: Reassessing the Claims of Consensus Democracy«. In: Comparative Political Studies 34/4 (429–452).

Aristoteles (1994). Politik. Reinbek: Rowohlt.

Arnim, Hans Herbert von (1977). Gemeinwohl und Gruppeninteressen: Die Durchsetzungsschwäche allgemeiner Interessen in der pluralistischen Demokratie. Frankfurt a.M.: Alfred Metzner.

– (1993). Demokratie ohne Volk: Plädoyer gegen Staatsversagen, Machtmißbrauch und Politikverdrossenheit. München: Knaur.

– (2000). Vom schönen Schein der Demokratie: Politik ohne Verantwortung – am Volk vorbei. München: Droemer.

Ast, Susanne (1999). Koordination und Kooperation im europäischen Mehrebenensystem: Regionalisierung europäischer Strukturpolitik in Deutschland und Frankreich. Köln: Omnia.

Atkinson, Michael M. & William D. Coleman (1989). »Strong States and Weak States: Sectoral Policy Networks in Advanced Capitalist Economies«. In: British Journal of Political Science 19 (48–67).

Auer, Andreas (2005). »The Constitutional Scheme of Federalism«. In: Journal of European Public Policy 12/3 (419–431).

Austermann, Dietrich (2003). »Schlimmste Tendenzen«. In: politik & kommunikation 11 (37).

Axelrod, Robert (1984). The Evolution of Cooperation. New York: Basic Books.

Badiello, Lorenza (1998). »Regional Offices in Brussels: Lobbying from the Inside«. In: Paul-H. Claeys, et al., eds., Lobbyisme, pluralisme et intégration européenne (328–344). Bruxelles: PIE.

Beetham, David & Christopher Lord (1998). »Legitimacy and the European Union«. In: Albert Weale & Michael Nentwich, eds., Political Theory and the European Union: Legitimacy, Constitutional Choice and Citizenship (15–33). London: Routledge.

Beisheim, Marianne (1997). »Nichtregierungsorganisationen und ihre Legitimität«. In: Aus Politik und Zeitgeschichte 43 (21–29).

Bennett, Robert J. (1999). »Business Routes of Influence in Brussels: Exploring the Choice of Direct Representation«. In: Political Studies XLVII (240–257).

Bentley, Arthur F. (1908). The Process of Government: A Study of Social Pressures. Evanston: Principia Press.

Benz, Arthur (1998). »Ansatzpunkte für ein europafähiges Demokratiekonzept«. In: Beate Kohler-Koch, ed., Regieren in entgrenzten Räumen (345–368). Opladen: Westdeutscher Verlag.

– (2003a). »Compounded Representation in EU Multi-Level Governance«. In: Beate Kohler-Koch, ed., Linking EU and National Governance (82–110). Oxford: Oxford University Press.

– (2003b). »Mehrebenenverflechtung in der Europäischen Union«. In: Markus Jachtenfuchs & Beate Kohler-Koch, eds., Europaische Integration (317–351). Opladen. Leske + Budrich.

Beste, Ralf, et al. (06.06.2005). »Europa im Jahr null«. In: Der Spiegel.

Beyme, Klaus von (1969). Interessengruppen in der Demokratie. München: Piper.

Bieling, Hans-Jürgen & Frank Deppe (2003). »Die neue europäische Ökonomie und die Transformation von Staatlichkeit«. In: Markus Jachtenfuchs & Beate Kohler-Koch, eds., Europäische Integration (513–539). Opladen: Leske + Budrich.

Bode, Thilo (2003). Die Demokratie verrät ihre Kinder. Stuttgart: Deutsche Verlags-Anstalt.

Bogaards, Matthijs (1998). »The Favourable Factors for Consociational Democracy: A Review«. In: European Journal of Political Research 33 (475–496).

Bolesch, Cornelia & Alexander Hagelüken (09.12.2003). Angriff auf die grauen Zellen. City:

Bolz, Norbert (27.01.2004). »Die fünfte Gewalt«. In: Frankfurter Rundschau.

Borrás, Susana & Kerstin Jacobsson (2004). »The Open Method of Co-ordination and New Governance Patterns in the EU«. In: Journal of European Public Policy 11/2 (185–208).

Bouwen, Pieter (2002a). A Comparative Study of Business Lobbying in the European Parliament, the European Commission and the Council of Members. Köln: Max-Planck-Institut für Gesellschaftsforschung.

– (2002b). »Corporate Lobbying in the European Union: The Logic of Access«. In: Journal of European Public Policy 9/3 (365–390).

– (2003). »A Theoretical and Empirical Study of Corporate Lobbying in the European Parliament«. In: European Integration online Papers 7/11; http:// eiop.or.at/eiop/texte/2003-011a.htm.

Bozóki, András (2004). »Mitgliedschaft ohne Zugehörigkeit?«. In: Aus Politik und Zeitgeschichte 5–6 (3–4).

Buholzer, René Paul (1998). Legislatives Lobbying in der Europäischen Union: Ein Konzept für Interessengruppen. Bern: Paul Haupt.

Bundesverfassungsgericht (1993). »Urteil des Bundesverfassungsgerichts vom 12.10.2003 (»Maastricht«)«. In: BVerfGE 89/17 (155–213).

Bundeszentrale für politische Bildung (2002). Erweiterung der Europäischen Union. Bonn: bpb.

Burns, Charlotte (2004). »Codecision and the European Commission: A Study of Declining Influence«. In: Journal of European Public Policy 11/1 (1–18).

Cassen, Bernard (11.07.2003). »Die fehlende Hälfte der EU-Verfassung«. In: Le Monde diplomatique.

Cassidy, Bryan (2000). European Lobbying Guide: A Guide on Whom and How to Lobby. Hawksmere: Thorogood.

Claeys, Paul-H., et al., eds. (1998a). Lobbyisme, pluralisme et intégration européenne. Bruxelles: Presses Interuniversitaires Européennes.

Claeys, Paul-H. & Pascaline Winand (1998b). »Conclusions: Key Issues in European Lobbying«. In: Paul-H. Claeys, et al., eds., Lobbyisme, pluralisme et intégration européenne (407–424). Bruxelles: PIE.

Coen, David (1997). »The Evolution of the Large Firm as a Political Actor in the European Union«. In: Journal of European Public Policy 4/1 (91–108).

– (1999). »The Impact of U.S. Lobbying Practice on the European Business-Government Relationship«. In: California Management Review 41/4 (27–44).

Cohen, Joshua & Joel Rogers (1992). »Secondary Associations and Democratic Governance«. In: Politics & Society 20/4 (393–472).

Committee of the Regions (2001). Opinion of the Committee of the Regions on »New Forms of Governance: Europe, a framework for citizens' initiative«. Brussels: Committee of the Regions.

Cooke, Philip (1996). »Policy-Netzwerke, Innovationsnetzwerke und Regionalpolitik«. In: Hubert Heinelt, ed., Politiknetzwerke und europäische Strukturfondsförderung: Ein Vergleich zwischen EU-Mitgliedsstaaten (58–74). Opladen: Leske + Budrich.

Costa, Olivier, et al. (2003). »Introduction: Diffuse Control Mechanisms in the European Union: Towards a New Democracy?«. In: Journal of European Public Policy 10/5 (666–676).

Crepaz, Markus M. & Arend Lijphart (1995). »Linking and Integrating Corporatism and Consensus Democracy: Theory, Concepts and Evidence«. In: British Journal of Political Science 25 (281–288).

Czada, Roland (1992). »Korporatismus«. In: Manfred G. Schmidt, ed., Die westlichen Länder (218–224). München: Beck.

– (1994). »Konjunkturen des Korporatismus: Zur Geschichte eines Paradigmenwechsels in der Verbändeforschung«. In: Wolfgang Streeck, ed., Staat und Verbände (37–64). Opladen: Westdeutscher Verlag.

– (2000). Dimensionen der Verhandlungsdemokratie: Konkordanz, Korporatismus, Politikverflechtung. Hagen: Institut für Politkwissenschaft FernUniversität Hagen.

– (2002). Der Begriff der Verhandlungsdemokratie und die vergleichende Policy-Forschung.

– (2003). »Konzertierung in verhandlungsdemokratischen Politikstrukturen«. In: Sven Jochem & Nico A. Siegel, eds., Konzertierung, Verhandlungsdemokratie und Reformpolitik im Wohlfahrtsstaat: Das Modell Deutschland im Vergleich (35–69). Opladen: Leske + Budrich.

Czada, Roland & Manfred G. Schmidt, eds. (1993). Verhandlungsdemokratie, Interessenvermittlung, Regierbarkeit: Festschrift für Gerhard Lehmbruch. Opladen: Westdeutscher Verlag.

Daalder, Hans (1971). »On Building Consociational Nations: The Cases of the Netherlands and Switzerland«. In: International Social Science Journal 23 (355–377).

Dahl, Robert A. (1961). Who Governs? Democracy and Power in an American City. New Haven: Yale University Press.

– (1982). Dilemmas of Pluralist Democracy. New Haven: Yale University Press.

– (1989). Democracy and its Critics. New Haven: Yale University Press.

– (1993). »Pluralism«. In: Joel Krieger, et al., eds., The Oxford Companion to Politics of the World (704–707). Oxford: Oxford University Press.

– (1998). On Democracy. New Haven: Yale University Press.

Dahrendorf, Ralf (1957). Soziale Klassen und Klassenkonflikt in der industriellen Gesellschaft. Stuttgart: Enke.

Darnstadt, Thomas, et al. (06.06.2005). »Die Macht vom anderen Stern«. In: Der Spiegel.

Daumann, Frank (1999). »Interessenverbände im politischen Prozess – Einflußnahme und Möglichkeiten der Begrenzung«. In: ORDO – Jahrbuch für die Ordnung von Wirtschaft und Gesellschaft 50 (171–206).

Decker, Frank (2002). »Governance Beyond the Nation-State. Reflections on the Democratic Deficit of the European Union«. In: Journal of European Public Policy 9/2 (256–272).

Dehousse, Renaud (2003). »Comitology: Who Watches the Watchmen?«. In: Journal of European Public Policy 10/5 (798–813).

Delanoë, Bertrand, et al. (13.10.2004). »Le »oui« au traité constitutionnel de sept maires de grandes capitales européennes«. In: Le Monde.

Directorate-General for Research (2003). Working Paper: Lobbying in the European Union: Current Rules and Practices. Luxembourg: European Parliament.

Donnelly, Martin (1993). »The Structure of the European Commission and the Policy Formation Process«. In: Sonia Mazey & Jeremy Richardson, eds., Lobbying in the European Community (74–81). Oxford: Oxford University Press.

Dryzek, John S. (1990). Discursive Democracy: Politics, Policy, and Political Science. Cambridge: Cambridge University Press.

Earnshaw, David & David Judge (2003). »No Simple Dichotomies: Lobbyists and the European Parliament«. In: Rinus Van Schendelen & Roger Scully, eds., The Unseen Hand: Unelected EU Legislators (61–79). London: Frank Cass.

Eberlein, Burkhard & Edgar Grande (2003). »Die Europäische Union als Regulierungsstaat: Transnationale Regulierungsnetzwerke und die Informalisierung des Regierens in Europa«. In: Markus Jachtenfuchs & Beate Kohler-Koch, eds., Europäische Integration (417–447). Opladen: Leske + Budrich.

Ebner, Elke (2000). Die Zeit des politischen Entscheidens: Zwischen medialer Unmittelbarkeit und institutioneller Lähmung. Wiesbaden: Westdeutscher Verlag.

Eder, Klaus, et al. (1998). »Regieren in Europa jenseits öffentlicher Legitimation? Eine Untersuchung zur Rolle von politischer Öffentlichkeit in Europa«. In: Beate Kohler-Koch, ed., Regieren in entgrenzten Räumen (321–344). Opladen: Westdeutscher Verlag.

Eichener, Volker (2000). Das Entscheidungssystem der Europäischen Union: Institutionelle Analyse und demokratietheoretische Bewertung. Opladen: Leske + Budrich.

Eigen, Peter (2003). Das Netz der Korruption: Wie eine weltweite Bewegung gegen Bestechung kämpft. Frankfurt: Campus.

Eising, Rainer (2001). »Interessenvermittlung in der Europäischen Union«. In: Werner Reutter & Peter Rütters, eds., Verbände und Verbandssysteme in Westeuropa (453–476). Opladen: Leske + Budrich.

Eising, Rainer & Beate Kohler-Koch (1994). »Inflation und Zerfaserung: Trends der Interessenvermittlung in der Europäischen Gemeinschaft«. In: Wolfgang Streeck, ed., Staat und Verbände (175–206). Opladen: Westdeutscher Verlag.

Elgström, Ole & Christer Jönsson (2000a). »Negotiation in the European Union: Bargaining or Problem-Solving?«. In: Journal of European Public Policy 7/5 (684–704).

Elgström, Ole & Michael Smith (2000b). »Introduction: Negotiation and Policy-Making in the European Union – Processes, System and Order«. In: Journal of European Public Policy 7/5 (673–683).

Ellwein, Thomas (1974). »Die großen Interessenverbände und ihr Einfluß«. In: Richard Löwenthal & Hans-Peter Schwarz, eds., Die zweite Republik (470–508). Stuttgart: Seewald.

Eschenburg, Theodor (1955). Herrschaft der Verbände? Stuttgart: Deutsche Verlags-Anstalt.

European Commission (2000). Commission Discussion Paper: The Commission and Non-Governmental Organisations: Building a Stronger Partnership. Brussels: European Commission.

– (2001). European Governance: A White Paper (COM (2001) 428). Brussels: European Commission.

- (2002a). Communication from the Commission: General Principles and Minimum Standards for Consultation of Interested Parties by the Commission (COM (2002) 704). Brussels: European Commission.

- (2002b). Communication from the Commission: On the Collection and Use of Expertise by the Commission: Principles and Guidelines (COM (2002) 713). Brussels: European Commission.

European Parliament (2006). Rules of Procedure of the European Parliament, 16th edition.

Falkner, Gerda (1994). Supranationalität trotz Einstimmigkeit? Entscheidungsmuster der EU am Beispiel Sozialpolitik. Bonn: Europa Union.

- (2000). »Problemlösungsfähigkeit im europäischen Mehrebenensystem: Die soziale Dimension«. In: Edgar Grande & Markus Jachtenfuchs, eds., Wie problemlösungsfähig ist die EU? Regieren im europäischen Mehrebenensystem (283–311). Baden-Baden: Nomos.

Fehr, Helmut (2004). »Eliten und Zivilgesellschaft in Ostmitteleuropa«. In: Aus Politik und Zeitgeschichte 5–6 (48–54).

Finer, Samuel Edward (1960). Die anonyme Macht: Der englische Lobbyismus als Modellfall. Köln: Westdeutscher Verlag.

Fischer, Klemens H. (1997). Lobbying und Kommunikation in der Europaischen Union. Berlin: Spitz.

Fishkin, James S. (1997). The Voice of the People: Public Opinion and Democracy. New Haven: Yale University Press.

Follesdal, Andreas (1998). »Democracy, Legitimacy and Majority Rule in the European Union«. In: Albert Weale & Michael Nentwich, eds., Political Theory and the European Union: Legitimacy, Constitutional Choice and Citizenship (34–48). London: Routledge.

- (2005). »Towards a Stable Finalité with Federal Features? The Balancing Acts of the Constitutional Treaty of Europe«. In: Journal of European Public Policy 12/3 (572–589).

Fouilleux, Eves, et al. (2005). »Technical or Political? The Working Groups of the EU Council of Ministers«. In: Journal of European Public Policy 12/4 (609–623).

Fraenkel, Ernst (1964). »Deutschland und die westlichen Demokratien«. In: Deutschland und die westlichen Demokratien (32–47). Stuttgart: Kohlhammer.

- (1972). »Der Pluralismus als Strukturelement der freiheitlich-rechtsstaatlichen Demokratie«. In: Franz Nuscheler & Winfried Steffani, eds., Pluralismus: Konzeptionen und Kontroversen (158–182). Piper: München.

- (1973). »Die Wissenschaft von der Politik und die Gesellschaft«. In: Reformismus und Pluralismus: Materialien zu einer ungeschriebenen politischen Autobiographie (337–353). Hamburg: Hoffmann und Campe.

Frankfurter Rundschau (07.01.2005). »Aufruf gegen Lobbyismus«.

Fritz-Vanahme, Joachim (28.04.2005). »Das schwarze Schaf«. In: Die Zeit.

Fücks, Ralf (2003). »Lobbyismus braucht demokratische Kontrolle«. In: Thomas Leif & Rudolf Speth, eds., Die stille Macht: Lobbyismus in Deutschland (55–59). Wiesbaden: Westdeutscher Verlag.

Fukuyama, Francis (1989). »The End of History?«. In: The National Interest Summer 1989/16 (3–18).

– (1992). The End of History and the Last Man. New York: Perennial.

Geißler, Ulrike (2002). Lobbying im E-Business. Lohmar: Josef Eul.

Gobin, Corinne (1998). »Syndicalisme européen et lobbies: une antinomie fondamentale!«. In: Paul-H. Claeys, et al., eds., Lobbyisme, pluralisme et intégration européenne (110–123). Bruxelles: PIE.

Gobin, Corinne & Isabelle Smets (1998). »Introduction: Reflecting on European Lobbying«. In: Paul-H. Claeys, et al., eds., Lobbyisme, pluralisme et intégration européenne (13–33). Bruxelles: PIE.

Goodman, James (1997). »The European Union: Reconstituting Democracy Beyond the Nation-State«. In: Anthony McGrew, ed., The Transformation of Democracy? Globalization and Territorial Democracy (171–200). Cambridge: Polity Press.

Grande, Edgar (1996). »The State and Interest Groups in a Framework of Multi-Level Decision-Making: the Case of the European Union«. In: Journal of European Public Policy 3/3 (318–338).

– (2000a). »Multi-Level- Governance: Institutionelle Besonderheiten und Funktionsbedingungen des europäischen Mehrebenensystems«. In: Edgar Grande & Markus Jachtenfuchs, eds., Wie problemlösungsfähig ist die EU? Regieren im europäischen Mehrebenensystem (11–30). Baden-Baden: Nomos.

– (2000b). »Post-National Democracy in Europe«. In: Michael Th. Greven & Louis W. Pauly, eds., Democracy beyond the State? The European Dilemma and the Emerging Global Order (115–138). Lanham: Rowman & Littlefield.

Grant, Wyn (1993). »Pressure Groups and the European Community: An Overview«. In: Sonia Mazey & Jeremy Richardson, eds., Lobbying in the European Community (27–46). Oxford: Oxford University Press.

Gray, Oliver (1998). »The Structure of Interest Group Representation in the EU: Some Observations of a Practitioner«. In: Paul-H. Claeys, et al., eds., Lobbyisme, pluralisme et intégration européenne (281–302). Bruxelles: PIE.

Graziano, Luigi (1998). »Lobbying and the Public Interest«. In: Paul-H. Claeys, et al., eds., Lobbyisme, pluralisme et intégration européenne (36–50). Bruxelles: PIE.

Greenwood, Justin & Ruth Webster (2000). »Are EU Business Associations Governable?«. In: European Integration online Papers 4/3; http://eiop.or.au/eiop/texte/2000-003a.htm.

Greffrath, Mathias (02.07.2003). »Europa muss sich europäisieren«. In: taz.

Greven, Michael Th. (2000a). »Can the European Union Finally Become a Democracy?«. In: Michael Th. Greven & Louis W. Pauly, eds., Democracy beyond the

State? The European Dilemma and the Emerging Global Order (35–61). Lanham: Rowman & Littlefield.

– (2000b). Kontingenz und Dezision: Beiträge zur Analyse der politischen Gesellschaft. Opladen: Leske + Budrich.

Grimm, Dieter (07.01.2004). »Auf ewig unverfasst? Europas Weg, juristisch und symbolisch«. In: Suddeutsche Zeitung.

Grote, Jürgen R. (1998). »Regionale Vernetzung: Interorganisatorische Strukturdifferenzen regionaler Politikgestaltung«. In: Beate Kohler-Koch, ed., Interaktive Politik in Europa: Regionen im Netzwerk der Integration (62–96). Opladen: Leske + Budrich.

Gustavsson, Rolf (1996). »The European Union: 1996 and Beyond – a Personal View from the Side-line«. In: Svein S. Andersen & Kjell A. Eliassen, eds., The European Union: How Democratic Is It? (217–226). London: Sage.

Gustavsson, Sverker (1998). »Defending the Democratic Deficit«. In: Albert Weale & Michael Nentwich, eds., Political Theory and the European Union: Legitimacy, Constitutional Choice and Citizenship (63–79). London: Routledge.

Habermas, Jürgen (1996). Die Einbeziehung des Anderen: Studien zur politischen Theorie. Frankfurt a.M.: Suhrkamp.

Hamilton, Alexander, et al. (2003, orig. 1787-88). The Federalist Papers. New York: Bantam.

– (2003, orig. 1787–88). The Federalist Papers. New York: Bantam.

Hart, Thomas (2003). »Mehr Transparenz für die stillen Mächtigen«. In: Thomas Leif & Rudolf Speth, eds., Die stille Macht: Lobbyismus in Deutschland (60–84). Wiesbaden: Westdeutscher Verlag.

Hayes-Renshaw, Fiona (1996). »The Role of the Council«. In: Svein S. Andersen & Kjell A. Eliassen, eds., The European Union: How Democratic Is It? (143–163). London: Sage.

Heclo, Hugh (1978). »Issue Networks and the Executive Establishment«. In: Anthony King, ed., The New American Political System (87–124). Washington D.C.: American Enterprise Institute.

Heinelt, Hubert (1996). »Die Strukturfondsförderung – Politikprozesse im Mehrebenensystem der Europäischen Union«. In: Hubert Heinelt, ed., Politiknetzwerke und europäische Strukturfondsförderung: Ein Vergleich zwischen EU-Mitgliedsstaaten (17–32). Opladen: Leske + Budrich.

Held, David (1993). »Democracy«. In: Joel Krieger, et al., eds., The Oxford Companion to Politics of the World (220–224). Oxford: Oxford University Press.

– (1995). Democracy and the Global Order: From the Modern State to Cosmopolitan Governance. Stanford: Stanford University Press.

– (1996). Models of Democracy. Cambridge: Polity Press.

Herder-Dorneich, Philipp (1979). Konkurrenzdemokratie, Verhandlungsdemokratie: Politische Strategien der Gegenwart. Stuttgart: Kohlhammer.

Héritier, Adrienne (1999). »Elements of Democratic Legitimation in Europe: an Alternative Perspective«. In: Journal of European Public Policy 6/2 (269–282).

– (2003). »Composite Democracy in Europe: the Role of Transparency and Access to Information«. In: Journal of European Public Policy 10/5 (814–833).

Herz, Dietmar (1999). Die wohlerwogene Republik: Das konstitutionelle Denken des politisch-philosophischen Liberalismus. Paderborn: Ferdinand Schöningh.

Hildebrandt, Antje (15.02.2006). »Kontrolle der »fünften Gewalt««. In: Frankfurter Rundschau.

Hindess, Barry (1991). »Imaginary Presuppositions of Democracy«. In: Economy and Society 20/2 (173–195).

Hirst, Paul (1992). »Comments on »Secondary Associations and Democratic Governance««. In: Politics & Society 20/4 (473–480).

– (1994). Associative Democracy: New Forms of Economic and Social Governance. Cambridge: Polity Press.

Hix, Simon (2003). »Parteien, Wahlen und Demokratie in der EU«. In: Markus Jachtenfuchs & Beate Kohler-Koch, eds., Europäische Integration (151–180). Opladen: Leske + Budrich.

Hooghe, Liesbet & Gary Marks (2001). »Types of Multi-Level Governance«. In: European Integration online Papers 5/11; http://eiop.or.au/eiop/texte/2001-011a.htm.

Höreth, Marcus (1998). The Trilemma of Legitimacy: Multilevel Governance in the EU and the Problem of Democracy. Bonn: Zentrum für Europäische Integrationsforschung.

Hrbek, Rudolf (1981). »Die EG ein Konkordanz-System? Anmerkung zu einem Deutungsversuch der politikwissenschaftlichen Europaforschung«. In: Roland Bieber, et al., eds., Das Europa der zweiten Generation: Gedächtnisschrift für Christoph Sasse (87–103). Baden-Baden: Nomos.

Huber, Peter M. (1992). »Die Rolle des Demokratieprinzips im europäischen Integrationsprozeß«. In: Staatswissenschaften und Staatspraxis 3 (349–378).

Hudon, Raymond (1998). »Lobbying et éthique démocratique: l'expérience canadienne«. In: Paul-H. Claeys, et al., eds., Lobbyisme, pluralisme et intégration européenne (184–207). Bruxelles: PIE.

Hull, Robert (1993). »Lobbying Brussels: A View from Within«. In: Sonia Mazey & Jeremy Richardson, eds., Lobbying in the European Community (82–92). Oxford: Oxford University Press.

Hurrelmann, Achim (2005). Verfassung und Integration in Europa: Wege zu einer supranationalen Demokratie. Frankfurt a.M.: Campus.

Imig, Doug & Sidney Tarrow (2003). »Politscher Protest im europäischen Mehrebenensystem«. In: Markus Jachtenfuchs & Beate Kohler-Koch, eds., Europäische Integration (121–149). Opladen: Leske + Budrich.

Immergut, Ellen M. (1992). »An Institutional Critique of Associative Democracy: Commentary on »Secondary Associations and Democratic Governance««. In: Politics & Society 20/4 (481–486).

Ismayr, Wolfgang (2004). »Die politischen Systeme der EU-Beitrittsländer im Vergleich«. In: Aus Politik und Zeitgeschichte 5–6 (5–14).

Jachtenfuchs, Markus (1997). »Democracy and Governance in the European Union«. In: European Integration online Papers 1/2; http://eiop.or.au/eiop/texte/1997-002a.htm.

– (1999). »Die Zukunft der Demokratie im Rahmen der Europäischen Union«. In: Max Kaase & Günther Schmid, eds., Eine lernende Demokratie: 50 Jahre Bundesrepublik Deutschland (263–281). Berlin: WZB.

Jachtenfuchs, Markus & Beate Kohler-Koch (1996). »Regieren im dynamischen Mehrebenensystem«. In: Markus Jachtenfuchs & Beate Kohler-Koch, eds., Europäische Integration (15–44). Opladen: Leske + Budrich.

– (2003). »Regieren und Institutionenbildung«. In: Markus Jachtenfuchs & Beate Kohler-Koch, eds., Europäische Integration (11–46). Opladen: Leske + Budrich.

Jetzelsperger, Christian & Marc Schattenmann (1999). »Agenda 2000: Die Erweiterung und Vertiefung der Union«. In: Dietmar Herz, ed., Die Europäische Union: Politik Recht Wirtschaft (293–328). Frankfurt a.M.: Fischer.

Jochem, Sven & Nico A. Siegel (2003). »Konzertierung, Verhandlungsdemokratie und wohlfahrtsstaatliche Reformpolitik«. In: Sven Jochem & Nico A. Siegel, eds., Konzertierung, Verhandlungsdemokratie und Reformpolitik im Wohlfahrtsstaat: Das Modell Deutschland im Vergleich (7–32). Opladen: Leske + Budrich.

Kaiser, Karl (1996). »Zwischen neuer Interdependenz und altem Nationalstaat: Vorschläge zur Re-Demokratisierung«. In: Werner Weidenfeld, ed., Demokratie am Wendepunkt: Die demokratische Frage als Projekt des 21. Jahrhunderts (311–328). Berlin: Siedler.

Kaiser, Robert & Heiko Prange (2004). »Managing Diversity in a System of Multi-level Governance: The Open Method of Co-ordination in Innovation Policy«. In: Journal of European Public Policy 11/2 (249–266).

Kenis, Patrick & Volker Schneider (1991). »Policy Networks and Policy Analysis: Scrutinizing a New Analytical Toolbox«. In: Bernd Marin & Renate Mayntz, eds., Policy Networks: Empirical Evidence and Theoretical Considerations (25–59). Frankfurt a.M.: Campus.

Kielmansegg, Peter Graf (2003). »Integration und Demokratie mit Nachwort zur zweiten Auflage«. In: Markus Jachtenfuchs & Beate Kohler-Koch, eds., Europäische Integration (49–83). Opladen: Leske + Budrich.

Knill, Christoph (2001). »Private Governance across Multiple Arenas: European Interest Associations as Interface Actors«. In: Journal of European Public Policy 8/2 (227–246).

Kohler-Koch, Beate (1998). »Organized Interests in the EU and the European Parliament«. In: Paul-H. Claeys, et al., eds., Lobbyisme, pluralisme et intégration européenne (126–158). Bruxelles: PIE.

Kröter, Thomas (25.11.2005). »'Transparenz auf der Kippe: Streit über Nebenverdienste«. In: Frankfurter Rundschau.

Laffan, Brigid & Michael Shackleton (2000). »The Budget: Who Gets What, When, and How«. In: Helen Wallace & William Wallace, eds., Policy-Making in the European Union (211–241). Oxford: Oxford University Press.

Lahusen, Christian (2002). »Commercial Consultancies in the European Union: the Shape and Structure of Professional Interest Intermediation«. In: Journal of European Public Policy 9/5 (695–714).

Lahusen, Christian & Claudia Jauß (2001). Lobbying als Beruf: Interessengruppen in der Europäischen Union. Baden-Baden: Nomos.

Lane, Edgar (1964). Lobbying and the Law. Berkley: University of California Press.

Lane, Jan-Erik & Svante Ersson (1997). »The Institutions of Konkordanz and Corporatism: How Closely Are They Connected?«. In: Swiss Political Science Review 3/1 (1–29); www.spsr.ch.

Laursen, Finn (1996). »The Role of the Commission«. In: Svein S. Andersen & Kjell A. Eliassen, eds., The European Union: How Democratic Is It? (119–141). London: Sage.

Lehmbruch, Gerhard (1969). »Konkordanzdemokratien im internationalen System«. In: Ernst-Otto Czempiel, ed., Die anachronistische Souveränität: Zum Verhältnis von Innen- und Außenpolitik (139–163). Köln: Westdeutscher Verlag.

– (1974). »A Non-Competitive Pattern of Conflict Management in Liberal Democracies: The Case of Switzerland, Austria and Lebanon«. In: Kenneth D. McRae, ed., Consociational Democracy: Political Accomodation in Segmented Societies (90–97). Toronto: McClelland and Stewart.

– (1975). »Consociational Democracy in the International System«. In: European Journal of Political Research 3 (377–391).

– (1979a). »Consociational Democracy, Class Conflict and the New Corporatism«. In: Philippe C. Schmitter & Gerhard Lehmbruch, eds., Trends Towards Corporatist Intermediation (53–61). Beverly Hills: Sage.

– (1979b). »Wandlungen der Interessenpolitik im liberalen Korporatismus«. In: Ulrich von Aleman & Rolf G. Heinze, eds., Verbände und Staat: Vom Pluralismus zum Korporatismus. Analysen, Positionen, Dokumente (50–71). Opladen: Westdeutscher Verlag.

– (1992). »Konkordanzdemokratie«. In: Manfred G. Schmidt, ed., Die westlichen Länder (206–211). München: Beck.

– (1996). Die korporative Verhandlungsdemokratie in Westmitteleuropa.

Lehner, Franz (1986). »Konkurrenz, Korporatismus und Konkordanz: Politische Vermittlungsstrukturen und wirtschaftspolitische Steuerungskapazitäten in modernen Demokratien«. In: Max Kaase, ed., Politische Wissenschaft und politische Ordnung: Analysen zur Theorie und Empirie demokratischer Regierungsweise: Festschrift zum 65. Geburtstag von Rudolf Wildenmann (146–171). Opladen: Westdeutscher Verlag.

Leif, Thomas & Rudolf Speth (2003). »Anatomie des Lobbyismus: Einführung in eine unbekannte Sphäre der Macht«. In: Thomas Leif & Rudolf Speth, eds.,

Die stille Macht: Lobbyismus in Deutschland (7–32). Wiesbaden: Westdeutscher Verlag.

– (2006). Die fünfte Gewalt: Lobbyismus in Deutschland. Wiesbaden: VS Verlag.

Lequesne, Christian (2000). »The Common Fisheries Policy: Letting the Little Ones Go?«. In: Helen Wallace & William Wallace, eds., Policy-Making in the European Union (345–372). Oxford: Oxford University Press.

Lequesne, Christian & Philippe Rivaud (2003). »The Committees of Independent Experts: Expertise in the Service of Democracy«. In: Journal of European Public Policy 10/5 (695–709).

Lewis, Jeffrey (1998). The Institutional Problem-Solving Capacities of the Council: The Committee of Permanent Representatives and the Methods of Community. Köln: Max-Planck-Institut für Gesellschaftsforschung.

Lijphart, Arend (1968). »Typologies of Democratic Systems«. In: Comparative Political Studies 1 (3–44).

– (1974). »Consociational Democracy«. In: Kenneth D. McRae, ed., Consociational Democracy: Political Accomodation in Segmented Societies (70–89). Toronto: McClelland and Stewart.

– (1984). Democracies: Patterns of Majoritarian and Consensus Government in Twenty-One Countries. New Haven: Yale University Press.

– (1993). »Consociational Democracy«. In: Joel Krieger, et al., eds., The Oxford Companion to Politics of the World (188–189). Oxford: Oxford University Press.

– (1999). Patterns of Democracy: Government Forms and Performance in Thirty-Six Countries. New Haven: Yale University Press.

Lijphart, Arend & Markus M. Crepaz (1991). »Corporatism and Consensus Democracy in 18 Countries«. In: British Journal of Political Science 21 (235–246).

Lincoln, Abraham (1995, orig. 1863). »Address Delivered at the Dedication of the Cemetery at Gettysburg, November 19, 1863«. In: Nina Baym, et al., eds., The Norton Anthology of American Literature (724). New York: W. W. Norton & Company.

Linsenmann, Ingo (2002). »Wirtschafts- und Sozialausschuss«. In: Werner Weidenfeld & Wolfgang Wessels, eds., Europa von A bis Z: Taschenbuch der europäischen Integration (361–363). Bonn: Institut für Europäische Politik.

Locke, John (1966, orig. 1689). Über die Regierung. Reinbek: Rowohlt.

Lodge, Juliet (1996). »The European Parliament«. In: Svein S. Andersen & Kjell A. Eliassen, eds., The Europen Union: How Democratic Is It? (187–214). London: Sage.

Lord, Christopher (1998). Democracy in the European Union. Sheffield: Sheffield Academic Press.

Lorwin, Val R. (1974). »Segmented Pluralism: Ideological Cleavages and Political Cohesion in the Smaller European Democracies«. In: Kenneth D. McRae, ed., Consociational Democracy: Political Accomodation in Segmented Societies (33–69). Toronto: McClelland and Stewart.

Luthardt, Wolfgang (1997). »Formen der Demokratie: Die Vorteile der Konkordanzdemokratie«. In: Eckhard Jesse & Steffen Kailitz, eds., Prägekräfte des 20. Jahrhunderts: Demokratie, Extremismus, Totalitarismus (41–57). Baden-Baden: Nomos.

Magnette, Paul, et al. (2003). »Conclusion: Diffuse Democracy in the European Union: the Pathologies of Delegation«. In: Journal of European Public Policy 10/5 (834–840).

Majone, Giandomenico (1998). »Europe's »Democratic Deficit«: The Question of Standards«. In: European Law Journal 4/1 (5–28).

Marin, Bernd & Renate Mayntz, eds. (1991). Policy Networks: Empirical Evidence and Theoretical Considerations. Frankfurt a.M.: Campus.

Marks, Gary (1993). »Structural policy and Multilevel Governance in the EC«. In: Alan Cafruny & Glenda Rosenthal, eds., The State of the European Community: The Maastricht Debates and Beyond (390–410). Boulder: Lynne Rienner.

Marks, Gary, et al. (1996). »European Integration from the 1980s: State-Centric vs. Multi-Level Governance«. In: Journal of Common Market Studies 34/3 (341–378).

Marques-Pereira, Bérengère (1998). »Mort du néo-corporatisme?«. In: Paul-H. Claeys, et al., eds., Lobbyisme, pluralisme et intégration européenne (51–57). Bruxelles: PIE.

Martens, Steffen (2004). »Das erweiterte Europa«. In: Aus Politik und Zeitgeschichte 17 (3–5).

Matláry, Janne Haaland (1995). »New Forms of Governance in Europe?«. In: Cooperation and Conflict 30/2 (99–123).

– (1998). »Democratic Legitimacy and the Role of The Commission«. In: Andreas Føllesdal & Peter Koslowski, eds., Democracy and the European Union (65–80). Berlin: Springer.

Mayntz, Renate (1991). Modernization and the Logic of Interorganizational Networks. Köln: Max-Planck-Institut für Gesellschaftsforschung.

– (1992). »Interessenverbände und Gemeinwohl – Die Verbändestudie der Bertelsmann Stiftung«. In: Renate Mayntz, ed., Verbände zwischen Mitgliederinteressen und Gemeinwohl (11–35). Gütersloh: Bertelsmann Stiftung.

Mazey, Sonia & Jeremy Richardson (1993a). »Conclusion: A European Policy Style?«. In: Sonia Mazey & Jeremy Richardson, eds., Lobbying in the European Community (246–258). Oxford: Oxford University Press.

– (1993b). »Introduction: Transference of Power, Decision Rules, and Rules of the Game«. In: Lobbying in the European Community (3–26). Oxford: Oxford University Press.

–, eds. (1993c). Lobbying in the European Community. Oxford: Oxford University Press.

McGrew, Anthony, ed. (1997). The Transformation of Democracy? Globalization and Territorial Democracy. Cambridge: Polity Press.

McRae, Kenneth D., ed. (1974). Consociational Democracy: Political Accomodation in Segmented Societies. Toronto: McClelland and Stewart.

Midgaard, Knut (1998). »The Problem of Autonomy and Democracy in a Complex Polity: The European Union«. In: Andreas Follesdal & Peter Koslowski, eds., Democracy and the European Union (189–203). Berlin: Springer.

Milbrath, Lester W. (1963). The Washington Lobbyists. Chicago: Northwestern.

Mill, John Stuart (1971, orig. 1861). Betrachtungen über die repräsentative Demokratie. Paderborn: Schöningh.

Montesqieu, Charles-Louis de Secondat, Baron de la Brède et de (1994, orig. 1748). Vom Geist der Gesetze. Stuttgart: Reclam.

Moravcsik, Andrew (2001). »Despotism in Brussels? Misreading the European Union«. In: Foreign Affairs 80/3 (114–122).

Müller, Burkhard (11.06.2004). »Wahl ohne Wähler: Europa funktioniert, weil es nicht demokratisch ist«. In: Süddeutsche Zeitung.

Muntean, Andrei M. (2000). »The European Parliament's Political Legitimacy and the Commission's »Misleading Management«: Towards a »Parliamentarian« European Union?«. In: European Integration online Papers 4/5; http://eiop.or.au/eiop/texte/2000-005a.htm.

Nentwich, Michael (1998). »Opportunity Structures for Citizens' Participation: The Case of the European Union«. In: Albert Weale & Michael Nentwich, eds., Political Theory and the European Union: Legitimacy, Constitutional Choice and Citizenship (125–140). London: Routledge.

Neunreither, Karlheinz (2003). »Elected Legislators and their Unelected Assistants in the European Parliament«. In: Rinus Van Schendelen & Roger Scully, eds., The Unseen Hand: Unelected EU Legislators (40–60). London: Frank Cass.

Neyer, Jürgen (2004). »Explaining the Unexpected: Efficiency and Effectiveness in European Decision-Making«. In: Journal of European Public Policy 11/1 (19–38).

Nohlen, Dieter (2004). »Wie wählt Europa? Das polymorphe Wahlsystem zum Europäischen Parlament«. In: Aus Politik und Zeitgeschichte 17 (29–37).

Obradovic, Daniela (1995). »Prospects for Corporatist Decision-Making in the European Union: the Social Policy Agreement«. In: Journal of European Public Policy 2/2 (261–283).

Offe, Claus (1972). »Politische Herrschaft und Klassenstrukturen«. In: Gisela Kress & Dieter Senghaas, eds., Politikwissenschaft (135–164). Frankfurt a.M.: Fischer.

– (1996). »Bewährungsproben: Über einige Beweislasten bei der Verteidigung der liberalen Demokratie«. In: Werner Weidenfeld, ed., Demokratie am Wendepunkt: Die demokratische Frage als Projekt des 21. Jahrhunderts (141–157). Berlin: Siedler.

– (2000). »The Democratic Welfare State in an Integrating Europe«. In: Michael Th. Greven & Louis W. Pauly, eds., Democracy beyond the State? The

European Dilemma and the Emerging Global Order (63–89). Lanham: Rowman & Littlefield.

Olsen, Johan P., et al. (2000). »Symposium: Governing in Europe: Effective and Democratic?«. In: Journal of European Public Policy 7/2 (310–324).

Olson, Mancur (1965). The Logic of Collective Action: Public Goods and the Theory of Groups. Cambridge: Harvard University Press.

– (1982). The Rise and Decline of Nations: Economic Growth, Stagflation, and Social Rigidities. New Haven: Yale University Press.

Papadopoulos, Yannis (2005). »Implementing (and Radicalizing) Art. 1-47.4 of the Constitution: Is the Addition of Some (Semi-)Direct Democracy to the Nascent Consociational European Federation Just Swiss Folklore?«. In: Journal of European Public Policy 12/3 (448–467).

Pappi, Franz Urban & Christian H.C.A. Henning (2003). »Die Logik des Entscheidens im EU-System«. In: Markus Jachtenfuchs & Beate Kohler-Koch, eds., Europäische Integration (287–315). Opladen: Leske + Budrich.

Peters, Anne (2003). »A Plea for a European Semi-Parliamentary and Semi-Consociational Democracy«. In: European Integration online Papers 7/3; http://eiop.or.au/eiop/texte/2003-003a.htm.

Peterson, John (1995). »Decision-Making in the European Union: Towards a Framework for Analysis«. In: Journal of European Public Policy 2/1 (69–93).

Pfister, Sandra (05.12.2002). »Interessenvertreter in Brüssel: Rasanter Zuwachs«. In: Die Zeit.

Pijnenburg, Bert (1998). »EU Lobbying by Ad Hoc Coalitions: an Explanatory Case Study«. In: Journal of European Public Policy 5/2 (303–321).

Pinzler, Petra (14.04.2005). »Europa nervt«. In: Die Zeit.

Pollack, Mark A. (1997). »Representing Diffuse Interests in EC Policy-Making«. In: Journal of European Public Policy 4/4 (572–590).

Preston, Mary E. (1998). »The European Commission and Special Interest Groups«. In: Paul-H. Claeys, et al., eds., Lobbyisme, pluralisme et intégration européenne (222–232). Bruxelles: PIE.

Rasmussen, Anne (2003). »The Role of the European Commission in Co-decision – A Strategic Facilitator Operating in a Situation of Structural Disadvantage«. In: European Integration online Papers 7/10; http://eiop.or.at/eiop/texte/2003-010a.htm.

Rawls, John (1971). A Theory of Justice. Cambridge: Harvard University Press.

Reif, Karlheinz & Hermann Schmitt (1980). »Nine Second-Order National Elections: A Conceptual Framework for the Analysis of European Election Results«. In: European Journal of Political Research 8 (3–45).

Reutter, Werner (2001). »Einleitung: Korporatismus, Pluralismus und Demokratie«. In: Werner Reutter & Peter Rütters, eds., Verbände und Verbandssysteme in Westeuropa (9–30). Opladen: Leske + Budrich.

Rhodes, R.A.W. (1990). »Policy Networks: A British Perspective«. In: Journal of Theoretical Politics 2 (293–317).

Richter, Carolin (1997). Lobbyismus und Abgeordnetenbestechung: Legitimität und Grenzen der Einflußnahme von Lobbyisten auf Abgeordnete. Aachen: Shaker.

Rothacher, Albrecht (2004). »Die EU 25: Chancen, Risiken und politische Folgen der Osterweiterung«. In: Aus Politik und Zeitgeschichte 5–6 (25–34).

Rousseau, Jean-Jaques (1977, orig. 1762). Vom Gesellschaftsvertrag oder Grundsätze des Staatsrechts. Stuttgart: Reclam.

Rudzio, Wolfgang (1977). Die organisierte Demokratie: Parteien und Verbände in der Bundesrepublik. Stuttgart: Metzler.

Saipa, Axel (1971). Politischer Prozeß und Lobbyismus in der Bundesrepublik und in den USA: Eine rechtsvergleichende und verfassungspolitische Untersuchung. Göttingen: Georg-August-Universität Göttingen, Juristische Fakultät.

Sannerstedt, Anders (1996). »Negotiations in the Riksdag«. In: Lars-Göran Stenelo & Magnus Jerneck, eds., The Bargaining Democracy (17–58). Lund: Lund University Press.

Sassen, Saskia (1999). A New Geography of Power?

Schaber, Thomas (1998). »The Regulation of Lobbying at the European Parliament: The Quest for Transparency«. In: Paul-H. Claeys, et al., eds., Lobbyisme, pluralisme et intégration européenne (208–221). Bruxelles: PIE.

Scharpf, Fritz W. (1970). Demokratietheorie zwischen Utopie und Anpassung. Konstanz: Universitätsverlag.

– (1988). »The Joint-Decision Trap: Lessons from German Federalism and European Integration«. In: Public Administration 66 (239–278)

– (1992). Versuch über Demokratie in Verhandlungssystemen. Koln: Max-Planck-Institut für Gesellschaftsforschung.

– (1993). »Versuch über Demokratie im verhandelnden Staat«. In: Roland Czada & Manfred G. Schmidt, eds., Verhandlungsdemokratie, Interessenvermittlung, Regierbarkeit: Festschrift für Gerhard Lehmbruch (25–50). Opladen: Westdeutscher Verlag.

– (1999). Regieren in Europa: Effektiv und demokratisch? Frankfurt a.M.: Campus.

– (2000). Notes Towards a Theory of Multilevel Governing in Europe. Köln: Max-Planck-Institut für Gesellschaftforschung.

Schieder, Siegfried (2004). »In guter Verfasstheit? Nutzen und Nachteil eines europäischen Verfassungsvertrags«. In: Aus Politik und Zeitgeschichte 17 (13–20).

Schimmelfennig, Frank (2003). »Osterweiterung: Strategisches Handeln und kollektive Ideen«. In: Markus Jachtenfuchs & Beate Kohler-Koch, eds., Europäische Integration (541–568). Opladen: Leske + Budrich.

Schindler, Jörg (25.02.2006). »Von Einflüsterern umgarnt«. In: Frankfurter Rundschau.

Schmidt, Hilmar & Ingo Take (1997). »Demokratischer und besser? Der Beitrag von Nichtregierungsorganisationen zur Demokratisierung internationaler

Politik und zur Lösung globaler Probleme«. In: Aus Politik und Zeitgeschichte 43 (12–20).

Schmidt, Manfred G. (2000a). Demokratietheorien: Eine Einführung. Opladen: Leske + Budrich.

– (2000b). »Der konsoziative Staat. Hypothesen zur politischen Struktur und zum politischen Leistungsprofil der Europäischen Union«. In: Edgar Grande & Markus Jachtenfuchs, eds., Wie problemlösungsfähig ist die EU? Regieren im europäischen Mehrebenensystem (33–58). Baden-Baden: Nomos.

Schmidt, Vivien A. (1997). »European Integration and Democracy: the Differences Among Member States«. In: Journal of European Public Policy 4/1 (128–145).

Schmitt, Carl (1972). »Die konkrete Verfassungslage der Gegenwart«. In: Franz Nuscheler & Winfried Steffani, eds., Pluralismus – Konzeption und Kontroversen (99–111). München: Piper.

Schmitter, Philippe C. (1979). »Still the Century of Corporatism?«. In: Philippe C. Schmitter & Gerhard Lehmbruch, eds., Trends Towards Corporatist Intermediation (7–52). Beverly Hills: Sage.

– (1993). »Corporatism«. In: Joel Krieger, et al., eds., The Oxford Companion to Politics of the World (195–198). Oxford: Oxford University Press.

– (1994). »Interests, Associations and Intermediation in a Reformed Post-Liberal Democracy«. In: Wolfgang Streeck, ed., Staat und Verbände (160–171). Opladen: Westdeutscher Verlag.

– (1998). »Is It Really Possible to Democratize the Euro-Polity?«. In: Andreas Follesdal & Peter Koslowski, eds., Democracy and the European Union (13–36). Berlin: Springer.

Schmuck, Otto (1993). Demokratiedefizit in Europa – Neue Herausforderungen für eine Politische Union. Bonn: Friedrich-Ebert-Stiftung.

Schneider, Volker (2000). »Organisationsstaat und Verhandlungsdemokratie«. In: Raymund Werle & Uwe Schimank, eds., Gesellschaftliche Komplexität und kollektive Handlungsfähigkeit (243–269). Frankfurt a.M.: Campus.

Schulten, Thorsten (1998). »Perspektiven nationaler Kollektivvertragsbeziehungen im integrierten Europa«. In: Beate Kohler-Koch, ed., Regieren in entgrenzten Räumen (145–168). Opladen: Westdeutscher Verlag.

Schumpeter, Joseph A. (2000, orig. 1942). Capitalism, Socialism & Democracy. London: Routledge.

Schütt-Wetschky, Eberhard (1997). Interessenverbände und Staat. Darmstadt: Wissenschaftliche Buchgesellschaft.

Sedelmeier, Ulrich & Helen Wallace (2000). »Eastern Enlargement: Strategy or Second Thoughts?«. In: Helen Wallace & William Wallace, eds., Policy-Making in the European Union (427–460). Oxford: Oxford University Press.

Smets, Isabelle (1998). »Les régions se mobilisent – quel »lobby régional« à Bruxelles?«. In: Paul-H. Claeys, et al., eds., Lobbyisme, pluralisme et intégration européenne (303–327). Bruxelles: PIE.

Smismans, Stijn (2000). »The European Economic and Social Committee: Towards Deliberative Democracy Via a Functional Assembly«. In: European Integration online Papers 4/12; http://eiop.or.au/eiop/texte/2000-012a.htm.

Stacey, Jeffrey (2003). »Displacement of the Council via Informal Dynamics? Comparing the Commission and Parliament«. In: Journal of European Public Policy 10/6 (936–955).

Staeck, Nicola (1997). Politikprozesse in der Europäischen Union: Eine Policy-Netzwerkanalyse der europäischen Strukturfondspolitik. Baden-Baden: Nomos.

Steffani, Winfried (1979). Parlamentarische und präsidentielle Demokratie: Strukturelle Aspekte westlicher Demokratien. Opladen: Westdeutscher Verlag.

Steinberg, Rudolf (1985). »Die Interessenverbände in der Verfassungsordnung«. In: Rudolf Steinberg, ed., Staat und Verbände: Zur Theorie der Interessenverbände in der Industriegesellschaft (228–255). Darmstadt: Wissenschaftliche Buchgesellschaft.

Steiner, Jürg (1974). »The Principles of Majority and Proportionality«. In: Kenneth D. McRae, ed., Consociational Democracy: Political Accomodation in Segmented Societies (98–106). Toronto: McClelland and Stewart.

Stenelo, Lars-Göran & Magnus Jerneck, eds. (1996). The Bargaining Democracy. Lund: Lund University Press.

Sterzing, Christian (12.07.2003). »Vom Unwort zur Normalität«. In: taz.

Streeck, Wolfgang (1994) »Staat und Verbände: Neue Fragen. Neue Antworten?«. In: Wolfgang Streeck, ed., Staat und Verbände (7–34). Opladen: Westdeutscher Verlag.

Telò, Mario (1998). »Analyse du lobbying et questions méthodologiques: quelques remarques et points d'interrogation sur le néo-institutionnalisme et le transnationalisme«. In: Paul-H. Claeys, et al., eds., Lobbyisme, pluralisme et intégration européenne (159–166). Bruxelles: PIE.

Teuber, Jörg (2001). Interessenverbände und Lobbying in der Europäischen Union. Frankfurt a.M.: Peter Lang.

The European Public Affairs Directory (2004). The European Public Affairs Directory: The Comprehensive Guide to Opinion-formers in the Capital of Europe. Brussels: Landmarks.

Thunert, Martin (2003). »Is that the way we like it? Lobbying in den USA«. In: Thomas Leif & Rudolf Speth, eds., Die stille Macht: Lobbyismus in Deutschland (320–334). Wiesbaden: Westdeutscher Verlag.

Traxler, Franz (1990). »Political Exchange, Collective Action and Interest Governance: Towards a Theory of the Genesis of Industrial Relations and Corporatism«. In: Bernd Marin, ed., Governance and Generalized Exchange: Self-Organizing Policy-Networks in Action (37–67). Boulder: Westview Press.

Treaty Establishing a Constitution for Europe (2005). Treaty Establishing a Constitution for Europe. Bagsvaerd: Jens-Peter Bonde.

Trenz, Hans-Jörg (2005). Europa in den Medien. Frankfurt a.M.: Campus.

Truman, David B. (1951). The Governmental Process: Political Interests and Public Opinion. New York: Knopf.

– (1985). »Group Politics and Representative Democracy«. In: Rudolf Steinberg, ed., Staat und Verbände: Zur Theorie der Interessenverbände in der Industriegesellschaft (17–63). Darmstadt: Wissenschaftliche Buchgesellschaft.

Tsebelis, George (1995). »Decision Making in Political Systems«. In: British Journal of Political Science 25 (289–325).

Tsebelis, George & Geoffrey Garrett (1997). »Agenda Setting, Vetoes and the European Union's Co-decision Procedure«. In: Journal of Legislative Studies 3/3 (74–92).

United Nations Department of Public Information (2004). NGOs and the United Nations Department of Public Information. http://www.un.org.

United Nations Non-Governmental Liaison Service (2004). Applying for Consultative Status with the United Nations Economic and Social Council (ECOSOC). http://www.unsystem.org.

Van Schendelen, Rinus (2002). Machiavelli in Brussels: The Art of Lobbying the EU. Amsterdam: Amsterdam University Press.

– (2003a). »Brussels: The Premier League of Lobbying«. In: Thomas Leif & Rudolf Speth, eds., Die Stille Macht: Lobbyismus in Deutschland (300–319). Wiesbaden: Westdeutscher Verlag.

– (2003b). »The In-Sourced Experts«. In: Rinus Van Schendelen & Roger Scully, eds., The Unseen Hand: Unelected EU Legislators (27–39). London: Frank Cass.

Van Schendelen, Rinus & Roger Scully, eds. (2003). The Unseen Hand: Unelected EU Legislators. London: Frank Cass.

Vandenberghe, Kurt (1995). »Lobbying in the European Union«. In: Government Relations 5.

Veit, Winfried (1989). Souveränität '93: Europa zwischen Integrationsdruck und Demokratiedefizit. Bonn: Friedrich-Ebert-Stiftung.

Verhofstadt, Guy (25.11.2003). »Die deutsch-französische Allianz ist gut für Europa«. In: Süddeutsche Zeitung.

Vertrag über eine Verfassung für Europa (2005). Vertrag über eine Verfassung für Europa. Luxembourg: Europäische Gemeinschaften: Amt für Veröffentlichungen.

Vieler, Alexander (1986). Interessen, Gruppen und Demokratie. Tübingen: Mohr.

Voelzkow, Helmut (2000). »Von der funktionalen Differenzierung zur Globalisierung: Neue Herausforderungen für die Demokratietheorie«. In: Raymund Werle & Uwe Schimank, eds., Gesellschaftliche Komplexität und kollektive Handlungsfähigkeit (270–296). Frankfurt a.M.: Campus.

Vowe, Gerhard (2003). »Interessenkommunikation: Lobbyismus als »Fünfte Gewalt« im Interaktionsfeld von Politik und Medien«. In: Ulrich Sarcinelli & Jens Tenscher, eds., Machtdarstellung und Darstellungsmacht: Beiträge zu Theorie und Praxis moderner Politikvermittlung (105–112). Baden-Baden: Nomos.

Waarden, Frans van (1993). »Über die Beständigkeit nationaler Politikstile und Politiknetzwerke: Eine Studie über die Genese ihrer institutionellen Verankerung«. In: Roland Czada & Manfred G. Schmidt, eds., Verhandlungsdemokratie, Interessenvermittlung, Regierbarkeit: Festschrift für Gerhard Lehmbruch (191–212). Opladen: Westdeutscher Verlag.

Wallace, Helen (1993). »Deepening and Widening: Problems of Legitimacy for the EC«. In: Soledad García, ed., European Identity and the Search for Legitimacy (95–105). London: Pinter Publishers.

– (2000a). »Analysing and Explaining Policies«. In: Helen Wallace & William Wallace, eds., Policy-Making in the European Union (65–81). Oxford: Oxford University Press.

– (2000b). »The Institutional Setting: Five Variations on a Theme«. In: Helen Wallace & William Wallace, eds., Policy-Making in the European Union (3–37). Oxford: Oxford University Press.

– (2000c). »The Policy Process: A Moving Pendulum«. In: Helen Wallace & William Wallace, eds., Policy-Making in the European Union (39–64). Oxford: Oxford University Press.

– (2003). »Die Dynamik des EU-Institutionengefüges«. In: Markus Jachtenfuchs & Beate Kohler-Koch, eds., Europäische Integration (255–285). Opladen: Leske + Budrich.

Wallace, Helen & William Wallace, eds. (2000). Policy-Making in the European Union. Oxford: Oxford University Press.

Wallace, William (2000d). »Collective Governance: The EU Political Process«. In: Helen Wallace & William Wallace, eds., Policy-Making in the European Union (523–542). Oxford: Oxford University Press.

Wallmeyer, Gerhard (2004). Fundraising bei Greenpeace: Funktion und Methodik. Hamburg: Greenpeace Deutschland e.V. (internal report).

Walther, Rudolf (06.05.2004). »Die Euro-Priester kennen Bürger nur als Statisten«. In: Frankfurter Rundschau.

Waschkuhn, Arno (1998). Demokratietheorien: Politiktheoretische und ideengeschichtliche Grundzüge. München: Oldenbourg.

Weale, Albert (1998). »Between Representation and Constitutionalism in the European Union«. In: Albert Weale & Michael Nentwich, eds., Political Theory and the European Union: Legitimacy, Constitutional Choice and Citizenship (49–62). London: Routledge.

Weber, Werner (1957). »Referat zur BDI Veranstaltung«. In: Wilhelm Beutler, et al., eds., Der Staat und die Verbände (19–26). Heidelberg: Verlagsgesellschaft Recht und Wirtschaft.

– (1970). »Das politische Kräftesystem in der wohlfahrtsstaatlichen Massendemokratie: Die Gruppeninteressen und ihre Einfügung in die Ordnung des öffentlichen Lebens«. In: Werner Weber, ed., Spannungen und Kräfte im westdeutschen Verfassungssystem (121–142). Berlin: Duncker & Humblot.

Weiler, J.H.H. (1997). »To Be a European Citizen – Eros and Civilization«. In: Journal of European Public Policy 4/4 (495–519).

Wendon, Bryan (1994). »British Trade Union Responses to European Integration«. In: Journal of European Public Policy 1/2 (241–261).

Wessels, Wolfgang (1996). »The Modern West European State and the European Union: Democratic Erosion or a New Kind of Polity«. In: Svein S. Andersen & Kjell A. Eliassen, eds., The European Union: How Democratic Is It? (57–69). London: Sage.

– (2003). »Beamtengremien im EU-Mehrebenensystem – Fusion von Administrationen?«. In: Markus Jachtenfuchs & Beate Kohler-Koch, eds., Europäischen Integration (353–383). Opladen: Leske + Budrich.

Williams, Shirley (1991). »Sovereignty and Accountability in the European Community«. In: Robert O. Keohane & Stanley Hoffmann, eds., The New European Community: Decisionmaking and Institutional Change (155–176). Boulder: Westview Press.

Young, Alasdair R. & Helen Wallace (2000). »The Single Market: A New Approach to Policy«. In: Helen Wallace & William Wallace, eds., Policy-Making in the European Union (85–114). Oxford: Oxford University Press.

Zick, Tobias (08.10.2003). »Die heimlichen Gesetzgeber«. In: Frankfurter Rundschau.

Zürn, Michael (1996). »Über den Staat und die Demokratie im europäischen Mehrebenensystem«. In: Politische Vierteljahresschrift 37/1 (27–55).

– (2000). »Democratic Governance beyond the Nation-State«. In: Michael Th. Greven & Louis W. Pauly, eds., Democracy beyond the State? The European Dilemma and the Emerging Global Order (91–114). Lanham: Rowman & Littlefield.

Zweifel, Thomas D. (2002). »... Who is without Sin Cast the First Stone: the EU's Democratic Deficit in Comparison«. In: Journal of European Public Policy 9/5 (812–840).

List of tables

List of abbreviations

BEUC	European Consumers' Organization
CAP	Common Agricultural Policy
CEEP	Centre of Enterprises with Public Participation and Enterprises of General Economic Interest
CFP	Common Fisheries Policy
COPA	Committee of Professional Agricultural Organisations
COR	Committee of the Regions
Coreper	Committee of Permanent Representatives
Council	Council of Ministers (Council of the European Union)
DG	Directorate-General
EAEC	European Atomic Energy Community (Euratom)
EC	European Community
ECA	European Court of Auditors
ECJ	European Court of Justice
ECSC	European Steel and Coal Community
EEB	European Environmental Bureau
EP	European Parliament
ESC	Economic and Social Committee
ETUC	European Trade Union Confederation
Eurochambres	Association of European Chambers of Commerce and Industry
MEP	Member of the European Parliament
MNC	Multinational corporation
NGO	Non-governmental organization
PHARE	Poland-Hungary: Assistance to Economic Restructuring
QMV	Qualified majority voting
SEA	Single European Act
UNICE	Union of Industrial and Employers' Confederations of Europe

Social Science

Stefani Scherer, Reinhard Pollak, Gunnar Otte, Markus Gangl (Hg.)
FROM ORIGIN TO DESTINATION
Trends and Mechanisms in Social Stratification Research
2007 · 323 p. · ISBN 978-3-593-38411-5

Johannes Harnischfeger
DEMOCRATIZATION AND ISLAMIC LAW
The Sharia Conflict in Nigeria
2007 · 260 p. · ISBN 978-3-593-38256-2

Helmut Willke
SMART GOVERNANCE
Governing the Global Knowledge Society
2007 · 206 p. · ISBN 978-3-593-38253-1

Michael Dauderstädt, Arne Schildberg (eds.)
DEAD ENDS OF TRANSITION
Rentier Economies and Protectorate
2006 · 249 p. · ISBN 978-3-593-38154-1

Magdalena Nowicka
TRANSNATIONAL PROFESSIONALS
AND THEIR COSMOPOLITAN UNIVERSES
2006 · 280 p. · ISBN 978-3-593-38155-8

Sonja Puntscher Riekmann, Monika Mokre, Michael Latzer (eds.)
THE STATE OF EUROPE
Transformations of Statehood from a European Perspective
2004 · 358 p. · ISBN 978-3-593-37632-5

campus

Frankfurt · New York